Party Influence in Congress

Party Influence in Congress challenges current arguments and evidence about the influence of political parties in the U.S. Congress. Steven S. Smith argues that theory must account for both the policy and electoral goals of congressional parties, as well as for sometimes conflicting collective party goals. These goals call for flexible party organizations and leadership strategies. They demand that majority party leaders seek to control the flow of legislation in their houses; seek to package legislation and time action in order to build winning majorities and attract public support; work closely with a president of their party; and, with some frequency, influence the vote choices for legislators. In making these arguments, Smith observes that the circumstantial evidence of party influence is strong, multiple collective goals remain active ingredients after parties are created, party size is an important factor in party strategy, both negative and positive forms of influence are important to congressional parties, and the needle-in-the-haystack search for direct influence will prove frustrating. Special emphasis is given to the need to incorporate the Senate more fully in theory about party influence.

Steven S. Smith is the Kate M. Gregg Professor of Social Sciences, Professor of Political Science, and the Director of the Murray Weidenbaum Center on Economy, Government, and Public Policy at Washington University in St. Louis. He has taught at George Washington University, Northwestern University, and the University of Minnesota, where he was the Distinguished McKnight University Professor of Political Science and Law. He is the author or coauthor of seven books on congressional politics, coauthored a book on Russian legislative institutions, and served as an editor of *Legislative Studies Quarterly*.

"*Party Influence in Congress* is required reading for students of Congress, parties, and national institutions more generally. Smith critiques a generation of scholarship on the impact of political parties on legislative behavior and outcomes, identifying both the strengths and shortcomings of existing theory and empirical work on parties in the House and Senate. Smith pushes scholars to acknowledge the limits of stylized treatments of party influence, and to build theory that provides a better match of analytical rigor and empirical reality. Smith's theoretical perspective – coupled with historical and empirical nuance – definitely moves the study of Congress forward."
– Sarah Binder, Brookings Institution and George Washington University

"In *Party Influence in Congress*, Steve Smith challenges current theories of party influence in Congress, and he rightfully criticizes these theories for being overly simplified and for focusing more on one chamber than on the other. In so doing, Smith marshals evidence that yields a more nuanced view of partisan influence – one that goes beyond roll call voting and takes into account the multiple collective goals of parties and their leaders. Specifically, Smith demonstrates that the pathways through which parties move legislation in the House and Senate are different and have varied over time. This finding, along with his argument that parties provide order to roll call voting in both chambers and that a party's likelihood of winning increases as its size increases, is a novel addition to the literature. Indeed, throughout Smith's book are important theoretical insights that, together with the empirical evidence that he provides, lay the foundation for the next generation of theories of legislative organization. As always, I admire Smith's ability to weave so much evidence into one coherent argument. As with his other books, this one is so well written that even undergraduate audiences will find it accessible and compelling."
– Mat McCubbins, Chancellor's Associates Chair in Political Science, University of California, San Diego and Visiting Professor of Law, University of Southern California

"A major work, an absolute must-read for scholars of Congress and parties. With his incisive analysis of prominent theories of party influence and his subtle and creative proposals for tackling the problems that a truly satisfactory theory must confront, Smith
decisively sets the direction for future work in this central domain of scholarship."
– Barbara Sinclair, Marvin Hoffenberg Professor of American Politics, University of California, Los Angeles

Party Influence in Congress

STEVEN S. SMITH

Washington University in St. Louis

CAMBRIDGE
UNIVERSITY PRESS

CAMBRIDGE UNIVERSITY PRESS
Cambridge, New York, Melbourne, Madrid, Cape Town, Singapore, São Paulo

Cambridge University Press
32 Avenue of the Americas, New York, NY 10013-2473, USA

www.cambridge.org
Information on this title: www.cambridge.org/9780521878883

First published 2007

Printed in the United States of America

A catalog record for this publication is available from the British Library.

Library of Congress Cataloging in Publication Data

Smith, Steven S., 1953–
Party influence in Congress / Steven S. Smith.
p. cm.
Includes bibliographical references and index.
ISBN 978-0-521-87888-3 (hardback) – ISBN 978-0-521-70387-1 (pbk.)
1. United States. Congress. 2. Political parties – United States.
3. Power (Social sciences) – United States. 4. United States – Politics
and government. I. Title.
JK1021.S65 2007
328.73–dc22 2007001306

ISBN 978-0-521-87888-3 hardback
ISBN 978-0-521-70387-1 paperback

For
Tyler and Shannon

Contents

Acknowledgments

Several colleagues encouraged me to write this book. Eric Lawrence and Forrest Maltzman, who coauthored Chapter 7, were partners in a project on party influence and were kind enough to allow me to pursue a book-length discussion of the subject. I am indebted to many colleagues and friends for their encouragement, ideas, reactions, and material contributions. Stanley Bach, Sarah Binder, Karen Hedin, Michael Lynch, Tony Madonna, Cindy Neis, Jason Roberts, Elizabeth Rybicki, Pamela Van Coevering, Ryan Vander Wielen, and Jennifer Victor were particularly important. Christine Moseley of the Weidenbaum Center assisted me in preparing the manuscript and helped me juggle several responsibilities. My other colleagues at the Weidenbaum Center – Murray Weidenbaum, Paul Rothstein, Dick Mahoney, Melinda Warren, Gloria Lucy, Alana Bame, and Cherie Moore – always provide the friendship and support that makes my work possible. I could not hope for a more encouraging and helpful editor than Lewis Bateman at Cambridge University Press. Lew and his colleague, Eric Crahan, were superb partners in the publication process. Research reported in this book is supported by the National Science Foundation (SES 0095787). Please do not blame any of my friends, colleagues, and associated organizations for any mistakes in this book.

I dedicate this book to Tyler and Shannon, my son and daughter, whose enthusiasm and love inspires me every day.

I

Introduction

We love to hate political parties in America. The parties in Congress, with their famous leaders and infamous gamesmanship, are particularly easy to dislike. In the view of many Americans, self-interest, not the public interest, motivates party behavior. Remarkably, the American Constitution is silent on the subject of political parties. Madison, Hamilton, and Jay argued in *The Federalist Papers* that parties were inevitable but their unfortunate effects would be minimized in a system in which governmental power is shared across two houses of Congress, a president, and a Supreme Court and across national and state institutions. Parties emerged quickly – even over the ratification of the Constitution. True to prediction, separation of powers and federalism limited party power, at least in comparison with parties that emerged in other democracies.

Legislative parties emerged in Congress's early years and were controversial from the start. They remain so. Critics dislike the way partisan considerations undermine genuine deliberation among legislators, generate conflict instead of finding a middle ground and building a consensus, and encourage gamesmanship and public relations efforts over real problem solving. Defenders insist that parties aggregate and lend order to the multiplicity of society's interests, provide a basis for organizing the large decision-making bodies of Congress, and create alternatives that give the electorate a basis for holding public officials accountable.

Critics and advocates of parties seem to agree on one thing – parties matter. That is, congressional parties affect policy choices by influencing the behavior of legislators. This is a dubious claim in the view of some scholars. It is suspect because congressional parties are created and governed by legislators themselves. It is asked, Why would legislators invent and tolerate parties that lead them to behave differently than they would otherwise? The answer to that question lies at the center of any explanation of the influence of congressional parties on legislative outcomes.

I seek to explain why congressional parties exist and to evaluate the evidence for their influence on legislative outcomes. In this book – which really is a set of essays – I proceed by

- establishing some foundations for a theory of congressional parties,
- reviewing and evaluating existing theories of congressional parties in light of those foundations,
- addressing the challenges of measuring the effects of parties on legislative outcomes and considering past efforts,
- scrutinizing the most recent claims about the nature of party influence in Congress, and
- providing an appropriately synthetic view of the role of parties in congressional decision making.

ANALYTICAL ISSUES

Party leaders are the most visible figures in the modern Congress. In recent decades, to know something about Congress meant knowing something about Speakers Thomas P. "Tip" O'Neill, Newt Gingrich, Dennis Hastert, and Nancy Pelosi and Senate leaders Bob Dole, Tom Daschle, Bill Frist, and Harry Reid. As heads of the four congressional parties – Democrats and Republicans, House and Senate – the elected leaders are frequently interviewed and mentioned in the media, and for good reason. Party leaders and the organizations they supervise are involved in every stage of the legislative process: adopting chamber rules, appointing committees, setting the floor agenda and organizing debate, naming conference committee members, and so on. They frequently discuss and often write or endorse legislation. They appear around the country at a wide variety of party and fundraising events. They worry about their parties' public images and consult with the president and administration officials on policy and political matters.

As leaders appeared to become more central to the legislative process in the 1980s, journalists and scholars began to give them more attention. Particularly in the House of Representatives, where the speaker began to more fully exploit his formal powers in response to demands from fellow partisans, studies began to report the importance of majority party leaders in setting the agenda, building majorities, and speaking for their parties. Political scientists returned to enduring analytical problems – how to conceptualize and measure the influence of party on legislators' behavior and legislative outcomes.

Theory about congressional parties and leadership has taken several steps forward in recent years. These theories usually have a central analogy in mind – parties are like teams, or firms, or cartels, or coalitions. As teams, firms, cartels, or coalitions, congressional parties form to pursue certain objectives or goals held in common by their members. Theorists propose somewhat different common goals for legislators and, consequently, theories emphasize different features of the legislative process and institutions.

Legislators, theorists variously propose, seek to win elections, win policy battles, or reduce uncertainty about the electoral or policy future. I share the view that congressional parties are motivated by the pursuit of both electoral and policy goals and, further, that these goals, while usually compatible, frequently force their leaders to make trade-offs in priorities. Legislators' common electoral and policy interests lead them to form party organizations and decision-making processes, to select leaders who are charged with setting strategy and coordinating their implementation, and to create mechanisms for holding leaders accountable. These features of congressional parties did not appear at once. Rather, they emerged in response to the changing interests and demands of partisans, evolving competition between parties, and changes in chamber rules and structures, which are determined by the membership, too. Moreover, while the parallels between House and Senate parties run deep, differences in members' goals, chamber size, and institutional setting produced differences in the organization of parties in the two houses of Congress, a consideration largely ignored in the current literature on party effects.

The search for evidence to test the various theories of congressional parties should involve many aspects of the legislative process and the use of a variety of methodological techniques. In fact, the political science literature properly reflects the complexity of the subject. Political scientists have been drawn most frequently to the roll-call voting record of Congress for evidence of party influence. The roll-call record is the most historically extensive record of quantifiable legislative behavior that we have for Congress. Legislators' votes on motions for final passage, conference reports, and veto overrides are the closest expressions of definitive policy choices that we have. Interpreting the record of roll-call voting is not easy, as I will emphasize, but it surely is a task that political scientists must take seriously in sorting out the effects of legislative parties on policy outcomes.

In the 1990s, measuring party effects in roll-call voting once again became a boom industry in political science – and for good reason. The introduction of spatial theory of legislative behavior forced reconsideration of claims about party influence, a subject considered in detail in the following chapters. Conceptual problems arise in the application of spatial theory to congressional parties, but this has not deterred analysts from applying it. The introduction of new statistical approaches and computational technology also has facilitated recent work. However, the new work has not given much attention to the interchamber differences and changing patterns of party effects that theoretical developments suggest should be important.

My purpose is a modest one – to sort through the theoretical arguments and evidence in the debate about party influence in Congress and offer a more nuanced argument that appears supported by the evidence. My working hypothesis is that the influence of congressional parties on the voting behavior of legislators and policy outcomes is a product of their efforts to achieve collective goals. The collective goals include both electoral and policy goals. These goals are not always compatible, at least in the context of a two-year Congress, which forces leaders to make controversial strategic choices for their party colleagues. The pursuit of the collective party goals entails multiple forms of party influence and varying degrees of influence on legislators' voting behavior and policy outcomes.

OUTLINE OF THE ARGUMENT

Everyday activity in Congress leads to the inescapable inference that congressional parties seek to advance both the electoral and the policy interests of their members. I support these inferences in Chapter 2 with accounts of several recent episodes on Capitol Hill. The episodes provide circumstantial evidence for a theory that explains the multifaceted activities of congressional parties. Existing studies of party effects fail to capture the quite varied forms of party influence that are frequently observed. Instead, we must reach beyond the single-goal studies, as insightful as they might be, to explain institutional features and the patterns in floor voting that we observe in the House and Senate.

For too long, party influence was described in terms of pressure and arm-twisting. In fact, it is a more complicated matter than that. Once the types of party influence are more fully detailed, as I do in Chapter 3, we discover that they may have different origins and historical patterns. Moreover, we learn that the methods for measuring party influence must vary with the form the influence takes. There is no single measure of party influence. Confirming or disconfirming propositions about party influence by a single test of any kind does not exhaust the range of party effects that a nuanced view of the role of parties suggests are present.

Beginning with A. Lawrence Lowell's "The Influence of Party upon Legislation," a paper written for the American Historical Association in 1901, scholars have made arguments about party effects in voting on the basis of quantitative evidence. Political scientists have moved from simple counts of the frequency with which voting aligns with party affiliation to statistical models in which the effects of other factors are taken into account in efforts to evaluate party effects. Moreover, many scholars have examined partisan processes in settings beyond roll-call voting. Many of these studies are very informative, but no one has digested them to provide an appropriately nuanced discussion of the role of congressional parties. I provide such a discussion in Chapter 4.

Recent theories of congressional parties have done a better job of identifying forms of party influence and their distinguishable consequences for legislators' behavior and policy outcomes. Two theories, known as conditional party government and cartel theory, have been important in recent years. In Chapter 5, I provide a critical review of the theories and find them wanting in a number of respects. They fail to take multiple goals into full account, place too little emphasis on party size as a variable in party strategy, and give inadequate consideration to one house of Congress, the Senate.

The major challenge to the entire "party effects" enterprise is Krehbiel's *Pivotal Politics* (Krehbiel 1998), in which it is argued that legislators' policy preferences and the rules of the legislative game, not legislators' party affiliations, explain legislative outcomes. Remarkably, the theoretical foundations and empirical claims of the book have not received much attention in the ten years since its publication. I address the key issues in Chapters 5 and 6. I argue, on the basis of another look at the evidence in *Pivotal Politics* and another recent paper, that party effects are readily discernible in Krehbiel's studies and that, given the theories of party influence that motivate our search, the effects are of the predicted size and kind. I find Krehbiel's conclusions from his own analysis misleading and suggest that his model serves as a poor standard for evaluating party effects in Congress.

My principle observations, reported in Chapter 7, are that parties give order to roll-call voting patterns in both houses and in all Congresses since the end of Reconstruction, the form of party structuring varies between the House and Senate in ways that reflect their differences in the parliamentary advantages granted the majority party, and the form of party structuring varies in important ways over time. Borrowing from collaborative work with Forrest Maltzman and Eric Lawrence, I show that majority and minority parties do not exhibit symmetrical behavior – that is, with the majority favoring and the minority opposing passage of legislation (Lawrence et al. 2006). Rather, the parties typically exhibit asymmetric behavior – the majority party showing more cohesiveness than the underlying policy positions of its members would suggest, while the minority party's members are more likely to show variation in voting that is readily predicted by their general policy positions.

In the end, the evidence for the presence of party influence in congressional policy making is strong but circumstantial. Recent theories – conditional party government and cartel theories – represent important progress in the science of policy making and yet both miss important features of party influence. Recent evidence based on aggregate analyses of the historical congressional voting record shows the traces of party influence. Most persuasive are a few studies that account for specific forms of party efforts. Even a few studies that make the case that legislators' preferences drive outcomes ultimately add to the accumulating evidence for party effects.

In sum, I develop several themes about the ingredients of a theory of congressional parties. The theory must allow for both policy and electoral goals and for sometimes conflicting collective party goals. These goals call for flexible party organizations and leadership strategies. They demand that majority party leaders seek to control the flow of legislation in their houses, seek to package legislation and time action in order to suit their needs to build winning majorities and attract public support, work closely with a president of their party, and, with some frequency, influence the vote choices of legislators. In the concluding chapter, I return to these themes:

Theme 1. The Circumstantial Evidence of Party Influence Is Strong
Theme 2. Multiple Goals Remain Active Ingredients After Parties Are Created
Theme 3. Collective Party Goals Require That We Account for Party Size
Theme 4. A Theory of Party Leader Strategies Is Needed
Theme 5. Negative Agenda Control Does Not Stand Alone
Theme 6. The Search for Direct Party Effects Will Prove Frustrating
Theme 7. The Senate Is Not Well Understood
Theme 8. The Majority and Minority Parties Are Not Mirror Images of Each Other

If I have persuaded you of the viability of these themes, I will have succeeded in making my arguments about the state of theory and empirical work on party influence in Congress.

FINAL THOUGHT

I am a little embarrassed by publishing the essays of this book. Much of what I argue is obvious to me and I have long resisted the temptation to put it down on paper. I realize that my background on Capitol Hill makes me a little impatient with the necessarily simplified constructions of theorists. The question is whether the simplification captures the essential features of a political process. As the reader will see, I have my doubts about the recent literature on the subject.

I realize that I am needling the scholarship of friends from whom I have learned a great deal. Some of these friends, such as John Aldrich, Gary Cox, Keith Krehbiel, Mat McCubbins, Keith Poole, David Rohde, and Barbara Sinclair have been engaged in an intellectual quarrel for some time. Their different theoretical stances have not been confronted squarely, it seems to me. So, while these quarrels produce a few laughs for many of their colleagues, I take these differences seriously. I hope to raise awareness of the consequences of our theoretical choices.

2

The Microfoundations of Theories of Congressional Parties

In the fall of 2005, House Majority Leader Tom DeLay (R-TX) was indicted by a Texas grand jury for violations of the Texas campaign finance law. As required by a House Republican Conference rule, Rep. DeLay temporarily gave up his leadership post. The rule, which Republicans had considered dropping at the beginning of the year but were compelled to reinstate to avoid further criticism, spared the party of having to vote to dethrone a leader who might prove to be embarrassing. Speaker Dennis Hastert (R-IL) appeared to have Rules Committee Chairman David Dreier (R-CA) in line to replace DeLay, but Republicans belonging to the Republican Study Committee, an unofficial group of about 100 conservatives, demanded that Roy Blunt (R-MO) take over because Blunt was a more faithful conservative than Dreier on social issues.

Blunt's appointment was temporary, but DeLay's problems led DeLay to resign from his leadership post in January 2006, leading to a contest to replace him. The contest, which generated a challenge to Blunt from John Boehner (R-OH) and John Shadegg (R-AZ), was affected by at least two important considerations. A scandal involving a lobbyist with connections to DeLay and former DeLay staff members that implicated several House Republicans led party members to worry about the electoral fallout and produced demands that lobbying reforms be enacted. Neither Blunt nor Boehner was directly involved in the scandal, but their connections with lobbyists were questioned. In addition, neither Blunt nor Boehner was closely connected to the

Republican Study Committee, so Shadegg, who once chaired the group, entered the race. Members of both the Republican Study Committee and the Tuesday Group, a more centrist group of Republicans, expressed concerns about the policy commitments of the candidates and demanded that the leadership candidates appear before them. Ultimately, Boehner won the race for majority leader.

The DeLay episode exposed to public view the competing forces at work in congressional parties. On the one hand, the need to minimize harm to his party's standing with the public led DeLay to step aside and others to urge him to do so. The concern about the lobbying scandal raised additional concerns about public support and the party's strategies for managing the crisis. On the other hand, given that DeLay had to be replaced, Republicans wanted a leader who shared their policy views. Speaker Hastert, seeking to balance these interests, quickly accepted DeLay's temporary resignation, bent to pressure to name Blunt as DeLay's replacement, and negotiated a hybrid leadership role for Dreier.[1] And the policy views of Blunt and Boehner played a conspicuous role in the calculations of their colleagues in the subsequent election.

FOUNDING THEORY ON MULTIPLE PARTY GOALS

The lessons of the DeLay episode and others like it are ignored by most recent political science. This is done for a good reason but with serious consequences. In order to deduce propositions about the behavior of party leaders and legislators, the theorist requires a single objective (a well-behaved utility function, the theorist would say) from which to predict the best strategies of the legislators. Multiple goals that cannot be translated into a common metric or utility function yield less precise predictions of expected behavior. Thus, if the conflicting electoral and policy demands placed on Speaker Hastert in the 24-hour period following DeLay's indictment are typical of the challenges party leaders confront, single-goal theories, whether grounded in parties' electoral or

---

[1] John Cochran, "Debacles, DeLay and Disarray," *CQ Weekly*, October 3, 2005, pp. 2636–41; Ben Pershing, "Conservative Revolt Pushes Dreier Aside," *Roll Call*, September 29, 2005, pp. 1, 26; Patrick O'Connor, "Blunt Takes Initial Lead," *The Hill*, January 11, 2006, p. 1.

policy goals, are likely to disregard many situations that party leaders are expected to manage.

This chapter begins with a consideration of the goals that serve as the foundation for theory about congressional parties and their influence. Too little attention has been given to this subject in recent theories of congressional parties. I begin with a couple of stories that serve to highlight legislators' expectations for their parties. I argue that the dominant theoretical approaches are wrong, as an empirical matter, about the motivational foundations of parties. Moreover, a fuller account of legislators' and parties' goals provides a stronger basis for explaining the existence and influence of congressional parties.

PARTY IN PRACTICE

Members of Congress form their own parties and choose their own party leaders. Neither the Constitution nor public law dictates that legislators organize themselves into legislative parties once in office, but they have done so. Over the decades, legislators have elaborated party organizations, added leadership posts, and altered party rules. These legislative parties have ties to the national and state party committees, but they remain independent organizations. Even House and Senate Democrats and House and Senate Republicans maintain separate organizations with only as much coordination as their leaders choose to provide.

I assume, with justification, that legislators develop their legislative parties for instrumental reasons. Legislators share certain goals that they seek to achieve through organized party action. In the modern Congress, newly elected legislators join long-standing party organizations, but these organizations remain subject to change by their memberships and are directed by elected leaders. The shared goals and the predictable strategies parties pursue to achieve them form a theory of rational action by the congressional parties. The theory serves as the basis for predicting variation in the influence of congressional parties on legislators' behavior and policy outcomes. Different assumptions about the nature of the shared goals often yield different predictions about party activity and influence.

Clues about the nature of congressional parties, and the sources of party influence, are scattered throughout the daily politics of Capitol

Hill. Such clues were plentiful in two recent episodes. The first concerns a contest for a party leadership post. We gain insight into what legislators want from their party leaders as the candidates for the post vie for the support of their party colleagues. The second story involves a prominent leader's effort to balance important policy and electoral objectives in a legislative battle. The story illustrates the tradeoffs that leaders are expected to make. The two stories suggest that (1) legislators look to their party leaders to address their common policy and electoral interests, (2) the strategies implied by collective policy and electoral goals are not always compatible, at least not in the short run, (3) party leaders pursue a variety of strategies in seeking to achieve party goals, including agenda setting, arm twisting, and promoting loyalty, and (4) the party strategies suggest that the observable consequences of party influence on the behavior of individual legislators will take several forms, even with respect to floor voting.

Expectations for Parties and Leaders: The Whip Contest

In October 2001, Rep. Nancy Pelosi (D-CA) was elected her party's whip, defeating Rep. Steny Hoyer (D-MD) by a 108–95 vote in the House Democratic Caucus. Democrats were the minority party so the whip was the second-ranking leadership post in the party. The whip is responsible for counting votes within the party and for disseminating information to party colleagues about party policy positions, the legislative schedule, and political events. The whip works with the party floor leader on virtually all facets of party strategy, including determining who gives the party's weekly radio address, allocating floor speaking time and organizing one-minute speeches, developing public relations efforts, and speaking for the party on television and radio and at major events. Pelosi was the first woman to be elected to such a high party leadership position in Congress and would be the favorite to be elected the top leader when Minority Leader Richard Gephardt (D-MO) retired, as he did in 2004. In fact, Pelosi was elected minority leader without serious opposition and was elected speaker in 2007 after the Democrats won a majority of House seats in the 2006 elections.[2]

---

[2] Sen. Barbara Mikulski (D-MD) served as Democratic Conference Secretary, making her the third-ranking party leader and the highest ranking woman before Rep. Pelosi

The 2001 race for Democratic whip was remarkable for several reasons. First, it was one of the longest leadership contests ever. Pelosi announced her intention to run for whip in 1999, nearly three years before the vote. At the time, she reasoned that the Democrats might achieve a majority in 2000, in which case Gephardt, the Democratic leader, would become Speaker and David Bonior (D-MI), the second-ranking leader, would become majority leader, leaving the whip's post open. Shortly after word spread of her intentions, Rep. John Lewis (D-GA), a veteran of the Civil Rights Movement, and Hoyer started their efforts to attract support. Lewis gave up in mid-2000, saying that a long race without a known end was too much for him. Lewis endorsed Hoyer.[3]

Second, the race was very expensive. In the 1999–2000 election cycle, Pelosi raised and spent $1.1 million on the campaigns of House candidates; Hoyer spent well over $900,000. Pelosi's total for the previous decade was $3.9 million; Hoyer's was $1.5 million. Both spent several hundred thousand dollars on colleagues' campaigns in 2001 before the fall election by the caucus.[4]

Third, the race was eventually conducted with the speakership on the horizon. In 2001, Bonior announced his intention to resign as whip in order to run for governor in Michigan. Democrats were optimistic about winning the 2002 elections, which would put Democratic leader Richard Gephardt (D-MO) in the speakership and likely make the winner of the whip race the majority leader. Gephardt, however, was viewed as a likely candidate for president in 2004, so the winner of the whip's race might soon take over as Speaker – easily the most powerful position in Congress. Thus, from the perspective of 2001, winning the whip's race might quickly lead to the top position in Congress.

With so much at stake and quality legislators competing for their colleagues' votes, the race generated an intense debate among Democrats about party strategy. Hoyer and Pelosi, their supporters, and their

was elected whip in the House. In the House, no woman had been higher than fourth-ranking party leader before Pelosi's election as whip. Rep. Jennifer Dunn (R-WA) ran unsuccessfully for House majority leader in 1998 against the incumbent leader.

[3] Karen Hosler, "Democrat Struggle Has Maryland History," *Baltimore Sun*, August 12, 2001, p. 1A.

[4] Juliet Eilperin, "The Making of Madam Whip," *Washington Post Magazine*, January 6, 2002, p. W27. Fundraising ability was cited as a major advantage of Roy Blunt (R-MO), who was elected as Republican whip in 2002. See John Bresnahan, "Blunt 'Understands the Value of Relationships,'" *Roll Call*, January 21, 2002, p. B14.

colleagues who were weighing the alternatives articulated a variety of criteria for evaluating the candidates. The arguments offer clues about what members want from the legislative party. Voting on the race was by secret ballot so systematic analysis of voting for Hoyer and Pelosi is not possible. Nevertheless, several propositions about Democrats' expectations for their party seem reasonable based on the statements made by legislators and close observers.[5]

First, the central theme of the campaign was how to win a Democratic majority in the House of Representatives. The *Washington Post* reported, "Impatient after seven years in the minority, House Democrats are searching for leaders who are best positioned to bring them back into power. 'It's about where do you go in the future to put a new face forward for the Democratic Party,' explained Rep. Tim Roemer (D-IN), who said he was 'agonizing' over the decision."[6] Hoyer's pitch to his colleagues was that he was a "legislative pragmatist" who would appeal to swing voters and moderate and conservative districts critical to gaining a majority of House seats. Pelosi, in contrast, emphasized that she would be a telegenic spokesperson for the party, would be the personification of diversity in the party, and would be an effective fundraiser for the party and individual Democrats.

Second, legislators' policy views, closely associated with the nature of their home districts, appeared to influence preferences about Hoyer

---

[5] In the following paragraphs, I draw on many newspaper accounts of the whip race. They include, in chronological order, Chris Matthews, "Show Her the Money," *San Francisco Chronicle*, July 29, 2001, p. D1; Karen Hosler, "Democrat Struggle," p. 1A; Marc Sandalow, "Push for House Leadership Job Pits Tauscher Against Pelosi," *San Francisco Chronicle*, August 20, 2001, p. A1; Juliet Eilperin, "House Whip Race Seen as Indicator of Democrats' Future," *Washington Post*, September 8, 2001, p. A1; Spencer S. Hsu, "Once More Hoyer Aims for the Top," *Washington Post*, October 7, 2001, p. C01; Juliet Eilperin, "Democratic Whip Hopefuls Rustle Up Votes," *Washington Post*, October 8, 2001, p. A19; Nick Anderson, "House Democrats to Pick Minority Whip," *Los Angeles Times*, October 10, 2001, p. A20; Juliet Eilperin, "Democrats Pick Pelosi as House Whip," *Washington Post*, October 11, 2001, p. A01; Karen Hosler, "California's Pelosi Chosen as House Democratic Whip," *Baltimore Sun*, October 11, 2001, p. 3A; Marc Sandalow, "Pelosi Breaks House Glass Ceiling," *San Francisco Chronicle*, October 11, 2001, p. A1; Caroline Marinucci, "Fund Raising Critical to Pelosi Win," *San Francisco Chronicle*, October 11, 2001, p. A15; Deirdre Shesgreen, "House Democrats Choose Nancy Pelosi for No. 2 Spot," *St. Louis Post Dispatch*, October 11, 2001, p. A16; Nick Anderson, "Pelosi's Message for Success: Organization," *Los Angeles Times*, October 12, 2001, p. A30; Juliet Eilperin, "Pelosi Finds Her Place in the House," *Washington Post*, November 13, 2001, p. A29; Juliet Eilperin, "The Making of Madam Whip," p. W27. Also see CQ, NJ.
[6] Juliet Eilperin, "House Whip Race," p. A1.

and Pelosi. Hoyer drew support disproportionately from moderate and conservative Democrats, while Pelosi drew support disproportionately from liberals. Hoyer represents a southern Maryland district, a moderate to conservative district that had voted for Republican candidates for president. Pelosi represents a district in the city of San Francisco, one of the most liberal districts in the country. Hoyer had a somewhat more moderate voting record than Pelosi and had established a pro-defense legislative reputation. Pelosi was a champion of women's rights, funding for AIDS research and treatment, and a prominent advocate for human rights in China. Thus, legislators' preferences for Hoyer and Pelosi reflected, at least in part, a judgment about which mix of messages was consistent with their own thinking.

Third, policy differences were entwined with judgments about how to win elections. A spat between Pelosi and her California colleague, Ellen Tauscher (D-CA), reflected these differences. Tauscher represented a conservative district west and north of San Francisco and is a member of the conservative "Blue Dog" caucus of Democrats. When explaining her support for Hoyer, Tauscher asserted, "I have made it very clear for a long time that who I support for my leadership is about the fact that I want to have a more fiscally responsible moderate in leadership... I believe that is the only way we achieve the majority. That is why I am supporting someone else."[7] An anonymous Democrat, identified as a conservative, complained that "my concern is that perception is bigger than reality. A woman from California who is a liberal, from my point of view, casts the wrong image for where the party wants to be. We want to be in the center."[8] For at least some legislators, then, preferences for Hoyer and Pelosi reflected a judgment about which mix of messages would work best in districts like their own.

Fourth, many Democrats believed that appealing to women and minorities was critical to the party's electoral interests. One supporter, Rep. Janice Schakowsky (D-IL), argued, "For the party that depends on women for most of our votes, I think putting a woman in one of the top two leadership jobs – or the failure to – that sends a message."[9] Just before the caucus election, Pelosi reported the support of 33 of

---

[7] Marc Sandalow, "Push for House Leadership," p. A1.
[8] Juliet Eilperin, "Democrats Pick Pelosi," p. A01. Also see the comments of Rep. Gene Taylor (D-MS), in Juliet Eilperin, "Pelosi Finds Her Place," p. A29
[9] Karen Hosler, "Democrat Struggle," p. 1A.

the 45 women in the caucus. Some observers thought that gender was a decisive consideration of some members, even male members. Rep. Barney Frank (D-MA) noted, "Everything else being equal, breaking what's been an all-male monopoly of leadership in both houses for both parties is a good thing. That's probably the major difference."[10] The moderately conservative Texan Ken Bentsen (D-TX) said, "It is terribly important for the Democratic Caucus, when you look at our base, to have a woman in the elected leadership."[11] In fact, Hoyer commented after the election that the outcome turned on Pelosi's gender and the size of the California delegation.[12]

Finally, it appears that some Democrats simply wanted to support the eventual winner.[13] Very early on, Lewis indicated to Hoyer that he wanted to go with a winner.[14] At the very least, going with a winner may improve a legislator's access to the inner leadership circle and gain more favorable consideration on matters the leaders control or influence – scheduling legislation, granting committee assignments, and so on.

Remarkably, press coverage of the contest leads us to believe that the issue of who would best perform the everyday tasks of the whip's job was not very important. Democrats, it seems likely, believed that both Hoyer and Pelosi had the skills to do the work. Both had served in the House for many years, both were ranking members on committees, and both were respected for their skill in both public and interpersonal relations.

Democrats' evaluation of Hoyer and Pelosi, and the arguments made in support of the two candidates, suggest that a mix of policy, electoral, and personal considerations influence the choice of party leadership. More than policy differences were at stake. Indeed, Pelosi received support from conservatives and Hoyer received support from prominent liberals. More than electoral strategies were at stake. Plainly, policy views dictated the choice for many members. The talents of the candidates were an issue, but neither candidate seemed to have much of an advantage on that score. Personal considerations were important

---

[10] Nick Anderson, "House Democrats," p. A20.
[11] Juliet Eilperin, "The Making of Madam Whip," p. W27.
[12] Karen Hosler, "California's Pelosi Chosen," p. 3A.
[13] Juliet Eilperin, "Democratic Whip Hopefuls," p. A19.
[14] Juliet Eilperin, "The Making of Madam Whip," p. W27.

to at least a few members. If we take these observations seriously and focus on the strategic interests of the party, we are led to believe that Democrats were divided over the blend of policy directions and electoral strategies that they pursued. The *mix* of policy and electoral strategies – of Pelosi's liberal policy views, the appeal to women, and upgraded fundraising and electioneering for the party – seem to best account for her success.

The Hoyer–Pelosi race was not unusual. Every race has its unique features, but Peabody demonstrates that a mix of electoral and policy concerns motivated many races for leadership posts during the mid–twentieth century (Peabody 1976). To be sure, personalities, friendships, and other considerations are given emphasis by Peabody. Yet, the most significant races, such as Charles Halleck (R-IN) unseating incumbent House Republican leader Joseph Martin (R-MA) after the 1958 election disaster for Republicans, and Gerald Ford's (R-MI) defeat of Halleck after the 1964 elections, illustrated how the task of balancing policy and electoral strategies is central to legislators' expectations of their parties.

The Strategies of Parties and Leaders: A Legislative Battle

The challenge of balancing policy and electoral demands is evident in the everyday flow of strategic choices made by congressional party leaders. The challenge was plain in the struggle over economic stimulus legislation in late 2001 and early 2002. My focus is on the strategies pursued by Sen. Tom Daschle (D-SD), the Senate's majority leader. Daschle had served as minority leader from 1995 until June 2001, when Sen. Jim Jeffords (I-VT) left the Senate Republican conference, became independent, and gave the Democrats a one-seat advantage. With the economy faltering in the aftermath of the terrorism of September 11, 2001, leaders of both parties urged the enactment of an economic stimulus package. The fight over the content of the legislation proved to be the first significant test of Daschle's service as majority leader.

The context of the battle over the economic stimulus package was exceptional. Democrats held a one-seat majority in the Senate and Republicans had an 11-seat edge in the House. Party control of the two houses could easily change in the next election. Nearly any advantage in public perceptions for either party might make the difference.

Republican President George W. Bush's popularity, which rose to record heights during the initial months of the war against terrorism, clearly advantaged his party, but, in late 2001, an economic recession seemed threatening to Republicans. The fate of the first President Bush in 1992 was mentioned frequently – Bush was blamed for inaction while the economy slumbered. Nevertheless, the Democrats were not in a strong position. They held the barest of majorities in the Senate, where the minority's opportunity to filibuster gave it substantial bargaining leverage. To make matters worse for Daschle, any stimulus package would likely violate existing budget restrictions that could be overcome only with 60-vote majorities, as required by budget rules. Given the rules and the polarization of the parties, it was immediately clear that getting any legislation out of the Senate would be difficult. Gaining enactment of favored legislation, attracting credit for the legislative effort, and avoiding blame for killing legislation proved to be a significant challenge in this context.

Economic issues, at least as much as any other domain of public policy, divided the two parties. Republicans pushed for a package of tax cuts for business and speeding up personal income tax cuts that were approved earlier in the year. Democrats favored some tax cuts but emphasized income and health coverage benefits for the unemployed. Partisan sensitivities on tax cuts are always present but in the fall of 2001 they were especially intense. Republicans successfully pushed tax-cut legislation earlier in the year. However, overt partisanship in the first few months of the war against terrorism seemed likely to be punished by the public.

From the start of discussions in late September 2001, the parties distrusted each other. Democrats insisted on an explicit agreement from President Bush that he would endorse the increased spending in a stimulus bill so that Republicans would not later claim that Democrats were seeking to bust the budget. Bush signed a letter indicating that there was "no disagreement" between the parties on overall spending in the bill. After a meeting at the White House on October 2, it appeared that the president and congressional leaders agreed on the overall size of the plan, and everyone agreed that mix of tax cuts and aid to the unemployed would be included, but no agreement was attempted on the specific mix of tax cuts and aid for laid-off workers. Daschle later insisted that the Bush administration had agreed that any tax cuts would be temporary. Congressional leaders and the White House agreed to continue to work jointly on a plan.[15]

Within days, the Bush administration announced that it would support a plan urged by congressional Republicans. The proposal, which provided about one-fifth of the funding for aid to the unemployed and dedicated the remainder to tax cuts for individuals and businesses, was unacceptable by most congressional Democrats, including Daschle. Democrats insisted that more of the $75 billion plan be devoted to unemployment insurance and health care assistance. Daschle charged that the president backed off from his commitments under pressure from Republican conservatives who wanted a heavier emphasis on tax cuts. At the same time, Republicans of the House Ways and Means Committee indicated that they planned to write their own bill, including tax provisions that the White House had set aside. Daschle said that he would oppose a plan that included permanent tax cuts or cost more than the administration suggested.[16]

In two weeks, the Ways and Means Committee swiftly produced, and the House approved, a $100 billion measure that was composed almost entirely of tax cuts. The House bill passed 216–214 with the support of only three Democrats and all but seven Republicans. The White House announced that it supported the bill, although it indicated that the president was willing to consider changes during Senate deliberations. Nevertheless, the president used his weekly radio address to urge the Senate to follow the lead of the House in approving a large tax cut. Daschle, giving the Democrats' response, expressed his hope that the president and Congress "rededicate ourselves to that spirit of bipartisanship." "It is not acceptable for either party to dust off pre-September 11 agendas and re-label them as 'economic stimulus,'" Daschle said.[17]

The distance between the president and Senate Democrats did not close during November. To the contrary, the president continued to

---

[15] Glenn Kessler and Juliet Eilperin, "Deal Reached on 8% Spending Boost," *Washington Post*, October 3, 2001, p. A01.

[16] Glenn Kessler and Juliet Eilperin, "GOP Forced Bush Change on Stimulus, Democrats Say," *Washington Post*, October 12, 2001, p. A12.

[17] Juliet Eilperin, "House Approves Economic Stimulus Package," *Washington Post*, October 25, 2001, p. A02; Janet Hook, "Bush Takes Bolder Line With Rivals," *Los Angeles Times*, October 28, 2001, p. A1.

endorse the House Republicans' tax-cut approach and demanded Senate action. Daschle insisted that the Senate bill include an extension of unemployment benefits and subsidies that would allow laid-off workers to maintain their health insurance. The administration indicated that the president probably would veto a bill that included health insurance subsidies. The impasse led Daschle to ask the Senate Finance Committee to proceed with a Democratic bill, which it did. Daschle and Finance Committee Chairman Max Baucus (D-MT) said that they would not accept key provisions of the House bill, such as acceleration of the tax cuts approved earlier in the year. When the bill reached the Senate floor in mid-November, all Republicans voted against the procedural motions, which required 60-vote majorities, to overcome budget enforcement restrictions on the bill. The Senate continued debate on the bill but further action was not possible without additional negotiations.[18]

Daschle indicated that further negotiations on the bill should include House Republicans and the White House so that a comprehensive agreement might be reached. Sen. Trent Lott, the Republican leader, agreed, but little happened. The White House demanded that the Senate pass a bill, implying that Senate Democrats should make concessions to the Republicans, and a business-backed group placed radio ads in Daschle's home state that criticized Daschle for a visit to Mexico while the stimulus bill was pending.

Both Republicans and Democrats, including Daschle, publicly expressed doubt that the other side was serious about enacting a stimulus package. It wasn't hard to see why. Republicans favored a sizable tax cut package for business and upper-income taxpayers that nearly all Democrats disliked, even many who supported Republican tax cuts earlier in the year. As a result, some Democrats, perhaps most, preferred no bill to the House bill. On the other hand, Democrats favored a large spending package for homeland security and health insurance subsidies for the unemployed as in their Senate bill. Many

[18] Richard W. Stevenson, "Bush Sets Nov. 30 Deadline for Economic Stimulus Plan," *New York Times*, November 1, 2001, p. B6; Glenn Kessler, "Hill Faces Big Divide on Stimulus Plans," *Washington Post*, November 8, 2001, p. A06; Adam Clymer, "Democrats' Stimulus Plan for Economy Dies in Senate," *New York Times*, November 15, 2001, p. B9.

Republicans made it plain that they favored no bill to the Senate Democrats' bill. The tax cuts versus spending choice was made clear by both sides – and both sides used phrases such as "clearly unacceptable," "it will never pass," and "they are not serious about negotiating," to describe the position of their opponents. Stalemate, and no legislation, seemed a real possibility, maybe even a likely outcome, at the end of November.

The bill might have died a natural death but more than policy was at stake. The Republicans did not want to be blamed for inaction during a recession – the fate of the first President Bush was still fresh in memory. The president was publicly committed to getting a bill. The Democrats did not want to be blamed for obstructionism. Almost inevitably, then, November ended and December began with a flurry of speculation about which party would bend and about which party would be blamed for inaction on the bill. While Daschle claimed that the Republicans were conducting a virtual filibuster in the Senate, Republican elected leaders, party officials, and administration spokesmen blamed Daschle. Members of both parties trotted out longstanding criticisms of the opposition – Republicans charged that the Democrats could not break their habits of taxing and spending, while Democrats claimed that the Republicans were the puppets of business and the rich. Outside observers noted that the president is blamed if government does not function, although the Republicans and their supporters among newspaper editors, radio talk show hosts, and others seemed to be making headway in pinning the blame on Daschle. Just how blame might fall remained in doubt, if for no other reason than uncertainty about where the economy was heading with or without a stimulus bill. The blame game did not let up through the next two months of action on the issue.[19]

At the end of November, two suggestions rekindled hope for a compromise. Daschle indicated his willingness to cut the bill's homeland security spending in half, which Republicans interpreted as a significant concession. Sen. Pete Domenici (R-NM) suggested a one-month

---

[19] For commentary on the predicament of the parties, see Norman Ornstein, "The Balancing Act, Cont.: With Midterms Looming, Bush Faces Big Decision on Daschle and the Best Use of His Political Capital," *Roll Call*, January 21, 2002, p. B4.

payroll (social security) tax holiday that would benefit workers and employers, an idea that seemed to appeal to nearly everyone. A meeting of congressional leaders and the president on November 27 in which these proposals were aired led to renewed discussions about a compromise.

Procedural obstacles slowed action. Leaders agreed to proceed as if they were conducting conference committee deliberations. Representatives from each house would be named by the top party leaders to work out the differences. Administration officials would participate. Senate Democrats wanted the House to name an Energy and Commerce Committee member to the committee, in addition to Ways and Means representation, in order to negotiate the Medicaid parts of the Senate bill. Furthermore, House Republicans worried that any compromise introduced in the Senate would be subject to amendment and perhaps extended debate (the Senate had not passed a bill so the compromise would be considered a new bill there). Within a few days, the top congressional party leaders agreed to have each chamber represented by two majority party members and one minority party member who would work on tax and unemployment issues, while a similar group would work on Medicaid matters. These members would constitute a "virtual conference committee" – virtual because no bill had passed the Senate that could be taken to an official conference. Senators Daschle and Lott pledged to oppose all amendments when any compromise was considered in the Senate.

Just as it appeared that substantive negotiations would finally get underway, the Republican chairman of Ways and Means, Rep. Bill Thomas (R-CA), cut off the discussions and flew back to his district for the weekend in protest to the news that Daschle would not agree to a package unless two-thirds of Senate Democrats agreed to it. Thomas and other House Republicans charged that it was pointless to negotiate if the Democratic leaders lacked the authority to make a deal. Daschle said the Republicans were overreacting and trying to shift blame for their own disinterest in compromise, but it appeared that Daschle had problems of his own. Daschle seems to have been compelled to make the commitment to his party colleagues because many of them were unhappy with the senior Democrat on the Senate Finance Committee, Max Baucus, who had negotiated another tax bill six months earlier. Substantive policy differences between the parties quickly overshadowed the issue of gaining enough Democratic support for a compromise.[20]

As the Christmas holiday approached, both the administration and Senate Democrats showed some signs of willingness to compromise on taxes and unemployment benefits. However, talks stalled on the issue of how to assist unemployed workers in need of health insurance. To turn up the heat on Democrats, House Republicans pushed through their chamber a revised version of their plan, one with more funding for the unemployed, which was intended to show their willingness to compromise. Three Senate Democrats indicated support for the new plan, but that still left Senate Republicans far short of the necessary 60 votes for cloture. As a result, Congress went home for the holidays without enacting a stimulus bill.

In the meantime, economic analysts began to argue that any stimulus bill would be little help because the economy was already showing signs of improvement. The news seemed to bolster the position of partisans on both sides that no bill was better than a compromise.[21] The situation seemed to expose the political objectives of the parties to scrutiny. If no bill was better than a compromised bill that favored the other side, then appearances and not policy substance was the reason for continuing negotiations. Neither side wanted to be responsible for killing the bill.

No material progress in negotiations occurred until the stimulus package was pronounced dead by Daschle in early February. In January, Daschle proposed that Congress pass a greatly pared-down bill that included only a few items on which the two parties seemed to have agreed – an extension of unemployment benefits and short-term investment incentives for business. The proposal stimulated some expressions

---

[20] Paul Kane, "Democrats Set Stimulus Hurdle: Senators Require Supermajority," *Roll Call*, December 6, 2001, p. 1; Glenn Kessler, "Stimulus Bill Stalls as Charges Fly," *Washington Post*, December 8, 2001, p. A07; Richard W. Stevenson, "Republicans Break Off Talks on Measures to Spur Economy," *New York Times*, December 8, 2001, p. B6.

[21] Glenn Kessler, "Two Issues Blocking Stimulus Agreement," *Washington Post*, December 13, 2001, p. A02; Glenn Kessler, "Talks Yield Little Progress in Dispute Over Stimulus," *Washington Post*, December 17, 2001, p. A02; Janet Hook, "Stimulus Bill Compromise Falls Short Over Health Care," *Los Angeles Times*, December 19, 2001, p. A1; Gail Russell Chaddock, "Why the Stimulus Stalled Out (Hint: 2002)," *Christian Science Monitor*, December 21, 2001, p. 2.

of hope from a few Republicans, but serious negotiations with House leaders and the administration were not restarted. Eventually, the Senate again voted down efforts to overcome procedural obstacles, 56–39, four votes short of the 60 votes required. Seven Republicans voted with the Democrats.

Daschle's experience shows the importance of tradeoffs among party goals. In this case, the demands placed on Daschle by fellow Democrats were remarkably homogeneous. On the policy side, the vast majority of Democrats appeared to agree on a stimulus package heavily weighted in favor of spending for unemployment benefits and health insurance subsidies, but at least a few Democrats were willing to accept a Republican plan emphasizing business tax cuts and moving forward personal income tax cuts that were enacted earlier in the year. Nearly all Democrats believed that the Republicans were overreaching in attempting to pass tax cuts under the guise of antirecession measures. On the electoral side, few Democrats expressed doubts about the Republicans' potential vulnerability for urging tax cuts for the rich and big business. Uncertainty about the effects of the war against terrorism on the president's popularity and the speed of economic recovery produced varied judgments about the viability of attacking the president. Still, nearly all Democrats appeared to believe that Daschle's effective style – he was low-key, nonconfrontational, articulate, and not overtly partisan – made it difficult for the Republicans to demonize him and make an issue of his effort to oppose tax cuts. This consistency in colleagues' expectations licensed Daschle to be proactive in the process, although party conference meetings and other venues were used to learn about his plans and influence his actions.

The test for Daschle was to adjust policy and electoral tactics over the course of negotiations with the Republicans and the administration. Gaining short-term policy objectives – extending assistance to the unemployed during a recession and opposing expansive, lasting tax cuts – was not always compatible with the objective of maintaining the party's majority in the 2002 elections. Policy sacrifices had to be evaluated and timed with care so as not to give up too much and yet avoid appearing unpatriotic, partisan, and obstructionist. And action on many other matters – antiterrorism legislation, campaign finance reform, farm legislation, and so on – had to be considered in the mix. Balancing goals under conditions of uncertainty was Daschle's everyday burden.

More Systematic Evidence

The two stories of congressional party leadership are hardly unique. The literature on leadership contests and performance provide a rich history that demonstrates the significance of electoral and policy goals, and the necessity of balancing goals, to congressional parties (Peabody 1976; Sinclair 1983, 1995b). The underlying political interests of rank-and-file legislators that generate demands on party leaders have not been tallied in a systematic way and, regrettably, I do not have systematic evidence to present here. It is worth noting several studies that report legislators' responses to questions about their motivations for taking committee assignments (Bullock 1976; Calvert and Fenno 1994; Deering and Smith 1983; Fenno 1973). Legislators mentioned electoral and policy interests in nearly equal frequency. Interest in some committees was more strongly based on policy interests than reelection concerns. It is improbable that legislators' expectations for their parties and leaders are based on a fundamentally different mix of motivations. To the contrary, the Pelosi and Daschle stories suggest that a similar mix of political motivations appears to drive legislators' expectations of their parties, too.

PARTY IN THEORY

My view is that we should not be satisfied with single-goal theories that do not capture central activities of congressional parties. Single-goal theories, I must hasten to add, have generated important insights. Single-goal theories permit the deduction of reasonably precise propositions about behavior while the tradeoffs of multiple-goal theory usually leaves the predicted behavior less fully determined. Nevertheless, as I argue in this section, multiple-goal theory is essential for explanation of some of the most powerful sources of party influence in Congress.

Party Goals and Collective Action

From observing many episodes of party and leadership action on Capitol Hill, I have found it useful to characterize congressional parties as seeking two collective goals – majority party status and policy. The goals are founded on the goals of individual legislators – reelection, good public policy, and power (Bullock 1976; Deering and Smith 1983;

Fenno 1973). For example, legislators seeking to enact certain policies are advantaged if their party wins majority control of Congress, its committees, and scheduling mechanisms. Legislators seeking reelection are advantaged if their party's record for policy achievement is viewed favorably by the public.

The collective electoral and policy goals of the congressional parties have the character of public goods.[22] A public good is a benefit that is nonexcludable and jointly supplied. That is, achievement of a party goal benefits all party members whether or not they have contributed materially to the collective effort (nonexcludable) and is not exhausted for some members as other members benefit from it (jointly supplied). These features deserve a little discussion.

Congressional parties have the ability to determine their own membership so, in principle, the benefits of membership are excludable. In practice, the parties accept everyone elected under the party's label unless there is some specific and substantial grievance that their party has against them. The only exception in modern times occurred in 2001 when Democrats took the step of expelling James Traficant (D-OH) after he voted for the Republican candidate for speaker (Traficant was indicted a few months later on corruption chargers and eventually expelled from the House).[23] After the 1932 elections, when four Republican senators supported Franklin Roosevelt for president, a senior Republican proposed excluding the four from the Republican conference, but no action was taken (*Washington Post*, March 1933, p. 1). Going back a few more years, the endorsement of the presidential candidate of the opposite party led the Senate Republican caucus in 1872 to invite only those who supported the party's platform and candidates that year, thereby excluding Charles Sumner (R-MA) (Donald 1996). Plainly, exclusion from the caucus is seldom a threat and for several

---

[22] Technically, public goods are nonrivalous and nonexcludable (Coase 1974). If the party wins a majority, has legislative success, and a favorable party reputation, the benefit that any senator enjoys from these achievements does not reduce the benefits that his party colleagues enjoy (nonrivalous, sometimes labeled jointness of supply) and, for all practical purposes, no legislator of the party can be excluded from enjoying the benefits even if he or she failed to contribute much to the effort of acquiring them (nonexcludability).

[23] Karen Foerstel, "Traficant May Get 'Beamed Out' of Democratic Caucus," *CQ Weekly*, October 21, 2000, p. 2449; Peter Cohn, "Traficant Thumbs a Ride With Republicans," *CQ Weekly*, January 6, 2001, p. 6.

good reasons – the party prefers to have more rather than fewer members for the purpose of determining majority status, prefers more to fewer members for setting party ratios on committees and conference committees, and would rather minimize the number of new members required to gain majority status in the future.

While caucus membership is nonexcludable in practice, the benefits of caucus membership are not. Parties have the ability to favor some legislators over others in distributing the benefits of enacted policy and majority party status. Perhaps most notable, parties have denied committee chairmanships to legislators who, by virtue of the norm of seniority, expected them. After they gained a new majority in the 1994 elections, for example, House Republicans passed over the senior Republicans on three committees when filling chairmanships.[24] The reasons for denying chairmanships to the senior party members have ranged from punishing someone for ethics transgressions, to lacking sufficient leadership skills, to being untrustworthy or disloyal on key policy issues. If chairmanships enhanced legislators' electoral prospects by giving them access to campaign donations or greater influence over policy important to them or their voters, as they might, denying chairmanships can be costly to the affected legislator. Thus, some of the benefits of party membership can be exclusive and exhausted for some members as others enjoy them. Consequently, parties have at least a few ways to motivate their members to support collective efforts by selectively manipulating incentives (Olson 1966).

The use of selective incentives often is a controversial matter. When a move to strip legislators of committee chairmanships or assignments is contemplated, it usually is opposed by partisans who do not like the precedent or fear that the affected colleagues will switch parties or leave Congress. Examples from recent decades include unsuccessful efforts in 1995 to depose Sen. Mark Hatfield (R-OR) from the Appropriations Committee chairmanship after he voted against his party on a constitutional amendment requiring a balanced budget and to strip freshman Rep. Mark Neumann of his seat on the House Appropriations subcommittee for his stand against his party and committee chair

---

[24] Jeffrey L. Katz, "Appropriations," *Congressional Quarterly Weekly Report*, November 12, 1994, p. 3254; Karen Foerstel, "Gingrich Flexes His Power in Picking Panel Chairs," *Congressional Quarterly Weekly Report*, November 19, 1994, p. 3326.

on the adoption of a conference report on an appropriations bill. In
Hatfield's case, the Republican leader, Bob Dole, is reported to have
been very upset with Hatfield but worried that taking away the chairmanship would lead Hatfield to switch parties. Others expressed concern that Hatfield would be less motivated to run for reelection and
put the seat at risk of being won by a Democrat.[25] In Neumann's case,
his fellow freshmen rallied to his defense and Neumann was promised
a seat on the Budget Committee in addition to keeping his post on
Appropriations![26] Republicans appeared to be particularly eager to
punish disloyal colleagues in 1995 just after they gained new majorities
in the House and Senate and were anxious to see their agenda enacted.
Nevertheless, other considerations weighed heavily in the calculations
of both leaders and rank-and-file members.

Leaders are far more likely to reward than to punish party colleagues. They may favor colleagues who have proven their willingness to take political risks for their party with campaign help, coveted
committee assignments, seats on commissions and special committees,
appointments to a variety of party positions – task forces, whip organ-
isation posts, and so on. Some of these incentives hold only modest
value, but major committee assignments and campaign assistance can
be highly valued. None of these inducements is powerful enough to
motivate a legislator to put his or her reelection at serious risk. Thus,
for most legislators most of the time, support for the leadership can be
useful in building a legislative career, but being *denied* caucus membership or *losing* valued benefits of caucus benefits unique to majority
party status is not a serious threat.

Certain features of party membership – such as the party's reputation and policy outcomes – truly are nonexcludable and jointly supplied
goods. A party's reputation for performing well or poorly in office is
likely to have implications for all members of the party. This serves as a
bond among fellow partisans, even across the House, Senate, and presidency. For this reason, legislators care about the public's evaluations
of the president, the actions of partisans in the other house of Congress,
and any events that are connected by voters to their party.

---

[25] "Keep the Rope Handy," *National Review*, April 13, 1995, p. 14.
[26] Donna Casata, "GOP Leaders Walk a Fine Line to Keep Freshmen on Board," *Congressional Quarterly Weekly Report*, October 14, 1995, p. 3122.

With respect to public policy, legislators vary in the policy domains that interest them, but there are policy domains (tax rates, overall spending, defense policy, and so on) that always attract the interest of all legislators. Legislation related to shared or similar preferences in salient policy domains serves as a public good. That is, once legislation is enacted, all legislators may benefit, and one legislator's benefit does not diminish another legislators' benefit.

Party efforts to acquire public goods – that is, to gain or maintain majority status or to enact or protect favored policies – are subject to collective action, coordination, and conflict-of-interest problems. The free rider problem arises because the successful achievement of party goals is not greatly influenced by the actions of any individual legislator. Consequently, the incentive for individuals to contribute a fair share to collective party efforts is small (Olson 1966). For example, the ordinary legislator cannot expect to materially affect the reputation of his or her party and would reason that personal electoral prospects are more likely to be improved by campaigning at home than by participating in time-consuming efforts on Capitol Hill to enhance the party reputation (Mayhew 1974). A legislator might even reasonably expect a net gain in votes from criticizing his or her own party.

Moreover, congressional parties, like other sizable groups, can suffer from the problems of coordination and transaction costs. The party's members must somehow coordinate their choices, or alternatively, create a mechanism that will choose one of the acceptable alternatives for them. Coordination is not a free commodity. The transactions required to coordinate the behavior of many people may be quite costly and even prohibitive (Coase 1960; North 1990). High transaction costs, relative to the expected gains from coordination, can prevent a collective choice and the realization of benefits from a public good.

Coordination among dispersed candidates for public office is a more daunting task than coordination among elected legislators who gather on Capitol Hill. It is not surprising, then, that coordination of national parties started among members of Congress. Still, transactions among legislators can be so time consuming that some collective decisions are not made. Meetings must be organized, responsibilities delegated, information disseminated, and leaders held accountable – all of which may be viewed as costly to busy legislators. Organizational innovations that improve the efficiency of collective choice by reducing transaction costs can be expected whenever rising transaction costs (or rising benefits of collective action) increase the incentives for doing so.

Thus, while the collective goals require coordinated action to be achieved, we would expect legislators to contribute less than their fair share to the effort. Party goals certainly would be pursued inefficiently if legislators operated independently. To one degree or another, all congressional parties probably experience such inefficiency from time to time, but, at least in the long run, substantial inefficiency is likely to be addressed. Both inside and outside observers are quick to observe and comment on it. Competitive pressures from the other party encourage legislators to invent new ways of organizing their party for collective action and successful innovations in one party are readily adopted in the other.

Parties address the competitive challenges by organizing (Gamm and Smith 2002). Parties create committees, task forces, and leadership positions and assign responsibility for achieving collective party goals to the legislators appointed or elected to those posts. Legislators need to be motivated to pursue these efforts, but the same mix of goals that motivate others – an increment of influence over policy outcomes, visibility useful in the pursuit of reelection or higher office, satisfaction from involvement – may motivate at least a few legislators to attend to the collective interests of the party.

Legislators may not fully trust their leaders and committees. After all, power delegated to committees and leaders to pursue party interests might instead be used in pursuit of personal interests. Like all organizations, congressional parties address this threat – called the principal-agent problem, or simply the agency problem – in a variety of ways, such as by limiting the jurisdiction of committees and leaders, assigning some decisions to multimember committees or leadership groups rather than to individuals, subjecting top leaders to periodic election, and requiring leaders to justify their strategies at caucus or other party meetings (Kiewiet and McCubbins 1991).

Not all costs of collective action are paid by legislators. Often forgotten is the fact that certain collective party efforts can be provided without costing the rank-and-file party member anything. This is accomplished by appropriating public funds to supplement leaders' salaries, hire party staffs, and provide financial support of office operations and studio facilities. These appropriations became substantial after the

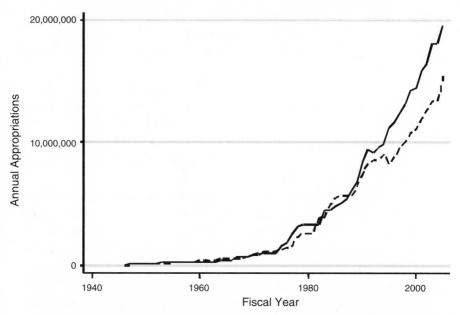

FIGURE 2.1. Annual appropriations in absolute dollars for party offices, 1946–2003: House (solid line) and Senate (dashed line). *Source:* Legislative Appropriations Bills.

1946 Legislative Reorganization Act created party policy committees and continued a rapid rise over the following decades (Figure 2.1).

The Relationship Between Electoral and Policy Goals

Does it make any difference that I emphasize *both* electoral and policy goals? I have two answers to the question. First, yes, it does matter, and most major theoretical statements on congressional parties in the last 20 years either remain silent on the matter or, at least implicitly, agree with me. Second, by failing to come to terms with the relationship between electoral and policy goals, the existing theoretical accounts lack key ingredients that are required to explain the creation and influence of congressional parties.

The Major Schools of Thought

One school of thought, I will call it the *electoral school*, follows in the footsteps of David Mayhew's book *Congress: The Electoral Connection* (Mayhew 1974). Mayhew explored the implications of an assumption about legislators' motivations – that legislators are single-minded seekers of reelection. Mayhew argued that reelection was the proximate goal of nearly all legislators, one that had to be achieved if they were going to achieve anything else. His book then explored the implications of the reelection goal for the behavior of individual legislators and for the organization of the policy-making process in the two houses. From this perspective, legislators do not have a personal or inherent interest in public policy or legislation. Rather, policy positions are advocated merely to serve the reelection goal, which entails a variety of nonlegislative strategies too.

An offspring of Mayhew's argument is the cartel theory of Cox and McCubbins (Cox and McCubbins 1993, 2005). The congressional party, like a cartel, seeks to control factors that affect its success. A cartel, an organization of producers seeking a profit, limits competition and supply to allow the producers to fix prices and guarantee profits. Similarly, a congressional party seeks to control the legislative process to enhance the party's reputation and win elections. Gaining control over key features of the legislative process, such as the floor agenda, allows the congressional party, when in the majority, to keep off the floor matters that would divide the party or otherwise harm the party's image. Legislators who share a party label and therefore share a common fate have an incentive to manipulate the legislative process through the coordinated action of their party. The party, in turn, is driven by the goal of maintaining or enhancing the party reputation with the electorate.

A second school may be called the *policy school*. In this view, legislators seek policy outcomes as close to their own most preferred outcome as possible. Legislators may acquire policy preferences to appeal to home constituencies, to attract campaign contributions from special interests, to satisfy their personal preferences, or for other purposes, but, at least in their behavior as members of Congress, they behave as if minimizing the distance between their own preferences and the legislative outcome is the only consideration driving their choices as legislators (Clausen 1973). The most fully developed version of the policy school is spatial theory, which provides for a geometric characterization of the location of legislators and yields predictions of outcomes from the location of legislators' policy positions and the rules of the legislative process (Krehbiel 1998).

It is tempting to say that it does not matter which school of thought we favor because the two motivations – electoral and policy – are strongly correlated with each other. We might argue that the process of electing legislators matches candidates' policy dispositions to the policy positions of the local electorates. Liberal districts elect liberal candidates to Congress; conservative districts elect conservative candidates. For elected legislators, then, electoral and policy motivations are fully reinforcing and cannot be separated. Behavior that can be predicted from electoral motivations can be predicted from policy motivations, and vice versa. This is the nature of representation. The schools are equivalent in all essentials, even if a little translation is required to see it.

I have noted that, as an empirical matter, I do not find this argument persuasive. Still, the distinct political motivations might predict identical behavior if the motivations are mutually reinforcing. Actually, most theorists say otherwise. Mayhew contends that the goal of reelection leads legislators to care little about mobilizing majorities for or against legislation, to give their attention to individualistic efforts to attract voters through position taking (announcing policy positions merely for home consumption), to ignore issues of general import and focusing on legislation with local benefits, to advertise themselves rather than engage meaningfully in the policy-making process, and to prefer individualistic activities over the teamwork of parties. In fact, Mayhew must allow for the existence of nonelectoral motivations – selective incentives – to explain why some legislators are willing to move beyond their own electoral needs to serve as party leaders. That is, nonelectoral motivations, such as additional influence or advantages in the policy process, must motivate at least some legislators (but not others). Mayhew plainly argues that the behavior generated by the goal of reelection is different from the behavior predicted by other goals.

Another relevant representative of the electoral school is Arnold's account of *The Logic of Congressional Action* (Arnold 1990). For Arnold, legislators' decisions, including voting decisions, are primarily a function of the policy preferences of the public that is likely to vote in future elections on the basis of a given issue. Whereas Mayhew cordons off the motivations of leaders, Arnold simply sets aside analysis of the motivations of "coalition leaders," party leaders, committee leaders, or other members who champion certain causes. Instead, Arnold explicitly assumes that such leaders want to win (pass or block legislation) and assumes that they are motivated "for reasons of their own" that, he also must assume, are fully compatible with the goal of passing or blocking legislation (Arnold 1990, 89). Had Arnold assumed otherwise, as we might (Smith 1984), then he could not have explained the strategies of coalition leaders on the basis of the electoral calculations of the "followers" alone, as he seeks to do.[27]

Within the policy school, the spatial theorist never addresses the issue. She assumes that *all* political forces that influence a legislator are captured by the concept of preferences, which is given a technical definition. A preference, in this view, is a legislator's most desired outcome at the moment of decision. The source of the preference is not relevant. The source could be personal policy commitments, campaign promises, interest group demands, or whatever, but the theorist focuses on the preference without concern about how it is formed. Party influence is not weighed against preference; rather, party influence, and any other political force, is incorporated in preference. With this definition, it is meaningless to speak of preferences versus other forces, such as partisan ones, because all direct influences on legislators' behavior are causally prior to preferences. Strictly speaking, spatial theory posits that no other motivations are relevant once the preference is set. Preferences, along with the rules of the legislative game, determine legislators' behavior (strategies), but the theory simply does not address what forces are at work in determining preferences. Thus, spatial theory is silent on whether electoral considerations – or any other – are determinants of preferences.

Another variation within the policy school, which can be called the electoral coalition account, assumes a powerful connection between the electoral and legislative arenas but treats policy positions as the immediate cause of legislative behavior. In this set of studies, legislators' general policy positions are imported with elected legislators after each election and are assumed to be a product of the matching of electorates and legislators that occurs in the election process

---

[27] The assumption that leaders lead because of the intrinsic value they attach to leading is discussed in a variety of positive theories of political action (Frohlick et al. 1971).

(Aldrich et al. 2002; Brady et al. 1989; Cooper and Brady 1981). Once legislators are in office, it is their policy positions, rather than prospective electoral considerations or other forces, that drive their behavior and determine the role of parties in the legislative arena.[28]

Explaining Parties

Reading between the lines, theorists do not want to complicate their theorizing by formally positing more than one goal as the basis for legislators' calculations. A simple assumption about individual behavior allows for more fully developed deductions about collective behavior; complex assumptions about individual behavior yield ambiguities about individual strategies and collective behavior (Coleman 1987). Unfortunately, the understandable preference for the parsimonious over the complex in building a theory of the collective behavior of legislators forces us to set aside some of the sources of ambiguity and uncertainty that underlie the need for parties and leaders in the first place. This is the decisive consideration: If the two collective goals yield identical predictions about collective party behavior, it will not matter whether we isolate the electoral or policy goals. I think it does matter and it is important to understand why.

Consider the implications of policy goals first. The creation of leadership authority and resources is not readily explained by legislators' policy goals, at least not in the short term. If legislators were solely concerned about policy outcomes, they would worry that leadership power would be used to force them to vote differently than they would otherwise. If legislators truly were single-minded in their pursuit of their policy objectives, sacrificing for the sake of party would yield no benefit. Sacrificing in order to join a coalition of like-minded legislators may make sense, but no party influence would be required to explain legislators' behavior. Rather, the party would be nothing more than a means for coordinating strategies among legislators with compatible policy interests.

---

[28] Long-term policy positions often are confused with the preferences of spatial theory – the former being viewed as a valid measure of the latter. From the perspective of "pure" spatial theory, the long-term policy positions imported from the election process are merely one input among many possible forces that shape legislators' preferences at the moment of decision.

Legislators might accept party influence because of the long-term benefits of party activity for policy outcomes (Schwartz 1989). By accepting the efforts of their party to coordinate policy proposals, limit choices, and influence individual legislators, legislators may be judging that party activity improves overall, or net, policy outcomes for them even if they sometimes are unable to get outcomes as favorable as they might without the involvement of the party on a few issues. This account requires legislators to perceive a multidimensional policy space. In a complex policy world filled with issues of varying salience to legislators, legislators may be willing to make sacrifices on some issues to acquire better outcomes on other issues. If legislators differ in the issues they care most about, it may be possible to make trades across issues that are arranged by party leaders. All party members are better off in the long run from this logrolling – the term used to describe bargaining across issues – even when compromises on policy preferences are required in the short run. Essential to realizing these gains from trade is persuading legislators to make the short-term sacrifices required to implement the long-term logroll. Leaders are empowered to use their influence to do so. Thus, according to this line of argument, legislators form parties as long-term, multi-issue policy coalitions.

As policy coalitions, parties contribute to the achievement of legislators' policy goals in several ways. By developing institutional features such as committees and leaders, which reduce transaction costs and enhance coordination, parties can generate economies in producing legislation. Because managing transaction costs and providing coordination requires an organization and replacing that organization consumes time and other resources, parties are not readily displaced. Moreover, by implementing logrolls across issues, parties do not require a high level of intraparty cohesiveness on issues. Individual legislators are generally free to pursue their own policy interests.

From the gains-from-trade perspective, policy goals are paramount and electoral objectives are merely instrumental. The party seeks to elect more like-minded legislators to reduce the short-term sacrifices required to build majorities and implement logrolls. Short-term trade-offs between policy and electoral objectives may be required, but the purpose is to enhance the long-term policy success of party members.

It bears emphasizing that, even from the gains-from-trade perspective, parties may have good reason to direct resources away from short-term legislative ends and toward campaign-related activities.

Congressional parties also might be treated as long-term electoral coalitions or cartels with features that parallel those of parties in the gains-from-trade perspective (Cox and McCubbins 1993, 2005). Legislative parties can produce economies in efforts to marshal electoral resources and effect a favorable party reputation. Policy cohesiveness may enhance the party's reputation, but allowing members to take policy positions suited to their own reelection needs is desirable. Policy and legislation are merely instrumental and logrolling allows members to pursue an independent course on legislation critical to their own reelection. Tradeoffs between short-term policy and electoral interests sometimes occur because some conflict between fellow partisans over the legislation best suited to individual needs is unavoidable.

Both single-goal theories have intuitive appeal. Both are parsimonious and appear to account for much of what we observe in everyday party politics in Congress. Particularly with respect to predicting the necessity of tradeoffs between short-term electoral and policy interests, the two theories may be observationally equivalent.

However appealing the single-goal accounts, they must meet two tests. First, they must explain why legislators are willing to sacrifice for the good of the party. Second, they must explain the "leadership premium" – what it takes to motivate leaders to provide collective goods or coordination for the party (Frohlich et al. 1971). The test results are mixed, it seems to me.

The long-term versions provide for the possibility that legislators are better off *in the long run* by being a part of an electoral or policy coalition than by operating on their own or in some other groups. Sacrifices are short-term; in the long term, there is no sacrifice. Does this explain sacrifices for party? It does only if legislators calculate on the basis of the long-term time horizon. Unfortunately, this view is contrary to most of the underlying arguments in the electoral and policy schools. Mayhew and followers assume that all electoral interests are wrapped up in the next election – after all, winning on average over the long run is hardly sufficient for a legislator who must win every election. The time horizon must be within the term of office, or just two years for members of the House. And yet the commitments to leaders are much longer than a single term. In the case of the Senate, parties do not even go through the motions of reelecting leaders at the start of a new Congress.

More persuasive is the argument for parties as long-term policy coalitions. While legislators surely discount policy gains in the distant future, the discount seems hardly as large as it is for reelection. Battles over major legislation often take several Congresses (or even generations) and legislators are well aware of that. Policies not only require enactment, but also must be defended over the long run, and coordinated party strategies to influence outcomes may aid the effort.

What about the second test that the theory must motivate leadership? Again, consider the electoral story first. Even a party caucus filled with single-minded seekers of reelection needs leaders who are willing to attend to the collective interests of the party. Such leaders might be motivated by the additional publicity, campaign contributions, and home favors they enjoy that enhance their personal reelection prospects. Still, other legislators would have reason to worry that leaders would abuse their power to enhance their personal reelection prospects at the expense of others, but competition for leadership posts and other means of accountability might limit the risk. And, it may be possible for leaders to exploit their positions to enhance their own electoral prospects without materially affecting the prospects of others. Thus, contrary to Mayhew's argument, it is conceivable that the goal of reelection could motivate the assumption of leadership responsibilities.

In contrast, if all legislators only care about policy outcomes, at least in the long run, then leaders must be rewarded with greater influence over policy outcomes. Empowering leaders is an unavoidable risk for other legislators who will have to sacrifice on policy outcomes if their policy preferences are different from their leaders. If the size of the "leadership premium" is large, then legislators are much less likely to tolerate collective party activity. In the competition for leadership posts, we can expect winners to be legislators for whom the premium required for service is small or zero, or whose policy views would cause few problems for most of their colleagues. If the premium is small or zero, then it is hard to argue that leaders care exclusively about policy outcomes. Other considerations – considerations that affect calculations about important career moves – must be important to at least a significant number of legislators for the legislative party to be sustained. If policy views are the critical consideration, then it is likely that participating in the policy coalition will prove unwise for at least some legislators.

Plainly, the complications of theorizing about leaders and their motivations are many. For this reason, if no other, theorists of congressional parties leave leaders' motivations unexamined and merely assume that parties have the resources to motivate someone to perform leadership functions. The bottom line is that we have not yet connected them to our theories about the organizations over which they preside.

The Interdependence of Party Goals

My observation is that we must take this analysis a step farther. I have argued that legislators' electoral and career goals, their general policy attitudes, and their party labels are interdependent and imported to Congress. Potential candidates for office choose a party and probably do so for both electoral and policy considerations. Furthermore, electoral success may reflect both policy and party considerations. And legislators' policy positions may reflect the influence of both electioneering and the need to appeal to fellow partisans. By the time a legislator arrives on Capitol Hill, these relationships – the triangulation of party, policy, and election – are established. Legislators do not choose their legislative party free of constraint in order to maximize utility in electoral or policy terms. Instead, the party label with which they ran for office dictates, with very few exceptions, the party with which they caucus in Congress. Thus, the most reasonable assumption appears to be that a set of interdependent goals are imported to Congress that bind legislators to their parties.[29]

Similarly, and less well understood, it seems, the electoral and policy goals of congressional parties are interdependent and often not fully compatible, at least in the short term. Winning elections helps create the

---

[29] We might argue that electoral or policy goals dominate the other, but, as far as we know, there is no empirical evidence to support such a claim. To the contrary, party activity external to Congress is often conceptualized as having both career and policy foundations (Aldrich 1995).

sizable House and Senate coalitions necessary for passing or blocking legislation, and legislative success helps generate the desired reputation essential to winning elections. The responsibility of the party leaders is to further both party goals while minimizing the severity of the trade-offs that are required. This responsibility is manifested in the everyday activities of party leaders – managing the party organization, coordinating with the president or leaders of the other chamber, speaking on behalf of the party for the media and other audiences, managing floor activity, negotiating legislation within the chamber and with leaders of the other policy-making institutions, and even taking the lead in writing legislation and building majorities.

Fellow partisans may differ among themselves about the best choices to make. These differences are rooted in the variation in individuals' electoral and policy objectives and in judgments about collective and personal interests made under conditions of uncertainty. Intraparty conflict over the best collective strategic choices are reflected in arguments articulated in contests for leadership positions and the everyday meetings of the parties. As I illustrated in the Pelosi and Daschle episodes, this is the crux of intraparty politics on Capitol Hill.

Efforts to influence the voting behavior of legislators are a part, an important part, of a larger set of party activities intended to achieve collective goals. Leaders manipulate incentives (by using committee assignments, appointments for party posts, campaign contributions, and so on) to gain the votes of targeted legislators. The party creates and funds a campaign committee and leaders provide a variety of other services (radio and television studios; fundraising activity; and staff support for research, publication, and other purposes) to enhance electoral prospects of partisans. Public relations activities and staff operations are designed to maintain or improve the party's reputation with the general public and to attract public support for the legislative objectives the party is pursuing.

Party goals are strongly implicated in floor activity. At the floor stage in the legislative process, legislators make policy choices for which they can be held accountable. Their actions are visible to their home electorates and often recorded for posterity. It is at this stage that it is most likely that a leader cannot simultaneously maximize the number of votes obtained, maximize the electoral value of the effort for party colleagues and candidates, and maximize the quality of the party's nationwide reputation. Choices are required and these choices motivate legislators to seek coordinated party strategies so that they do not work at cross purposes.

The complexities involved in pursuing electoral and policy goals are reflected in legislators' floor behavior. Policy goals are most obviously affected by the outcome of floor votes, although even floor votes do not always have much relevance to party goals. When a floor vote is relevant to a party's electoral or policy goals, party leaders may be involved in building majorities for and against legislation by structuring and influencing choices (Sinclair 1983). Structuring choices is setting the agenda, while influencing choices once the agenda is set involves the manipulation of incentives to gain compliant behavior from individual legislators. Concern about majority party status and the party's reputation may alter the agenda-setting and direct-influence strategies that are chosen. For example, a legislator's electoral prospects may be harmed by voting with the party, which may force a party leader to choose between enhancing the chances of maintaining or gaining majority party status and winning a roll-call vote. Or a party's reputation may be adversely affected by a loss and cause a leader to be more averse to risk in forcing a vote.

The strategic challenges motivate a collective response from party leaders. Party members demand it. Leaders are expected to create and use tools for minimizing the severity of the tradeoffs that they and their party colleagues must make. In her account of majority party leaders' tasks, Sinclair emphasizes the structuring of choice – controlling the flow of legislation to the House floor and, by using special rules for major legislation to limit debate and amendments, manipulating the alternatives over which legislators are forced to make choices (Sinclair 1983, 1995b, 2000). By controlling the agenda, leaders can reduce the frequency with which they and their colleagues must choose between a preferred policy position and the position dictated by electoral concerns. They might be able to ensure that the opposition cannot offer an amendment that would split the party and create a public relations problem for the leadership. Parties may grant leaders other sources of influence that can be used to structure choices. Standing committee and conference committee members may be appointed for the purpose of generating policy proposals that suit the party's collective goals, which might be achieved by packaging legislation in certain ways. Thus, whether directly through floor scheduling or indirectly through the appointment of, or influence over, other agenda setters, control over agenda setting is expected to be a highly prized capacity of majority parties in Congress.

Sinclair's argument is an important one that is not fully incorporated in other discussions of agenda setting and parties (Cox and McCubbins 2005). Agenda control by the majority party leadership not only helps the majority party establish a winning record that is useful for reelection, it also allows the majority party to diminish the severity of the tradeoffs it confronts when balancing electoral and policy objectives. These necessary tradeoffs are unlikely to be made in a satisfactory way unless skilled leaders give careful thought to them and are allowed to implement corresponding strategies.

The interdependence of parties' collective goals implies that even if party members are single-minded seekers of policy or reelection, as the single-goal theories assume, then fellow partisans share an interest in both collective goals. It appears that the assumption of multiple party goals is unavoidable, involves tradeoffs between the goals at times, and serves as a realistic basis for developing expectations about the influence of parties in floor voting.

CONCLUSION

An economist friend of mine complains about the way his discipline tends to favor theorizing and the indirect test of derived propositions over the direct question. He tells the story of an economist who notices that a neighbor is in the backyard with a flashlight and shovel in the middle of the night. He theorizes about the strange behavior and installs a rooftop camera to record the neighbor's behavior to test his ideas. One night, as he is powering up his expensive video system for the first time to start gathering data, the economist's daughter calls over to the neighbor and is told that a fishing trip is planned for the weekend and the neighbor needs night crawlers for bait.

Some political science on congressional politics seems to share the bias of economists in favoring theorizing and indirect tests over the direct question. I have advocated asking direct questions and building an enriched theory of congressional parties that more fully captures the strategic challenges that parties and their leaders confront. As we will see, the complexities of multiple goals create some indeterminacy in predicting party strategies. In my view, such indeterminacy is precisely what intraparty struggles over strategy are about. The purpose of our consideration of party goals and associated strategies has been to provide a foundation for understanding when and how parties may influence policy outcomes.

If we take seriously the electoral and policy interests of congressional parties, we must question how far single-goal accounts of parties can take us. There will be times when party leaders sacrifice policy objectives for electoral reasons and other times when well-established policy preferences seem to account for outcomes perfectly. There will be times when leaders insist that colleagues take an electoral risk in order to pass a priority element of the party's legislative program and other times when leaders make no effort to directly pressure legislators to vote their way. Internal fights in party leadership and committee chairmanship contests and on everyday legislative battles reflect the tradeoffs that legislative parties face. Party leaders, more than anyone else, are expected to address these tradeoffs.

Floor voting, the focus of most political science on party influence, is important but is only one of many activities to which parties and their leaders devote time and material resources. The public's evaluations of the president may affect legislators' electoral prospects and their willingness to support the president (Bond and Fleisher 1990; Kernell 1997), so party leaders are expected to advise the president in the interest of their congressional colleagues. Nonlegislative options, such as agency rule making and executive orders, for achieving policy objectives may be available and party leaders may seek to influence the executive branch in their use. And nonlegislative activity, such as work with campaign committees, public relations and fundraising organizations, and interest groups, long has been central to the pursuit of electoral goals. Once parties and leaders are in place, their efforts to achieve collective party goals range widely across the spectrum of political activity. Thus, party influence is likely to extend in directions seldom studied systematically by political scientists.

3

The Types and Sources of Party Influence

The image of Lyndon Johnson browbeating a Senate colleague into supporting the party is familiar to most members of Congress and to all students of congressional politics. From time to time, party leaders use force of personality, appeals for loyalty, strong-arm tactics, and threats to gain compliance from difficult-to-persuade colleagues. Johnson relied on the technique – the "Johnson treatment," it was called – more than other leaders, but pressuring individual legislators to gain pivotal support has a long history in Congress.

The political science literature is in a second phase. In the first phase, which ran into the 1970s, much of the political science research on Congress was a search for the direct influence of partisan forces on legislators' voting decisions. Unfortunately, while many stories can be told, and I will do some of that again in this chapter, finding systematic effects of this kind of party influence is unlikely and even contrary to expectation, at least for the most common approaches. Too few legislators on too few votes are involved for statistical estimates of this kind of party influence to show anything meaningful. I demonstrate this in the next chapter, where I consider old and new arguments that the old statistical findings are not trustworthy. In this chapter, I reestablish, if it is needed, the importance of this form of party influence in voting.

As both insiders and political scientists have observed, direct pressure on legislators hardly exhausts the forms that party influence may take. Equally or even more effective forms of party influence may be far more indirect. Recent literature, which can be considered a second phase in the study of party effects, has emphasized the role of party leaders in determining the form and content of legislation that is considered in committee and on the floor. The power to set the agenda is a potentially important type of indirect influence, but indirect influence can come in many forms. I consider these indirect forms in this chapter, too.

Understanding the forms that party influence may take is important for three reasons. First, existing accounts of party influence tend to emphasize direct or indirect influence and ignore the other – to the detriment of a realistic understanding of the way party leaders use their resources interactively. Second, the political forces causing variation in party influence over time may be relevant to one form of influence but not the other. Third, the methods required for measuring different forms of influence vary. I consider the first two issues in this chapter and leave the third for the next chapter.

PARTY INFLUENCE AT WORK

In late 2005, the editorial writers of a major newspaper opined, "The wheels wobble on the Republican legislative juggernaut, but they're staying on – at least for now. Passage of a budget plan in the House restored some sense of agenda-setting to a party set back in recent days on Alaska oil drilling and a deficit-control bill that would have cut deeper into assistance programs than the broader budget plan."[1] The observation was made just after the House passed a budget reconciliation bill on a 217–215 vote after delaying the vote for days because a majority could not be obtained initially. The episode bears some scrutiny because it illustrates important features of party influence.

The legislation at issue was a bill providing for about $50 billion in budget cuts (over five years), including cuts in funding for college student loans, Medicaid, child support enforcement, food stamps, and foster care programs. As the bill emerged from committee, the measure included provisions to allow oil drilling in the Arctic National Wildlife Refuge and outer continental shelf. Many of these cuts were unpopular with moderate Republicans. Under the direction of Speaker Dennis Hastert (R-IL), the oil drilling authorization was removed from the bill as it was being prepared for floor consideration. Nevertheless,

---

[1] "Politics Toning Down GOP Budget," *Buffalo News*, November 22, 2005, p. A8.

moderates resisted appeals to support the bill because of their continuing objections to cuts in some domestic programs. Conservatives complicated matters by objecting to the removal of oil drilling authorization provisions and threatening to vote against final passage. These objections left the Republican leadership without a majority just as they were about to take up the bill on the floor and the leadership abruptly postponed action. The failure to gain enough Republican votes to pass the bill was reported to be an embarrassment to President George Bush, who endorsed the budget cuts, and to the Republican House leadership.[2]

After several days of wrangling over provisions of the bill and pressuring individual legislators, the bill was returned to the floor with new provisions that the leadership believed would attract majority support. The roll-call vote on the budget measure, which occurred at 1:42 A.M. and took twelve minutes longer than the fifteen minutes officially allotted for a roll-call vote, may have proved more difficult than the leadership anticipated. A reporter for *Roll Call*, a Capitol Hill newspaper, described the action in the final minutes:

[The Republican] "no" votes helped ensure that when the 15-minute clock reached zero the budget measure was trailing by roughly a dozen votes. The GOP was soon able to gain ground, however, as some Republicans who hadn't voted finally registered their support and others switched their vote from no to yes, including Reps. Steve LaTourette (Ohio) and Wayne Gilchrest (Md.).

[Committee on] Resources Chairman Richard Pombo (R-Calif.), who was upset that the leadership removed the ANWR provision from the measure, held back his vote but eventually voted yes after conversing with Hastert and Rep. Tom DeLay (R-Texas).

When the tally was 215–215, Rep. Mark Kennedy (R-Minn.), who is running for Senate, walked up to the voting machine with Majority Leader Roy Blunt (R-Mo.) right behind him and voted aye to put the bill in the positive column.

---

[2] James Kuhnhenn, "GOP Rift in Congress Stymies Budget Priorities," *Buffalo News*, November 11, 2005, p. A9; Janet Hook and Richard Simon, "Shy Votes, GOP Puts Off Budget," *Los Angeles Times*, November 11, 2005, p. 15; Richard Simon and Joel Havemann, "Senate, House Differences Complicated Spending Bill," *Los Angeles Times*, November 19, 2004, p. A16; Steven T. Dennis, Susan Ferrechio, Liriel Higa, and Michael Teitelbaum, "Savings Bill Heads to Conference Battle," *CQ Weekly*, November 21, 2005, pp. 3128–9; Ben Pershing, "House Passes Budget Bill With Two-Vote Margin," *Roll Call*, November 18, 2005, p. 1; Jonathan Weisman, "Republicans in House Pass $50 Billion in Budget Cuts," *Washington Post*, November 19, 2005, p. A6.

Then, as the vote was about to close, Energy and Commerce Chairman Joe Barton (R-Texas) [who was unhappy with drilling provisions] ended a conversation with [fellow Texan and former Majority Leader Tom] DeLay and walked to the well to register his own yes vote. The move prompted hearty cheers from the Republican side.

Barton, who like Pombo was upset about the ANWR change, looked tired and unhappy after the vote, refusing to comment to reporters chasing him to the elevator.[3]

Central to this story were efforts to directly influence individual legislators and to control what was subject to a vote on the House floor. As the *Roll Call* and other accounts attest, leaders appeared to squeeze out the last few votes by direct personal appeals to a handful of legislators. We know that policy concessions were made to gain the support of some moderates, but the public record does not tell us much about the nature of the appeals made to the last few legislators whose votes tipped the balance.

As usual, the agenda-setting powers of the Speaker were left unstated in journalistic accounts of the budget battle. Speaker Hastert took the bill to, from, and back to the floor, modified its provisions, and limited floor amendments. This was done with the swift approval of the Rules Committee, whose majority party members he nominated. The special rules for both the initial and the renegotiated version included these provisions: "The amendment printed in the report of the Committee on Rules accompanying this resolution shall be considered as adopted. All points of order against provisions in the bill, as amended, are waived."[4] The provisions made the revised versions the text of the bill without a separate vote on any of them and protected them from points of order that they violated the standing rules of the House in some way. A majority of the House had to approve the special rules, but the initiative rested with the Speaker and his agents in the Rules Committee.

The 2005 episode illustrates two key features of party influence. First, direct and indirect influence – arm-twisting and agenda setting – were used in tandem. Political scientists are tempted to say that one is more important or more decisive than the other to legislative outcomes, but the budget battle suggests that it is difficult to make that call. Generally, direct influence is difficult for outsiders to view. It is seldom as

[3] Ben Pershing, "House Passes Budget Bill," p. 1.
[4] H. Res. 542 and H. Res. 560, 109th Congress.

visible as it was in the wee hours of that morning in 2005 and so is particularly difficult to gauge. And even in that episode no one questioned the Speaker's direct control over the majority party members of the Rules Committee whose support was essential to the tactical adjustments made throughout the process.

Second, the use of special rules to set the floor agenda was vital to the promotion of some policy proposals and the avoidance of others. On the negative side, the majority party leadership barred alternatives to the negotiated provisions from floor consideration. Thus, the members concerned about the negotiated provisions were assured that their agreement would not be picked apart on the floor. On the positive side, a package of $50 billion of cuts affecting dozens of programs in hundreds of ways was enacted without a separate vote on any of them. The negotiated provisions that concerned the moderate Republicans were among them. The negotiated provisions did not originate in a standing committee and were not favored by committee members, but were placed in the bill under the direction of the Speaker and packaged so as to prevent separate votes on them or other parts of the bill.

Plainly, the negative and positive uses of the Speaker's agenda power were not readily distinguishable. A basic tool of floor agenda setting in the House, a special rule from the Rules Committee, was used to bring the budget measure to the floor, package provisions in creative ways, add legislative matter that was not considered in committee, provide for the automatic adoption of amendments to legislation upon the adoption of the rule, prevent points of order that might be raised against bills under the standing rules and precedents of the House, and protect legislative provisions that otherwise would be amended on the floor.

Finally, political and procedural constraints on the exercise of agenda-setting powers limited the options of the majority party leadership. Withholding the legislation from floor action was not a viable option for the majority party. The budget-cutting bill – technically, a budget reconciliation bill – was ordered by a previous budget resolution, was a central part of the president's agenda, and could not readily have been avoided without serious consequences. In this case, it was essential to pass the budget cuts before the fiscal year became too old and to make room for the tax cuts, which, for political reasons, were planned for a subsequent bill (Republicans did not want tax cuts for the wealthy and program cuts for the poor to be in the same bill). Much important legislation is of this kind in the modern Congress. Budget and appropriations measures, defense and other reauthorization bills, trade agreement legislation, and other matters are considered must-pass measures that are sometimes given privileged status in statute or chamber rules. In other cases, the legislation is central to the president's program and critical to the party's reputation. Thus, for some legislation, withholding action because the majority party leadership might lose a vote is not a viable option, at least not for long. It is reasonable to speculate that direct influence becomes more important to party success as indirect influence, such as agenda control, becomes weaker.

The 2005 episode illustrates the possibility of distinguishing direct and indirect forms of influence, along with both negative and positive applications of influence. It also demonstrates that party leaders, as they seek to influence outcomes under political and institutional constraints, mix and match their assets to particular circumstances, often in a freewheeling fashion. In the remainder of this chapter, I use these distinctions among types of influence to explore how and when party influence is exercised.

DIRECT AND INDIRECT INFLUENCE

Legislative party influence, direct or indirect, exists when the strategies of party leaders and rank-and-file members yield behavior on the part of at least some rank-and-file members that is more supportive of the party than it would be otherwise. As I have implied, direct influence corresponds to "pressure," "arm-twisting," and "leveraging" members. The subjects of direct influence are aware of the incentives to comply with requests to support the party or its leaders. Incentives might be tangible considerations, such as committee assignments and chairmanships, favorable scheduling of legislation, and campaign assistance, or less tangible considerations, such as the promise of continued convivial relations with party colleagues.

Direct influence usually is targeted at individuals. It is retail, custom-tailored politics – designed with the individual's interests and vulnerabilities in mind. From time to time, direct influence may be brought to bear on groups or factions of legislators, such as a state delegation that covets a committee assignment or piece of legislation. Direct influence also is implicated when committee chairs are informed by leaders and other colleagues that party loyalty is expected from them in their management of committee affairs and on major issues. Generally, direct influence involves an exchange, maybe an implicit one, between party leaders and individual legislators in which the individual legislators provide support for the party that they would not provide without the incentive provided by the party and its leadership. The match of parties' resources to legislators' interests determines the level of leaders' potential direct influence.

Indirect influence is simply all nondirect or nonpersonal forms of influence. The means for exercising indirect influence includes a somewhat disparate set of activities. These include, among other things, motivating other political actors to influence legislators on behalf of the legislative party, serving in a third-party role for deals arranged among fellow partisans, and setting the agenda in a way that favors certain policy outcomes. This is such a wide range of activities that it is difficult to generalize about. It is important to note that the indirect influence of leaders may not be obvious to members whose choices are constrained or altered by the action of party leaders. In fact, the source of indirect influence often is deliberately hidden from those legislators who are the targets of it. Indirect influence is frequently targeted at the House and Senate as a whole or at groups of legislators. Wholesale, rather than retail, politics is most frequently involved.

Party leaders seek to influence the electoral calculations of fellow legislators through public relations campaigns and appearances in the mass media. "Message" efforts, often organized with task forces or committees of legislators and sometimes organized for particularly important legislative battles, are now standard features of party efforts. Furthermore, leaders work with lobbyists, campaign contributors, presidents, local party officials, and others to orchestrate pressure on colleagues.

An important form of party leaders' indirect influence is to facilitate bargaining among fellow partisans in numerous ways, such as by

- arranging for meetings that would not occur otherwise,
- offering incentives for colleagues to work together,
- offering compromises or logrolls that otherwise would not have been proposed, or
- offering incentives to colleagues to adhere to agreements they have made with each other.

In more technical terms, leaders reduce or compensate for the trans-action and opportunity costs associated with bargaining and enforce agreements (compromises and logrolls) among their colleagues.

Setting the agenda, the one kind of indirect influence that is given considerable attention by political scientists, may take several forms. The most commonly observed is manipulating the policy choices that are available for consideration on the floor by determining the bills to be considered and the rules under which bills are debated and amended. This form of influence over the agenda is most transparent in the House, where control over the Committee on Rules allows the majority lead-ership to determine the timing and content of special rules, resolutions that give legislation the right-of-way for floor consideration and set limits on debates and amendments (Bach and Smith 1988; Cox and McCubbins 2005; Sinclair 1983). More indirect forms include inducing others, such as standing or conference committee members, to approve, block, or otherwise structure the agenda in a favorable way.

The distinction between direct and indirect influence is not without ambiguity. Party leaders frequently work with presidents and lobbyists to devise a common strategy for influencing the behavior of rank-and-file legislators. More important, some forms of indirect influence are built upon or coincident with direct influence. The Speaker's ability to control the floor agenda relies on his power to recognize legislators to make motions (without appeal) and his control over the Rules Com-mittee. The right of recognition is important to controlling the floor agenda while also giving the Speaker the ability to do favors for legisla-tors who seek to gain or avoid floor action on certain bills. In the case of the Rules Committee, the Speaker's ability to nominate the majority party members of the committee gives him a source of direct influence with those members who sit on the committee or seek appointment to it, an influence that serves as the foundation for setting the floor agenda on major legislation that passes through that committee. More generally, the manipulation of coveted committee assignments may be used as a source of leverage with individual legislators and as a way to affect the composition of committees so as to shape the form in which key legislation emerges and sets the floor agenda.

Plainly, the direct and indirect forms of influence do not operate in separate worlds. Having strong sources of one form of influence is likely to give party leaders influence of the other form, too. It seems likely that the strength of direct influence and the strength of indirect influence are positively correlated and, to some extent, interdependent. Each is sometimes put in the service of the other. If so, a theory of party strategy that focused on one form of influence to the exclusion of the other would be missing a central feature of the legislative world that party leaders inhabit.

Still, because the sources of direct and indirect influence are not identical, the two forms are not fully equivalent or interchangeable. Leaders' influence over committee assignments, which is a source of direct influence over individual legislators, comes from party rules governing the committee assignment process. Their influence over the floor agenda, which is a source of indirect influence, originates, in the case of the House, in chamber rules that create and empower the Committee on Rules to write resolutions governing floor debate and get the resolutions considered on the floor, in a chamber precedent that gives the Speaker the authority to recognize members on the floor to make motions, and in party rules that give the top party leaders the authority to nominate members to Rules. Plainly, it is possible to improve leaders' resources in one category without a large, immediate effect in the other category. If so, then direct influence and indirect influence are likely to be positively but not perfectly correlated with each other.

Until recent studies, direct influence has been the focus of empirical studies. Generally, party influence was juxtaposed to other sources of direct influence, primarily constituency influence, but sometimes to the influence of personal ideology, other colleagues, interest groups, and presidents. I consider these empirical studies in Chapter 4. More recent studies account for agenda control but downplay the importance of sources of direct influence and other forms of indirect influence. I take up these studies in Chapter 5.

POSITIVE AND NEGATIVE INFLUENCE

Political scientists have noted the utility of distinguishing positive and negative forms of influence in the legislative arena. Negative power is the ability to defend the status quo in the face of a majority that favors change; positive power is the ability to change the status quo in the face of a majority that opposes change (Smith 1989). Negative power usually involves preventing a decisive vote on a bill that would

TABLE 3.1. *Types of Party Influence*

	Direct	Indirect
Positive	X	
Negative		X

receive majority support. "Gatekeeping" is the term often applied to committees to reflect this form of indirect influence. It also may involve the application of direct influence to win votes against the passage of bills or amendments that would otherwise lead to a change in the policy status quo. Positive power includes the ability to force a vote on a particular proposal, as when a conference committee tucks new provisions to a bill that will not receive a separate vote later in either parent chamber. It includes the ability to protect bills from amendments, as when a bill is considered on the House floor under special rules limiting amendments or under suspension of the rules. Or it may simply involve buying votes by offering side payments (that is, special considerations unrelated to the policy at issue) to a few legislators to muster a majority in favor of a bill.

In principle, direct and indirect influence can be exercised for both negative and positive purposes. Four categories of influence are possible, as shown in Table 3.1, with most studies emphasizing either the direct, positive form (upper left) for majority party leaders or, more recently, the indirect, negative form (lower right), particularly agenda control. We must account for the full array of possibilities to accurately capture the nature of party influence on legislative outcomes.[5]

Two stories illustrate the importance of considering the empty cells in Table 3.1. Direct influence may play a role in preventing a policy proposal from getting a vote on the floor of the House of Representatives (lower-left cell in Table 3.1). In 1994, the House majority leadership prevented a measure to change the House rules from coming to a vote. At stake was a budget deficit reduction bill called the "A-to-Z" bill after its chief sponsors, Robert Andrews (D-NJ) and Bill Zeliff (R-NH).

---

[5] Recent theories of congressional parties vary in their emphases. Cartel theory emphasizes indirect, negative party influence in the form of restricting the floor agenda (Cox and McCubbins 2005). Conditional party government accounts give greater emphasis to positive, direct influence (Aldrich et al. 2002), as do most of the accounts discussed in Chapter 4.

Sponsored by a majority of the House, most minority party Republicans and some Democrats, the bill would guarantee every member the right to offer floor amendments that would reduce spending in any federal program. The leadership of the majority party Democrats opposed the bill because it would undermine their ability to set the floor agenda. The chief sponsors of the bill filed a discharge petition, which requires 218 signatures to force floor action on a bill, but were unable to persuade at least 33 of the cosponsors to sign the petition.

Press accounts, confirmed by subsequent systematic analysis (Binder et al. 1999), indicate that Democrats were persuaded by their leadership not to sign the petition. Leaders pursued extensive negotiations with key legislators and factions whose support of the leaders' position was in doubt. Only after agreeing to bring up a separate entitlement reform bill did the Democratic leadership persuade wayward party colleagues not to sign the discharge petition.[6] The majority party leadership, it turned out, was compelled to bargain, make personal appeals and concessions, and use positive agenda-setting tools to prevent discharge. Direct influence and a promise to approve floor action on a new bill were required to prevent discharge of the A-to-Z bill.

An illustration of indirect influence enabling the enactment of legislation that otherwise would be killed (upper-right cell in Table 3.1) is the strategic use of packaging. An everyday strategy on Capitol Hill is to package into larger bills provisions that would not gain approval by both houses or the president as stand-alone measures. In the House, a packaged measure can be protected by a special rule, written under the direction of the leadership, that bars or limits floor amendments related to the unpopular provisions as long as a majority of the House supports the special rule. In the Senate, packaging provisions in reconciliation bills, which are considered under time limits set in law, protects the measures from filibusters that might otherwise arise. And a president, who cannot veto individual provisions in bills, may be persuaded to sign a large bill that includes provisions he dislikes.

Plainly, studies that focus on direct influence with a positive effect and studies that emphasize indirect influence with a negative effect do not exhaust common applications of party leaders' influence.

---

[6] "Up and Down the Hill: Showtime in the Magic Budget Kingdom," *National Journal,* June 25, 1994.

SOURCES OF PARTY INFLUENCE

To this point, I have failed to be systematic in my discussion of the *sources* of party influence on legislative outcomes, whether the influence is direct or indirect, positive or negative. In the remainder of this chapter, I turn to the factors that may cause party influence to vary. I suggest that we can gain a better understanding of the forces at play by keeping in mind the distinction between types of influence. Political science has generated a wealth of propositions and hunches about the forces that condition the strength of party influence in voting, but little of it is guided by the differences between types of influence. I attempt to be somewhat more systematic about that here.

The conceptualization of party influence represented in Table 3.1 provides guidance about the changes in the environment of congressional policymaking that may increase or decrease party influence. Party influence flows from (a) incentives (rewards and punishments) the leaders can use to acquire the support of legislators, (b) incentives (rewards and punishments) that others can use to acquire the support of legislators on behalf of party interests, and (c) agenda-setting powers that enable leaders to pass (or block) legislation that would otherwise fail (or pass). The sources of change in potential party influence reside either in the resources of party leaders or in factors that determine legislators' susceptibility to the incentives offered. Leaders' resources originate in chamber or caucus rules. Legislators' susceptibility to influence is rooted in their personal political goals and the relevance of leadership resources to them, which may vary over time. Here I focus on the resources of party leadership. These resources vary widely across the House and Senate and across the majority and minority parties. They also have varied widely over time.

Because many sources of influence, such as party leaders' control of committee assignments, may be used for both negative and positive purposes, there is no tidy way to organize a discussion of the changing sources of negative and positive influence. I organize the discussion under the headings of direct and indirect influence and incorporate discussion of positive and negative uses in each section. I then turn to the external developments that might drive internal changes in the role of parties. We will see that many of these developments affect both direct and indirect forms of influence.

Sources of Direct Influence

Congressional party leaders have a few resources at their disposal that provide direct political benefits to their colleagues and can be used to reward loyalty and punish disloyalty. Moreover, parties have developed organizational capacities to assist leaders in identifying targets for and applying direct influence. The incentives at the disposal of leaders have waxed and waned over the decades, but the organizational capabilities of leaders show a more linear, cumulative pattern.

Group Identity

Before turning to tangible incentives that party leaders can offer as incentives for cooperation, it pays to note a feature of party life in Congress that scholars have recognized as important: Supporting the party appears to be a default voting strategy for most legislators. Scholars Charles O. Jones (Jones 1961) and David Truman (Truman 1959), studying the mid–twentieth century Congress, observed a widespread proclivity to support the party line when other significant pressures were not present, creating a significant baseline of support for the party. Studies offer at least three distinct stories about the origin of this minimum level of partisanship.

First, legislators may arrive in Congress with a strong psychological identification with their parties. Many of them have long experience working for and within their parties in their home states, state legislatures, and elsewhere. This is reinforced in everyday life with their party colleagues on Capitol Hill. A disposition to "go along" with the party position, in the absence of other influences, is the product. Identification with party colleagues creates the opportunity for "peer pressure," which political scientists may overlook but legislators do not. Barber Conable (R-NY), once the senior Republican on the Committee on Ways and Means, observes that "peer group pressure is of considerably greater significance than presidential blandishments."[7] Leaders exploit legislators' predispositions by frequently appealing to party loyalty when soliciting votes (Kingdon 1973; Ripley 1967).

Second, legislators often look to fellow partisans for guidance when they cast votes on the floor. Because legislators cannot make themselves

---

[7] Quoted in Martin Tolchin, "When Members Change Their Votes," *New York Times*, September 22, 1982, p. A24.

well informed on all of the issues on which they must cast votes, they must look to trusted colleagues for cues about how to vote without making a political or substantive mistake. Familiar colleagues, such as fellow partisans from the same state or sitting on the relevant committee, are natural sources of advice. These are the colleagues who are most likely to be trusted, have useful expertise, and share the same political background. Members of Congress can be observed consulting with colleagues or, in the House, scanning the electronic voting board, before stepping up to vote (Fiellin 1962; Kessel 1964; Kingdon 1973; Matthews and Stimson 1975; Truman 1956).

Third, leaders are proactive in the efforts to earn the personal support of their party colleagues. In fact, most leaders won their posts by gaining the confidence of their party colleagues. Hardly any account of leaders' success fails to emphasize the importance of developing strong personal bonds with colleagues. Socializing, learning about the personal and family interests, doing small favors, and deploying old-fashioned charm help a leader build a reservoir of goodwill with colleagues that works to the party's advantage. Personal persuasiveness can be important, too (Caro 2002).

We have no systematic evidence that the default level of partisanship varies over time, although it is reasonable to speculate that it does. In recent decades, congressional observers have noted changes in identification with parties generally, the rise of candidate-centered rather than party-run campaigns, the intensification of lobbying and increasing burdens of fundraising from special interests, and the decline of camaraderie among legislators as they spend less time with each other. These developments seem likely to reduce the base level of partisanship we observe among legislators.

Tangible Incentives

Party leaders lack the control and command over their fellow partisans that we often see elsewhere in the world of legislatures. In the case of the U.S. Congress, leaders cannot strip legislators of their membership in the legislative party caucus or deny them a place on the ballot in the next election, as can party leaders in many other national parliaments. The assets of leaders are not as likely to be decisive factors in the calculations of rank-and-file legislators as are control over ballot access and caucus membership in other systems.

Nevertheless, it would be foolish to argue that congressional leaders are without tools with which to influence their colleagues. Leaders' assets for direct influence may vary over time, vary in effectiveness among their party colleagues, and vary in relevance across the issues and stages in the legislative process. Moreover, the assets are likely to be applied in ways that are difficult to observe – either as a general threat for disloyal legislators, lingering in the unspoken background of legislative battles, or targeted, often privately, at a few individuals whose support is required to muster majorities for or against specific parliamentary motions.

An asset for direct influence in which these features are visible is committee assignments. Committee assignments have great value for most legislators and probably are the most valuable institutional benefit that the average legislator receives (Bullock 1976; Deering and Smith 1983; Fenno 1973; Maltzman 1997; Shepsle 1978). An assignment to a committee with jurisdiction over legislation important to a member's home constituency or to well-financed special interests may be important to the member's reelection prospects. The issues within the jurisdictions of committees often are of personal interest to legislators. In some cases, the committee is so important to most legislators that its members have special influence and prestige within the chamber. Because their colleagues value committee assignments, party leaders who exercise special influence over the allocation of assignments have an asset that generates direct influence. The value of any particular committee assignment is probably smaller in the Senate than in the House because, in the smaller Senate, legislators receive more assignments and have more opportunities for meaningful participation on the floor (Smith and Deering 1990). Consequently, the potential leverage a leader may gain from manipulation of committee assignments is likely to be greater in the House than in the Senate.

Leaders' influence over committee assignments has varied over time. In late nineteenth-century House, Speakers appointed committees, taking the list provided by the minority leader for minority party members and using their own discretion in naming majority party colleagues to committees. Both Democratic and Republican Speakers used the authority to advantage (Follett 1909), particularly after the Civil War when two-party system emerged. In the 1870s, Speaker James G. Blaine (R-ME), with a divided party, designated committee chairs and appointed committees to make certain that they would report legislation on the party agenda. Members who proved to be trustworthy were given the important committee assignments; others were appointed to committees that did nothing. His successors followed suit.

The manipulation of committee assignments by Republican Speaker "Uncle Joe" Cannon (R-IL), who served as Speaker from 1903 to 1911, produced serious objections from the progressive faction within his own party and contributed to a revolt in 1909 and 1910 that reduced the power of the Speaker in several ways (more on this later). Cannon had deposed committee chairs and reassigned other legislators on a scale that had not been seen before (Chiu 1928). Democrats, as they had promised in the 1910 campaign that produced a new Democratic majority in the House, moved the power to make committee assignments for the party's members on the Committee on Ways and Mean, thereby creating a new committee on committees for the party. Republicans created a separate committee on committees in 1917 (Brown 1922). These developments undermined the Speaker's unilateral control of committee assignments.

As a result of moves made to strengthen the hand of top leaders in granting committee assignments and to increase the accountability of legislators to their parties, modern House party leaders now play a major role in their parties' committees on committees. In 1974, liberal Democrats, led by Richard Bolling (D-MO), who openly advocated a stronger speakership and more party discipline (Bolling 1974), persuaded their caucus to transfer responsibility for committee assignments from Ways and Means Committee Democrats to a revitalized Steering and Policy Committee. The Steering and Policy Committee was chaired by the party leader and included several party leaders and elected representatives of regional groups. The result was a committee assignment process led and directly influenced by the Speaker (Ray and Smith 1983).

Until 1994, House Republicans gave each medium and large state with any Republican members a representative on their committee on committees with votes equal to the number of Republicans from that state; small states were represented collectively. In 1994, the Republicans assigned five votes to the top party leader and two votes to the second-ranking leader, and one vote to all other members, including other ex officio party leaders, with the collective leadership vote total constituting 25 percent of the vote total. In multilegislator contests for coveted committee assignments, the leadership vote is essential to success.

Appointments to the House Committee on Rules are a special case because of the committee's important role in approving resolutions, special rules, that structure floor debate on major legislation. The committee, created in 1880 in its modern form, was chaired and appointed by the Speaker until the revolt against Speaker Cannon in 1910 led to the adoption of a rule prohibiting the Speaker from membership on Rules and providing for direct election of the committee by the House, making the appointments to Rules subject to the same party-based committee on committees process as other committees. That remained the case until the early 1970s, when the majority party Democrats gave their top leader the authority to nominate the party's members for Rules. Republicans followed suit a few years later. Since that time, the Rules Committee has been considered a "leadership committee," even called the "Speaker's committee," reflecting the Speaker's control of majority party members of the committee.

Committee chairmanships also were at stake in the changes in House party practices and rules. The revolt against Cannon left nominations for standing committee chairmanships to the committee on committees, which observed seniority in preparing committee lists. In the 1970s, House Democrats made committee chairs stand for reelection in the party caucus, which created the opportunity for deposing several chairs and putting all others on notice that the party expected cooperation from committee leaders on important legislation. Democratic Speakers did not personally engage in threats to committee chairs, but there is evidence the committee chairs became more supportive of party policy positions after the new process was adopted (Crook and Hibbing 1985). House Republicans followed the Democrats' lead in allowing separate votes on ranking committee leaders and in 1992 set six-year term limits on committee chairs. The term limits were made a House rule after the Republicans gained a majority in the 1994 elections. Terms limit stimulate frequent contests for committee leadership posts and create a powerful incentive for committee leaders and prospective leaders to cater to the interests of fellow partisans. Explicit warnings to committee leaders have been expressed within majority party caucuses in both houses from time to time since the 1970s (Lawrence and Smith 1997; Smith 1982).

Senate parties lagged behind House parties in strengthening the hand of leaders in naming committees. Senate Democrats have not changed their mechanism for appointing members to standing committees since 1845 – election by a steering committee of one to two dozen senators, each with one vote, who are appointed by the floor leader (Gamm and Smith 1998, 2000). Some Democratic leaders, such as Lyndon Johnson (D-TX), were known for their aggressiveness in appointing friendly senators to the committee and in influencing individual assignment decisions, but even the leader's influence is limited by the tradition of allowing senators appointed to the steering committee to continue to sit on the committee for as long as they like. In moving to guarantee even junior senators a top committee assignment (referred to as the Johnson rule), Johnson created appointment opportunities for himself but limited his successors degrees of freedom.

Senate Republicans also created a committee on committees at an early point. They experienced a period of quite centralized allocation of assignments at the turn of the twentieth century when its committee on committees was dominated by a group of senior leaders working in consort to control the composition of the major committees. The group, centered in Nelson Aldrich (R-RI) and William Allison (R-IA), the latter being the caucus chair who appointed the committee on committees, dominated Senate Republican caucus affairs for nearly a decade starting in the mid-1890s. No single senator, however, dominated the process; the Senate Republicans did not have a regular floor leader at the time. Since then, Republicans have resolved conflicting requests for assignments by applying seniority as the decisive criterion. The result is that the Republican committee sometimes has not even met to ratify the decisions. The leader exercised little influence when seniority is applied in a ministerial fashion, usually by staff. Leaders could encourage more senior senators to apply for certain assignments, but their influence generally was marginal. In 2004, Senate Republicans adopted, by a vote with a one-vote margin, a rule that allows their floor leader to appoint at least half of the members of the top committees – Appropriations, Armed Services, Finance, and Foreign Relations. Proponents of the change described their purpose of enhancing the influence of the leader with individual senators, a lesson they drew from their House experiences.[8]

To review, the influence of top party leaders over committee assignments and chairmanships were strong at the turn of the twentieth century, weak during most of the twentieth century, and, in the case of the House Democrats, strengthened in the early 1970s when liberals asserted themselves. Leadership control over assignments is now much stronger in the House than the Senate, where direct leadership involvement is of very recent vintage, enhanced only for one party, and limited to a fraction of all committee assignments.

Tangible incentives come in many other forms, although few are as important as committee assignments to most legislators. Appointments to conference committees, party task forces, minor party positions, commissions, and foreign travel delegations are valued by legislators and so can be used to reward loyalists. As the party organizations have become more elaborate, the number of these appointments has increased. And leaders have become increasingly involved in colleagues' campaigns – attending fundraising events, directing the allocation of party campaign dollars, providing contributions of their own, and, in a few cases, intervening in local politics to discourage primary challenges to incumbent colleagues.[9] Particularly noteworthy about the broad but fragmented incentives that leaders draw upon is that they have increased in supply in recent decades. In contrast to the cycling on and off and on again, as for control of committee assignments, many discretionary favors and appointments that current leaders deploy are of recent vintage. Assignments to committees and chairmanships may remain more important than other incentives for good behavior, but leaders have a broader range of incentives now than at any other time.

Implementation

Leaders have acquired organizational support to assist them in exploiting their assets for influencing legislators. Whips were initially appointed to assist the top leaders in ensuring the attendance

---

[8] Mark Preston, "Frist Gains Committee Appointment Power," *Roll Call*, November 18, 2004; Carl Hulse, "Larger Majorities and the Itch to Stretch G. O. P. Muscles," *New York Times*, November 19, 2004, p. 18.

[9] Damon Chappie, "GOP Leaders Try to Quash Primary Challenge to Kelly," *Roll Call*, July 1, 1996, p. 7.

of legislators on important votes. Over time, with the assistance of
party staff, whips began to aid leaders in identifying how fellow partisans were likely to vote, monitor floor activity and substitute for floor
leaders, distribute scheduling information and communicate persuasive messages to colleagues, and work with administration officials
and lobbyists to apply pressure on legislators. The whip systems and
staffs grew by leaps and bounds in the last half of the twentieth century.
The appointment of assistant whips not only enhanced the capabilities
of the leadership, it also provided a means to reward loyal colleagues
with appointed positions in the leadership hierarchy.

The first formally designated House Republican whip was appointed
in 1897 by the Speaker, followed by appointment of the first House
Democratic whip and assistant whip by the floor leader in 1900. Whips
quickly acquired offices in the Capitol, were allowed to hire one or two
staff assistants, and, at several points in the first half of the twentieth
century, appointed colleagues as assistant whips. By 1963, the Republican whip had a deputy whip, three regional whips, and twelve assistant whips and the Democratic whip had a deputy whip, six appointed
assistant whips, and twelve regionally elected zone whips. By the turn
of the twenty-first century, the Republican system had grown to a
chief deputy whip, seventeen appointed deputy whips, and nearly fifty
regionally elected assistant whips. Democrats had as many as seven
chief deputy whips, twelve deputy whips, and seventy at-large whips,
all appointed, along with twenty-four regionally elected whips (Brown
1922; Galloway 1969; MacNeil 1963; Ripley 1964; Sinclair 1995b;
Smith and Gamm 2002; Smith et al. 2006).

Whips and other party operatives may exaggerate their importance,
but there is some systematic evidence and plenty of circumstantial evidence that, at least from time to time, they are important to the effective application of direct influence (Burden and Frisby 2004; Dodd
and Sullivan 1981; Ripley 1964; Sinclair 1981b). An example is a 2005
account by Sen. Trent Lott (R-MS) about his time, years earlier, as the
House Republican whip. At the time, Lott and his fellow minority party
partisans needed to win the votes of a few majority party Democrats
to carry their president's program through the House. Lott explains:

To pass the Reagan agenda – particularly the foundation legislation for what
became known as Reaganomics – I recruited a young and gung-ho team of

seventeen deputy whips and carefully trained them to wring votes out of the frostiest of Democrats. But first we took our targets apart and put them back together again. We psychoanalyzed them and studied their congressional lives to the nth degree. We identified their friends and enemies, located their key supporters back home, tracked their voting records back to the day they'd first set foot in the House, and put their political philosophies under a microscope...

My first deputy, Dave Emery, was something of a computer whiz, and he skillfully programmed every member of the House of Representatives into our database... I kept the computer in the small whip room just off the floor. Any of us in the whip operation could dash in and, say, call up a given congressman from Pennsylvania, and look at his voting records, the names of his big contributors and supporters, or the economic strength of his district – how much of it depended on manufacturing, on agriculture, on defense spending. For instance, when we were trying to pass the bill to allow President Reagan to post Pershing cruise missiles in Western Europe, we learned that some key backers of three local congressmen had graduated from the U.S. Military Academy at West Point. We talked these pro-defense, pro-Reagan politicos into calling the local representatives they had bankrolled and talking them into voting with us. (Lott 2005)

The former whip goes on in this vein at greater length. It is noteworthy that party influence was applied to opposition partisans, a possibility seldom addressed in political science accounts of party influence.

The first Senate whips were appointed later than the first House whips and the whip systems remain much smaller organizations in the smaller Senate. The first Senate whips were appointed in 1913 for the Democrats and 1915 for the Republicans. Senate whips gained Capitol office space in the 1950s. Deputy, or assistant, whips were first appointed in late 1960s. Deputy and assistant whips have numbered as many as a dozen or more in a few Congresses since then, but three or four deputy and assistant whips is more typical (Huitt 1961; Oleszek 1985; Ritchie 1998; Smith and Gamm 2002). With few exceptions, Senate deputy whips do little for the leadership. Instead, staff and bill managers assist the top two leaders in head counts and other party business.

Party staff personnel are difficult to count but the budgets allocated to party leadership and party committee offices are good surrogates (Figure 3.1). After the Legislative Reorganization Act authorized new party organs, legislative appropriations bills began to provide annual funding for party leadership staffs. Since the 1960s, these staffs grew

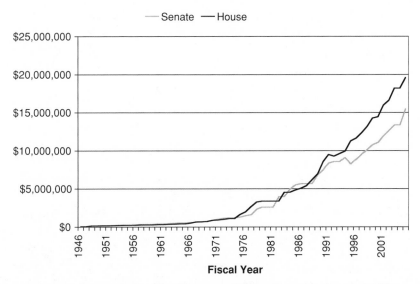

FIGURE 3.1. Appropriations for House and Senate Party Leaders and Offices, 1946–2005.

very rapidly, in part because new leadership posts were created but primarily because most leaders expanded their office operations.

Sources of Indirect Influence

The written rules of the House and Senate, a few statutes, and the rules of the congressional parties assign formal powers that leaders may exploit on behalf of their parties. In the modern Congress, leaders play a direct role in setting legislative priorities and scheduling legislation for floor consideration; proposing changes in the rules of their chambers; assigning their colleagues to standing committees, commissions, and party committees and task forces; overseeing the staff administrators of their chambers; and receiving official notices and briefings from the executive branch. These functions were acquired or assigned to leaders over many decades. Some of these functions give leaders control, or at least strong influence, over decisions that are valued by their colleagues and therefore can be used selectively to create incentives for cooperative behavior.

The formal rules of the House and Senate were not fixed in the first Congress. To the contrary, the two houses, using their constitutional authority to determine their own rules for proceedings, quickly evolved different rules. The House, which grew quickly in size and workload and assumed responsibility for initial action of legislation, developed more formal procedures to lend order to its proceedings and frequently changed its rules. These changes may be the product of changes in the composition of parties, as I discuss in a later section, but they may outlast the change in partisan circumstances that produced them and ultimately have an independent effect on party influence (Cooper and Brady 1981). The Senate, in contrast, seldom changed its basic rules, often because a minority could prevent a vote on resolutions to effect the change. As a result, the formal rules of the two houses are different in important ways – ways that may influence the form that party influence is most likely to take.

For the period since the modern two-party system of Democrats–Republicans emerged in the mid–nineteenth century, the procedural history of the House can be divided into four eras or regimes. The first House regime is the period between the Civil War in 1865 and the start of the period of strong House speakers in early 1889 with the election of Speaker Thomas Reed. During this period, the majority party struggled to get House action on much of its legislation, in part because of successful minority obstructionism. The regime of strong speakers begins with the election of Reed as speaker in 1889 and the adoption of the "Reed Rules" in 1890, and continues until the revolt against Speaker Joseph "Uncle Joe" Cannon in 1909–1910. The rules proposed by Speaker Thomas Reed ended disappearing quorums by allowing the speaker to count members on the floor, reduced the quorum in the Committee of the Whole to 100, prohibited dilatory motions, and changed the order of business to advantage standing committees. These rules, combined with the practice of using the Rules Committee to write special orders that began in 1883, gave the Speaker considerable influence over the floor agenda. The 1910 revolt led to the creation of Calendar Wednesday to ease committee access to the floor, guaranteed opponents to legislation a motion to recommit before votes on final passage, barred the Speaker from serving on the Rules Committee, stripped the Speaker of his ability to appoint the Rules Committee and other committees, and created a discharge rule by which a House majority could force floor action on a bill. The reforms affecting the Rules Committee were the most important and lasting because they separated the

Speaker from the committee that had direct responsibility for setting the floor agenda on major legislation.

The third House institutional regime extends from 1910 until the early 1970s, a period in which the Speaker's control of the floor agenda was constrained. During most of the twentieth century, the Speaker was a servant of the committees, had limited influence over the Rules Committee, and, for the Democrats, did not sit on the committee on committees that made committee assignments for the party. The "postreform" regime began with Democratic caucus reforms in the early 1970s that gave the Speaker the power to nominate Rules Committee members, made the Speaker the head of the party's committee on committees, and granted the Speaker the power to refer legislation to multiple committees. At the same time, House reforms weakened the influence of full committee chairs. The postreform regime of greater power for the Speaker continued under Republican majorities of the 1990s and early 2000s.

Worthy of special notice is that House reforms associated with the 1909–1910 revolt against Speaker Cannon and the early 1970s response to a conservative power structure involved both the direct and indirect influence of the Speaker. In the earlier period, the Speaker lost both his ability to manipulate committee assignments to reward friends and punish enemies and his control over the floor agenda through the Rules Committee. In the latter period, he regained a strong hand in committee assignments while he took charge of the Rules Committee. Direct and indirect influence, hand in hand, were viewed by legislators as tandem sources of the Speaker's power.

Senate procedures were different from those of the House in important ways from an early point and, consequently, the procedural path taken by the Senate is not parallel with the path of the House (Binder 1997; Roberts and Smith Forthcoming). The Senate path does not involve the substantial changes in majority party leadership agenda-setting power that were experienced in the House. The reason is that the Senate minority generally can prevent a vote on any new rule that enhances the influence of the majority party leadership. Still, three periods can be distinguished for the Senate.

The first period, the pre-1917 regime, ends with the adoption of Rule 22, which created the cloture mechanism permitting a two-thirds majority of senators voting to force a vote on a measure. Prior to 1917, a small number of senators could retain control of the floor and prevent a vote (a single senator would eventually tire and be forced to give up the floor). The effect of the Rule 22 was to specify a two-thirds majority as the threshold for cloture whenever a limit to debate is sought. Rule 22 was adopted soon after the Senate parties elaborated their leadership positions (Gamm and Smith 2002). Not until Sen. Joe Robinson (D-AR) became majority leader in 1933 did the Senate's majority leader assume the full range of modern leadership responsibilities – constructing unanimous consent agreements, monitoring the floor, serving as party spokesman, and so on. Soon thereafter the majority leader gained the right of first recognition on the floor. The developments ended the interim regime and initiated the modern regime in which the majority leader assumed responsibility for the Senate's agenda and had modest tools with which to attempt to do so. Although the Senate adopted changes in Rule 22 in 1949 and 1975, no significant chamber or party rule changes altered the formal agenda-setting powers of party leaders since the 1930s.

External Forces: Party Regimes, Electoral Coalitions, and Presidents

Many scholars argue persuasively that the character of the partisan environment external to Congress influences the nature of partisan activity internal to Congress. Whole books can, and have been, written on how the congressional environment has changed and influenced American politics. For recent decades, extensive commentary on campaigns, lobbying and the interest group community, congressional districting, and the polarization of political elites is available elsewhere. Here, I focus on those features of the environment that directly shape the powers of party leaders in Congress over the longer term.

Party Regimes

Legislators arrive in Congress having mastered, to a substantial degree, the challenges of nomination and election. They have found ways to attract votes, manage the multiple interests of their constituencies, and adapt to or overcome obstacles to election presented by their local parties. Legislators' expectations of their congressional parties, it is reasonable to suppose, are influenced by how they have navigated local political waters. The margin election victories, the nature of policy commitments made, the role of local and state party organizations in their nomination and elections, and other factors may influence what they need from, and their willingness to sacrifice for, their legislative parties. Widespread change in the mix of political forces in legislators' districts and states may produce systematic change in legislators' relationships to their legislative parties.

The rise and fall of state party machines in the late nineteenth and early twentieth centuries reflect significant changes in the party relationships legislators imported to Congress. According to Rothman (1966, 159–90), the Senate of the period was dominated by the rise of professional politicians running state party machines. Patronage-oriented Republican parties, sometimes with heavy financial backing of major economic interests, came to dominate state and local governments and the selection of legislators in the decades following the Civil War. As the Civil War generation passed away, the new breed of "party men" populated that Senate, where they continued the struggle to control patronage and support the interests that funded their home party organizations. Legislators were beholden to local party leaders and benefactors, and often were the top leaders themselves. They placed a high value on teamwork to control government appointments and public policies, such as tariffs, that were vital to local economic interests. In Rothman's view, these senators "were devoted to the exercise of power" and "were willing to pay obeisance in order to share in it" (190). While senators often led their state parties, Rothman's argument about the local political milieu fits representatives as well as senators.[10]

Democratic party machines did not emerge in most southern and new western states (Rothman 1966). In the one-party South, deep factionalism often surfaced between those advocating industrial progress and those adhering to traditional ways. The factionalism constrained the development of hierarchically ordered machines. In the new western states, populism undermined the emergence of machines.

The power of Republican state parties and the interests that backed them was undercut by the political reforms that were implemented

---

[10] The significant differences between the regions in the strength of party machines is largely neglected by Rothman (Shefter 1983), although he surely is right to emphasize the east and south in describing national politics in the decades immediately following the Civil War.

over a period of more than two decades and by the eventual election of progressives who advocated the reforms. In the 1890s, ballot reform, which introduced the Australian ballot in most states, reduced the frequency of straight-ticket voting and encouraged candidates to develop an identity independent of their parties. The old-party list ballots encouraged voters to cast ballots with the most important office in mind, which left candidates to depend on the parties and top leaders to conduct campaigns (Albright 1942; Katz and Sala 1996; Ludington 1911). Beginning in the early 1890s, states began to adopt mechanisms that translated popular will into senator selections by state legislators. Then the direct primary, which determined which major party candidates would be placed on the general election ballot, was adopted by all states during the first two decades of the twentieth century. Other reforms, such as civil service and nonpartisan commission reforms, voter registration requirements, and initiative, referenda, and recall procedures, were adopted during these decades to reduce the influence of party machines. By the time the Seventeenth Amendment providing for popular election of senators was adopted and implemented in the 1910s, the grip of state parties and associated industrial and financial interests on elected officials had been weakened considerably. Thus, the bonds between members of Congress and state parties that became strong in the late nineteenth century loosened again in the early twentieth century as the effect of progressive reforms was realized.

If Rothman is right, party voting should have been strong in the last two or three decades of the nineteenth century, and continued to be strong into the twentieth century, when, beyond the period about which he wrote, party voting would have declined. His argument applies to both parties – both had party machines backed by major economic interests. We might wonder whether the state parties were strong everywhere – they certainly were not equally strong (Shefter 1983) – and we know that states adopted progressive reforms at different times. Therefore, legislators are likely to vary in the strength and timing of change in their state–party connections. Still, Rothman's argument is that developments in state party politics had a pervasive effect on Congress, where the key issues of the tariff and currency brought the same economic and partisan interests that dominated state politics to bear on the membership.

The progressive reforms altered the role of state and local parties in electing members of Congress in fundamental ways. At a time when serving a career was becoming more attractive because of the prominence of federal policy and improvements in transportation made travel to and from Washington, D.C., less troublesome, the reforms made campaigns more candidate-centered and less party-centered. Party endorsements and support remained valuable, even essential in many places, but the iron grip of local parties was loosened considerably. In the second half of the twentieth century, the rise of modern media campaigns, campaign consultants, and polling further reduced reliance on parties and strengthened the independence of most candidates for Congress (Agranoff 1972; Nimmo 1970; Sabato 1981). Late in the century, parties regained some footing in campaigns by more aggressively recruiting, funding, and training candidates, but candidates continued to organize their own campaigns with parties remaining as service organizations in most places.

Electoral Coalitions
The most widely cited account of the ebb and flow of party influence is an essay by Cooper and Brady (1981) on the determinants of party voting in the House. The source of partisan voting patterns in Congress, in the Cooper–Brady argument, lies in the electorate. When a party's legislators are elected from states and districts with similar policy interests, the legislators will vote alike on the House and Senate floors. Put differently, the degree of homogeneity in the electoral coalition determines the legislative party's cohesiveness. When the other party has a homogeneous electoral coalition but with opposing interests, the legislative parties will exhibit polarized voting behavior in Congress. Homogeneous parties, in turn, empower strong leaders with more direct and indirect influence, to use my terms. Leaders' influence reinforces the cohesiveness of the party to produce more disciplined voting on the floor. If partisan differences weaken in the electorate and in Congress, the formal powers of party leaders are pared back and policy making becomes more decentralized. Similar arguments are offered by Brady and colleagues about the Senate (Brady et al. 1989; Brady and Epstein 1997).

The translation of electoral coalition polarization into congressional party polarization and stronger leadership is a process emphasized by other scholars (Rohde 1991, Sinclair 1983, 1995b). The perspective is now recognized as *conditional party government* (CPG) (Aldrich et al. 2002). We might call the theory the "Polarization-Plus Theory" to capture the idea that increasing polarization yields increasing returns for the majority party because its leaders gain more influence as the congressional parties become more polarized. Most members of the majority party benefit from improved coordination and the exercise of direct and indirect influence by leaders who aggressively employ the resources and procedural tools granted them.

Presidents

During most of the twentieth century and to the present, it appears to me, it is very difficult to separate presidential and party influence for the president's party in Congress. Analytically, we can distinguish presidential and legislative party influence from each other, but, as a practical matter, a president and party leaders of the president's party are likely to seek to influence legislative outcomes in mutually compatible ways and, typically, with an explicit sense of teamwork. A legislative victory is a win for the presidential party team. Unfortunately, while there is substantial literature on presidents and Congress, most of the political science of "party effects" ignores the president. Party effects may be presidential effects or, more likely, teamwork effects.

The issue is addressed in David Truman's study, *The Congressional Party*, which remains one of the two or three most nuanced studies of legislative parties, their leaders, and the president (Truman 1951, 1959). The study focuses on the House and Senate in a single Congress at the midpoint of the twentieth century in which Democrats had majorities in both houses and President Harry Truman, a Democrat, was in the White House. Truman argues that party leaders cannot command colleagues to yield to them but rather that leaders influence outcomes by "improvising effective combinations among fragments of power of the most varied sorts" (Truman 1959, 294). However, when a leader is of the president's party special responsibilities and opportunities are created. This is the reason, Truman hypothesizes, that the Democratic leadership was more effective than Republican leadership in the Congress he examined and that the Democrats were more cohesive than the Republicans. Truman argues

that the "program" of the President had a centripetal effect upon the majority Congressional parties that gave coherence to their leadership structures and meaning to the roles of the leaders, especially those in the principal "elective" positions. In other words, and somewhat more extreme ones, the Democratic majority parties in the Congress worked as groups because of and in response to the initiatives of a Democratic Administration. (Truman 1959, 289–90)

The common policy and partisan interests motivate presidents and party leaders to coordinate their legislative strategies. Because of partisan ties, Truman observed, a president and his congressional party leaders are interdependent; congressional leaders, as their party colleagues expect, assume responsibility to develop strategy jointly with the president. Congressional leaders are not always supportive of the president, but serving as the president's lieutenant is often an explicitly accepted role of party leaders (Bond and Fleisher 1990).

In Truman's account, the president has an effect that is not unlike that claimed for polarization – the president's party has a stronger motivation and more resources to draw upon to win legislative battles. Truman's conjecture was that even congressional leaders are more assertive and more effective because of the responsibilities and capabilities that materialize when they have a president of their own party. Former House Whip Trent Lott's experience, described above, seems to illustrate this. And biographies and the political science literature on twentieth-century party leadership makes leaders' role as an intermediary between the congressional party and the president a central theme.

Two sources of variation in leaders' relationships with presidents are particularly important. First, presidents were not always the preeminent policy makers, but Presidents Theodore Roosevelt, Woodrow Wilson, and Franklin D. Roosevelt transformed the policy-making role of presidents, which, in turn, led party leaders on Capitol Hill to view their relationship very differently. In the modern era, legislators and the general public expect the president to set the legislative agenda, presidential popularity and coattails affect legislators' reelection prospects, and presidents control innumerable resources (patronage, agency decisions, campaign support, and so on) that may be used to influence legislators. Put differently, presidents may exercise direct and indirect influence that augments, and probably exceeds, the legislative influence of congressional leaders. Consequently, while leaders may not follow the president's lead on unpopular proposals, their working assumption is that a president sets the agenda of his congressional party and, beyond the party's size in the House and Senate, controls the most important assets for enacting his program (Bond and Fleisher 1990; Covington 1987; Edwards 1984, 1989; Light 1983; Ripley 1967).

Second, congressional majorities serve at times with a president of the same party and at other times with a president of the opposite party. The tools of the majority leadership, whether deployed for negative or positive purposes, may be used to the president's advantage or disadvantage, to reinforce or counter his efforts to win legislative battles. It is reasonable to hypothesize that reinforcing efforts are more likely to produce legislative outcomes acceptable to the majority leadership and that opposing efforts are more likely to produce stalemate or even less acceptable outcomes. Circumstantial evidence supports this hunch. The support of congressional leaders is more strongly correlated with presidential success in floor votes when the leaders are in the majority than when in the minority (Bond and Fleisher 1990). Moreover, divided party control of the White House and Congress increases the likelihood of stalemate on important issues (Binder 2003).

MISSING ELEMENTS: THE SENATE AND THE MINORITY PARTY

The overwhelming emphasis of studies of party effects in congressional policy making is the House majority party. The power of the House Speaker, more than anything else, serves as the centerpiece of the study of party influence on legislators and legislative outcomes. In fact, most studies focus on the House majority leadership's influence on House majority party legislators. Yet, it is plain to see, parties organize the Senate and, depending on the size and cohesiveness of the majority party, the behavior of minority party legislators can be critical to legislative outcomes. Any fair account of party influence must account for the Senate and for minority parties, which, in turn, requires that we account for the rules of the two houses and the strength of the two parties.

Rules and the Strategic Context

Legislative parties operate in an institutional context defined by constitutional specifications (bicameralism, separation of powers), statutory requirements (sunset provisions, budget process), and intrachamber rules. Parties can influence or determine some of these rules but not others. The internal rules of the House and Senate are determined by majority vote so legislative parties have an opportunity to influence those rules. Over the decades, the two houses have developed quite different rules, rules that affect the short-term influence that party leaders may exert. Three differences between the House and Senate influence the agenda-control exercised by majority party leaders in the two houses – the absence of a powerful presiding officer, of a limit on debate, and of a general germaneness requirement in the Senate. Each of these considerations deserves brief discussion (Gamm and Smith 2000).

In the House, a powerful presiding officer emerged in the nineteenth century. The Speaker became the leader of the majority party and enjoyed the resources of party leadership granted to him by his party. He appointed committees. In 1853, the Speaker of the House became a member and chairman of the Rules Committee. In 1880, Rules became a standing committee and, in 1883, Rules began to report resolutions, dubbed special orders and later special rules that bring bills to the floor and set the terms of debate. In 1910, the Speaker lost the Rules membership and the power to appointment committees in the revolt against Speaker Joseph Cannon. In 1975, Democrats returned to their Speaker the authority to name their party's Rules Committee members, and in 1989 Republicans gave their leader the same authority. In the 1880s, Speaker Carlisle of the House successfully asserted the right to recognize members to make motions or speeches without appeal. Control over the Rules Committee, granted by the parties, combined with the right of recognition, granted by the House, gives the modern Speaker substantial control over the House schedule and the manner in which legislation is considered for amendment on the floor.

The agenda control of the House majority party leadership is not airtight. The leadership must gain a majority vote for resolutions from the Rules Committee. The discharge petition gives a House majority the opportunity to force floor action on a measure. And, it is theoretically possible for a majority of the Rules Committee to report a resolution that authorizes consideration of a bill without the sanction of the majority party leadership. Still, if a cohesive majority party backs its leadership, the party will be able to set the floor agenda – blocking legislation, determining eligible amendments, and so on. The House minority party, confronted with a cohesive majority party, would be unable to contribute to the structuring of the agenda. In this way, the House is fairly labeled "majoritarian."

Unlike the House, the Senate's majority parties have never empowered the chamber's presiding officer. The Constitution provides that the vice president serve as president of the Senate and nineteenth-century vice presidents generally served faithfully. Vice presidents need not be of the same party as the Senate majority, and, even if they were, were not beholden to senators. Presidents pro tempore, who were elected in the absence of the vice president, also proved feeble vessels for majority leadership – nineteenth-century senators believed that the term of a president pro tempore ended abruptly upon the return of the vice president, and they also believed that the Senate lacked the constitutional authority to remove a president pro tempore from office under any other circumstance, including a shift in majority control.

An important feature of the Senate's rules and precedents is that the presiding officer is not given authority to exercise discretion in recognizing senators to speak. The presiding officer is obligated to call on the senator who first seeks recognition, except when the floor leaders of the two parties are seeking recognition. While the Senate experimented occasionally with the assignment of some powers to its presiding officer, the Senate emerged from the nineteenth century with a presiding officer with very little authority, even over routine floor proceedings.[11] The Senate, therefore, lacked a formal leader who could combine the powers of the presiding officer with the influence of a party leader, as did the Speaker of the House.

Also unlike the House, where majorities could impose rules changes, Senate majorities have historically faced a filibuster of any rules change that might disadvantage a minority (Binder and Smith 1997). Until 1917, the Senate had no way to limit debate as long as senators sought recognition to speak. Consequently, in spite of repeated appeals by Senate majority parties for some limit on debate, minority party members regularly killed any hope of such a rule. The immediate consequence of this was that Senate majority parties that might have wanted to enhance the formal power of its leadership did not have the ability to do so. Consequently, the Senate floor, unlike the House floor, has been an inhospitable place for establishing majority party prerogatives.

The possibility of a filibuster means that the Senate's majority leader cannot guarantee a vote on most measures (budget measures are an

---

[11] The Senate's use of the presiding officer to maintain order, make committee assignments, and enforce unanimous consent agreements is discussed in Gamm and Smith (2000).

important exception since 1974) unless cloture can be invoked by a supermajority. Prior to 1917, there was no way to force a vote if senators continued to seek recognition to speak. In 1917, Rule 22 was adopted and empowered two-thirds majorities to invoke cloture. The threshold was reduced to a three-fifths constitutional majority in 1975, except for changes in the rules, for which the two-thirds majority requirement was retained.

Finally, and unlike the House, the Senate lacks a general rule that requires amendments to bills to be germane. In the House, the germaneness rule prevents unrelated legislation from being considered as an amendment to a bill. The absence of such a requirement in the Senate means that the text of an entire bill can be offered as an amendment to another bill. Consequently, Senate party leaders have a difficult time preventing a bill from being considered as an amendment. Generally, amendments can be filibustered, but a filibuster also prevents action on the underlying bill and thus often is not a viable option for a leader seeking action on the bill. The result is that Senate majority leadership has much more difficulty keeping legislation off the floor than do their House counterparts.

Still, the modern Senate majority leader has an important advantage. A procedural precedent dating to the 1930s gives the majority leader the right to be recognized before other senators. This gives the majority leader the opportunity to attempt to set the agenda, although most motions to proceed or other procedural actions can be filibustered. Thus, the right of first recognition is a right to propose an agenda.

A consequence of inherited Senate rules is that the majority party leadership generally has quite imperfect control of the chamber's agenda even when all party members back the leadership's procedural moves. The minority party can force compromise on the agenda through threatened or actual use of its procedural prerogatives. This possibility has led the Senate to develop informal devises, such as the practices of bill clearance and holds, to facilitate floor action (Smith 1989).

The institutional contexts in which congressional parties operate create asymmetries in the indirect influence of the four parties. A fair ranking of the agenda influence exercised by the four congressional parties, in descending order, is the House majority party, Senate majority party, Senate minority party, and House minority party. The ability to structure the agenda to further party goals is strongest for the House majority party and weakest for the House minority party. The Senate parties are more evenly matched, although the majority leadership has the important advantages of the right of first recognition and party size. Therefore, we expect the House majority party, more than the Senate majority party, to be able to structure votes in a favorable way. The House majority party leaders should be able to use this capacity to minimize the tension between electoral, policy, and party pressures on their party members as they seek to pursue the collective goals of their party.

Party Strength and the Strategic Context

Beyond the procedural context in the two houses, the size and cohesiveness – in combination we might refer to party strength – of the majority and minority parties will affect party strategies (Binder 1997; Jones 1970). A large majority party can win votes without the support of some of its members. A very cohesive majority party can win votes without having to ask its members to vote differently than they would otherwise. A large *and* cohesive party makes life particularly easy for the majority party leadership. Party influence will be exercised when the party's small size or lack of cohesiveness puts floor victories at risk. Weakness in the majority party generates the need for party influence.

The minority party can make little difference if the majority party is large or cohesive, particularly in the House, but minority party leaders may have opportunities to influence outcomes when the majority party is not large or cohesive. When majority party weakness creates the opportunity, minority party strength becomes important. If the minority party is sizable and cohesive, its leaders' strategic problem is to attract the support of some majority party members without demanding too much sacrifice from fellow partisans. If some sacrifice is required to win, minority leaders may need to influence fellow partisans to retain their support.

A weak majority party and strong minority party – that is, nearly equal relative party strength – is the strategic condition that will generate the greatest effort to influence legislators' voting behavior. Shaping agendas and pressuring legislators are likely to be decisive when the majority party cannot easily carry votes with its own members and the minority can win legislative battles with the support of just

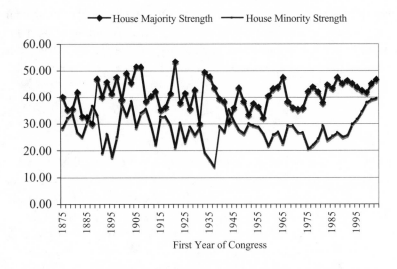

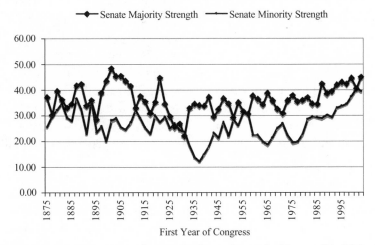

FIGURE 3.2. (a). Majority and Minority Party Strength, House. (b). Majority and Minority Party Strength, Senate.

a few majority party members. Figures 3.2(a) and 3.2(b) show party strength – party size multiplied by the average proportion of partisans voting with their party majority – for House and Senate parties over the period since the Civil War. Because the roll-call votes may reflect direct and indirect party influence, the measure of party cohesiveness used for the figure cannot be taken as a very accurate indicator of true cohesiveness. Nonetheless, the figure gives some indication of the periods in which intense party competition is likely to have occurred in the two houses and therefore generated particularly intense leadership efforts to influence outcomes. Remarkably, there are no studies that systematically examine the relationship between party strength and party influence.

CONCLUSION

For many years, political scientists conceived of party influence as one of several "forces" in the social psychology of the congressional decision maker. It weighed in against other forces, such as personal ideology or constituency interests, and the task of the political scientist was to estimate the relative importance of these forces and to identify the conditions that might cause those estimates to vary. Those studies dominated the 1950s and 1960s "behavioral" era of political science and carried into the 1970s. The capstone of these studies was two books, Kingdon's *Congressmen's Voting Decisions* and Clausen's *How Congressman Decide*, one using interviews and the other using the roll-call voting record (Clausen 1973; Kingdon 1973). I consider these empirical studies and more recent variants in the next chapter.

The events of the 1970s and 1980s, along with the introduction of game-theoretic concepts in studies of politics, sensitized political scientists that the direct influence reflected in the first generation of studies

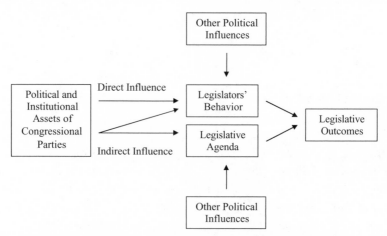

FIGURE 3.3. Summary of Sources and Types of Party Influence.

did not capture the indirect ways in which party leaders sought to influence outcomes. The new uses of House special rules, more than anything else, led several scholars to emphasize control of the agenda as a tool of the majority party leadership (Bach and Smith 1988; Davidson and Oleszek 1977; Rohde 1991; Sinclair 1983; Smith 1989) and eventually to a broader understanding of the role of indirect influence on floor voting. This understanding serves as the basis of cartel theory (Cox and McCubbins 2005), which I take up in Chapter 5.

This literature has motivated my outline of direct and indirect, negative and positive, forms of party influence in this chapter. I summarize the relationships between the sources of party influence and outcomes in Figure 3.3. While political scientists tend to emphasize one form of influence or another, leaders seem to use them in tandem – influencing a few legislators to set the agenda, buying the support of some legislators with new proposals while preventing consideration of others, and so on. The analytical clarity we gain by focusing on one kind of influence at a time is not duplicated in the practice of politics on Capitol Hill, where party leaders must mix and match strategies to a bewildering array of coalition-building challenges.

4

The Search for Direct Party Effects

In the first systematic study of congressional voting, A. Lawrence Lowell (1902) reported on the frequency with which 90 percent or more of one party opposed 90 percent or more of the other party on congressional and British House of Commons roll-call votes, finding far more party voting in the House of Commons than in the houses of Congress. Lowell wrote of party influence but was just as likely to more properly refer to the frequency of "party lines." Indeed, Lowell was quite aware of the limitations of his approach. He noted how rules (such as those affecting the ease of getting roll-call votes or the treatment of public and private bills) might influence his measure of party voting. And he was quite aware that the limited capacities of American electoral parties in formulating a policy program, determining candidates, and controlling incumbents' behavior prevented "government by party" in the United States. Still, Lowell's emphasis was that party influence was stronger in the House of Commons than in the House of Representatives and others followed in his footsteps.

Lowell, who graduated from Harvard College in mathematics and then from Harvard Law, joined Harvard's government department in 1897 and became Harvard's president in 1909, the year he also became president of the American Political Science Association. Between 1897 and 1909, he wrote four books (two of them in two volumes). At Harvard, he remains well known for inventing the system of concentrations (majors) and the reading period before exams (Yeomans

1948).[1] In more recent years, Lowell's legacy at Harvard has become controversial – he set a quota for Jewish students and established racially segregated dormitories.[2] Nevertheless, Lowell set a standard as an effective university administrator with solid scholarly credentials that few others, even at Harvard, have matched.

Much of today's journalistic discussion of partisanship in Congress has not advanced beyond Lowell's treatment of the subject. To this day, Congressional Quarterly calculates "party unity scores" based on votes on which more than 50 percent of one party opposed more than 50 percent of the other party, which are regularly reported in standard textbooks on Congress. The annual stories on the party scores in *CQ Weekly Report* and the *CQ Weekly* frequently refer to the ebb and flow of party influence. For example, in CQ's story on 2005 scores, the writer observes that "one manifestation of the leaders' demand for loyalty is a rising number of roll call votes on which a majority of Republicans line up against a majority of Democrats." The writer continues, "An utter lack of Democratic support, for example, required Republican leaders to twist arms and make promises to preserve very narrow victories in both chambers on a spending cut bill that still must survive one more test in the House early this year."[3] The funny thing is that the outcome of that arm-twisting had no impact on the subject of the story – whether or not a vote is a party vote – because overwhelming majorities of the two parties opposed each other anyway.

My discussion of party influence in the previous chapter emphasized that party influence comes in several forms – direct and indirect, negative and positive – and that the sources of these forms of party influence are quite varied. Starting with Lowell and continuing through today,

---

[1] Lowell reported that reading period was originally designed for professors, not students. Lowell was seeking to create time for professors' own research and writing. Typically, students were assigned heavy reading during the period and could not study for exams. Gaston De Los Reyes, "Reading Period Designed for Profs," *The Harvard Crimson*, May 13, 1994 (http://www.thecrimson.com/article.aspx?ref=224809).

[2] "Story Ignores Pres. Lowell's Racist Policies," *The Harvard Crimson*, February 8, 1994 (http://www.thecrimson.com/article.aspx?ref=242090); Andrew D. Fine, "An Exceptional Class," *The Harvard Crimson*, October 28, 2005 (http://www.thecrimson.com/article.aspx?ref=509366); also see Karabel (2005).

[3] Martin Kady II, "Party Unity: Learning to Stick Together," *CQ Weekly*, January 9, 2006, p. 92.

the literature on party influence emphasizes direct influence on legislators' behavior and, until recently, ignored indirect influence and
influence on legislative outcomes (see Figure 3.3). It is the empirical
literature on direct party influence on legislators' behavior that is the
subject of this chapter. While it has not been easy, political scientists
have, in recent years, generated considerable evidence for the frequent
and successful deployment of direct influence by congressional parties.

THE WEAK FORCE AND THE STRONG FORCE: WHERE TO LOOK
FOR DIRECT PARTY INFLUENCE

Estimating the effect of party influence, even direct party influence,
is a challenge that political scientists have not quite mastered. This is
no surprise, given the variety of ways in which direct influence can
be exercised, the multiplicity of its sources, the difficulty of measuring
the assets, efforts, and effects of legislative parties, and the remarkable
range of other forces that must be taken into account when evaluating
party influence. It pays to be clear about the kind of direct party effects
that we expect to observe before appraising the political science on the
subject.

In my discussion of direct influence in the last chapter, I noted that
several of observers of congressional politics argue that a minimum
level of party support can be expected as a by-product of group membership – the weak force in partisan politics. Fellow partisans asso-
ciate with each other and the party and seek to satisfy each other's
expectations. Party leaders frequently appeal to loyalty, presumably
because they think that they can stimulate an emotional response from
colleagues. This minimum level of party support costs the leaders little and appears to apply to nearly all members of a legislative party.
The result should be that two legislators of opposite parties who, as a
product of all other forces, have similar voting preferences should, as
a result of the partisan tendency, vote somewhat differently in favor of
the positions of their respective parties.

A stronger force in partisan politics, one for which leaders devote
more tangible resources, is one targeted at individuals or factions. It is
likely to be present only when required – that is, only when other forces
do not produce a legislative victory for the party. Even then, it is likely
to be focused on the legislators whose votes are required to win, which

may be no more than several legislators. Furthermore, the few legislators who are targeted may be approached and persuaded before legislation reaches the floor. When committee action, whip counts, experience, and other sources of information indicate which legislators will be troublesome, leaders can focus the exercise of influence early. The scene of the leadership strong-arming colleagues during a roll-call vote on the floor is atypical. Moreover, the targeted application of influence may be made conditional on how others' vote – having votes "in the pocket" if they are needed. And the targets may change from one legislative battle to another as the issues at stake vary.

Measuring the weak and strong forms of direct influence poses serious challenges to the political scientist. The weak force is probably a small effect. Statistical techniques intended to identify relationships that are stronger than expected by chance may or may not pick up weak force effects. Interviewing legislators is unlikely to yield many comments about predispositions to support that party about which legislators may not be fully conscious. Similarly, the few legislators who are the target of the strong direct influence are like needles in a haystack. Showing statistically significant effects of influence of that kind is possible only if the same legislators are the targets repeatedly. If legislators vote on a variety of issues with even slightly different divisions among legislators, it is not likely that any legislator is frequently a target. Because the typical legislator is seldom the target of direct leadership influence, even interviews with a cross section of legislators are unlikely to turn up many instances of targeting.

The implication of these observations is that direct party effects should be difficult to find when studying the behavior of individual legislators even when present. And yet the marginal effects of party of the weak or strong form may be critical to explaining legislative outcomes. A legislative battle, after all, is about assembling majorities; it is not about averages and explaining variance around the mean, as is the logic of statistical techniques and the implicit logic of most interview-based studies.

A BRIEF HISTORY OF FIRST-STAGE STUDIES OF PARTY EFFECTS

Stuart A. Rice, a sociologist who played a prominent role in advancing the role of statistics in political science and sociology and worked for some time at the Bureau of the Budget, made roll-call voting his early professional focus.[4] In his 1925 article on the analysis of roll-call votes, Rice observed that legislators' recorded roll-call votes are "the most tangible and measurable units of political behavior" (Rice 1925). Rice was aware of some of the complexities of drawing inferences from roll-call behavior, but, like political scientists today, he found roll-call votes an irresistible source of data about politics. His primary concern was to use the voting record to characterize the internal cohesiveness of, and distances between, legislative groups like parties, factions, and blocs. He proposed an index of cohesion (based on the extent of agreement among fellow partisans) and an index of likeness (based on the extent of agreement across party lines), applied them to both parties and within-party blocs, and compared group cohesiveness across several issue areas. The Rice index of party difference (the extent of disagreement) followed in his book (Rice 1924, 1925, 1928).

Lowell and Rice focused on group behavior and could offer only hunches about the forces operating on individual legislators that aggregated to produce the group behavior that was measured. A high frequency of "party votes" in Lowell's study and high cohesion in Rice's study implied strong party forces, the authors intimated, but, as Rice seemed to recognize in his discussion of multivariate cross-tabulation and political scientist Aage Clausen made explicit, "a variety of factors can have a cumulative effect in the direction of producing agreement among a group's members" (Clausen 1967). Consequently, political scientists, including Clausen, moved to studies that attempted to sort out the effects of the multiple factors that could influence individual legislators' vote choices.[5]

The general method of investigating individual legislators' voting behavior is to develop a score of voting behavior for each legislator,

---

[4] As a sociologist, Rice became a frequent author of articles appearing in political science journals that focused on government statistics. Stuart A. Rice, "The Role and Management of the Federal Statistical System," *The American Political Science Review* 34, no. 3 (1940):481–8, Stuart A. Rice, "Co-Ordination of Federal Statistical Programs," *American Journal of Sociology* 50, no. 1 (1944):22–8; Stuart A. Rice and Florence DuBois, "Statistics in Relation to Recent Social Trends in the United States," *Social Forces* 11, no. 4 (1933):511–13; Stuart A. Rice and Joseph W. Kappel, "Strategic Intelligence and the Publication of Statistics," *The American Political Science Review* 45, no. 4 (1951):1058–68.

[5] Rice's work stimulated scholars to propose alternative measures of group cohesion and intergroup similarity (Brams and O'Leary 1970; Grumm 1965).

usually on the basis of a scaling analysis of a set of roll-call votes (MacRae 1965; Weisberg 1972). Scale scores for all legislators are correlated with other characteristics, such as party affiliation, composition of home constituencies, and electoral circumstances. Studies vary in how voting behavior is scaled and scored, in the other characteristics that are correlated with the scale scores, and in the statistical methods for evaluating the independent strength of relationships.

Political scientist Julius Turner initiated the modern era of systematic studies of individual roll-call voting in Congress (Turner 1951). Turner's primary contribution was his effort to demonstrate that differences in legislators' constituencies were sometimes more strongly related to voting than party differences. His argument supported a pluralistic view of American and congressional politics – the coalitions and lines of conflict vary from issue to issue, with partisan lines central to many but not all important issues (Truman 1951). Turner was treated harshly by his critics, although it took some time for their concerns to be registered in print (Crane 1960; Greenstein and Jackson 1963; Shannon 1968b). The reviews criticized Turner for inferring influence, pressure, or loyalty from the correlation between legislators' party membership and aggregate voting records. Turner made the additional mistake of relying on a chi-square test, which tests for the *existence* of a statistically significant relationship between a vote and party labels to measure the *strength* of party influence.

Turner is not given due credit for articulating, however briefly, the first theory of congressional roll-call voting found in political science. He asserted that

with the exception of those few members on each roll call who have studied the merits of the legislation, the votes of the members are an excellent reflection of the individuals or groups on whom each member is most dependent for advice. The roll call record is, therefore, an accurate summation of the effectiveness of the pressure of various groups on each congressman, on those issues which are important enough or controversial enough so that a part of the membership wants a record kept of the vote for an ensuing election campaign. (Turner 1951, 19–20)

In equating advice with pressure, Turner failed to distinguish potentially different political circumstances. Still, he suggested that incomplete information is the normal condition of the average member on the average vote, which generates reliance on others for advice and creates vulnerability to pressure.

Incomplete information later became a core feature of the decision-making contexts in the theories of Truman (1956), Kingdon (1973), and Matthews and Stimson (1975), all of whom proposed that legislators necessarily and inevitably take cues from trusted colleagues or others as guidance in voting. Party colleagues are a common source of those cues. In each of these studies, similarly situated colleagues – such as party colleagues in one's own state delegation – are found to be common sources of cues. In this way, "party voting" is a cue-taking, decision-making shortcut – hardly reflective of the "pressure" emphasized by Turner. But, as these scholars have emphasized, cues originating in a legislator's party often have the same valence as constituency and interest groups cues, so separating party influence from other types of influence is a difficult empirical problem.

The full range of the direct effects of party that I mentioned in the previous chapter – pressures, cues, group loyalty, and so on – are discussed in this first generation of roll-call analyses. Even with the limitations of Turner's study, Turner's theme – the relative importance of party and constituency forces in roll-call voting – remained the predominant theme in voting studies through the early 1970s. Variations on the theme included the varying strength of party and constituency effects across policy areas and across legislators of varying degrees of electoral marginality and constituency types (Brady and Lynn 1973; Deckard 1976; Fiorina 1974; Kuklinski 1977; Kuklinski and Elling 1977; Shannon 1968a; Sullivan and Uslaner 1978). Measurement issues, particularly in the area of measuring constituency political attitudes, motivated many studies. With all that work, the presence of both party and constituency effects was confirmed many times. A fair generalization of the findings of these studies is that legislators tend to vote with their parties unless there is clear constituency (electoral) reason to deviate from the party line.

Two studies, each published in 1973 and each concerned with the mix of forces that influence the voting behavior of legislators, served as a capstone of the first-stage studies of roll-call voting. I mention Kingdon's *Congressmen's Voting Decisions* first because it did not involve a multivariate analysis of scale scores but rather was based on interviews with fifteen House members about fifteen roll-call votes, yielding 225 cases of voting. Kingdon provides a nuanced discussion of the relationship among the several forces that legislators take into account, at least some of the time, such as party leadership, other party colleagues, constituencies, presidents, and lobbyists. For the 225 (nonindependent) cases, Kingdon determined whether the legislator mentioned the various actors spontaneously and asked each legislator about the importance of each group of actors.

Party leaders were a last-place finisher in Kingdon's findings, with other legislators and the home constituency being the most important. Because the other legislators are fellow partisans in the vast majority of cases, there remains plenty of room for party effects, when aggregated over their several sources, to be important overall. More important, Kingdon's findings concern the experience of fairly average legislators on fairly typical issues. It is likely that none of them were pivotal to the outcomes on the issues at hand and so it is unlikely that party leaders would have given any of them special attention.

Clausen (Clausen 1973; Clausen and Cheney 1970; Clausen and Van Horn 1977; Wilcox and Clausen 1991) posits that legislators categorize the motions on which they must vote into a limited number of policy domains (social welfare, agriculture, foreign policy, etc.), within which legislators readily acquire stable policy positions. Each domain is conceived as a single dimension (e.g., pro- to antiagricultural subsidies) along which legislators can be arrayed on the basis of their voting record. Legislators' policy positions are postulated to be the product of a variety of political forces. The domains' scale scores, which serve as estimates of legislators' policy positions, can be correlated with each other to estimate the degree to which a single dimension captures all voting behavior. The scale scores also can be correlated with other factors, such as party affiliation and constituency characteristics, to estimate the relative importance of political forces that may vary in strength across the policy domains. Variation across domains is the focus of Clausen's analysis.

Clausen's findings about party influence appear to be straightforward (it varies across domains) but reflect the difficulties characteristic of the first generation of studies. While party affiliation is easily measured, constituency political attitudes are not and district demographic characteristics are used as a surrogate. Because only a few demographic characteristics are examined and the relevant demographic characteristics are likely to vary across policy domains, the surrogate may not be valid for all domains. Nevertheless, the claims that parties care about some policies more than others and that parties are more likely to be divided on some issues than others seem quite credible. Less credible are Clausen's claims that constituents pay less attention to issues related to government management of the economy (taxes, balancing the budget, economic policy) than to others.

Clausen's discussion of party and ideology gives a hint of the trouble to come. The primary evidence of ideology as a force influencing legislators' decision making is that legislators' voting behavior yields only a limited number of clusters of legislators on the scales associated with the several policy domains. That is, there is great regularity in the way legislators align themselves in floor voting across issues:

> Ideology, as a source of policy positions and as a mechanism of reinforcement of policy views, needs further investigation. We simply cannot ignore the fact that one-half of the members of the house can be classified as liberals or conservatives on the basis of their positions on four domestic policy dimensions. I find it hard to reject the existence of two political orientations, one liberal and one conservative, which predicate policy positions on a number of domestic questions. (Clausen 1973, 117)

It is patterned behavior, cutting across party lines, at least at the margins, that impresses Clausen – and most of his readers.

After the publication of the Clausen and Kingdon studies, investigations of congressional voting moved in two directions. The first direction was to extend the application of aggregate party voting measures over long historical periods to evaluate changes in the role of party in Congress. These studies increased the field's awareness of potential variation in the strength of party influences over time and suggested a number of propositions about the forces at work, the most important of which I discussed in Chapter 3. But a weakness of the Lowell-Rice approach, first noted by Clausen, applies to these studies. The "party position" is determined by observing the voting record, such as by using the position taken by a majority of partisans. The same voting behavior is used to measure a legislator's support for the party. The advantage of the approach is that the party position can be determined objectively for all votes, but the disadvantage is that a mathematical dependency exists between the existence of a party position and the measure of legislators' party support (Clausen 1967; Cox and McCubbins 1991; Jackson 1971).

The other direction taken by political scientists was to apply the spatial model, just emerging in the consciousness of the discipline, to the study of congressional voting behavior. The role of the spatial model in motivating new theory and empirical studies requires a little background, which I provide in the next section.

FOUNDATIONS OF THE SECOND-STAGE STUDIES OF PARTY EFFECTS: SPATIAL THEORY OF VOTING AND METHODS OF IDEAL POINT ESTIMATION

Clausen's 1973 book may be seen as a transitional work because it provided an explicit spatial characterization of legislators' policy positions. His emphasis, like that of most of his predecessors, on explaining the location of legislators' policy positions differed from the emphasis of spatial theorists, who place more emphasis on what outcomes are produced by legislators (and other players) with certain policy positions under certain rules. The spatial theorist does not worry about why legislators hold the policy positions they do and so treats the policy positions as exogenously determined preferences. The preferences can be characterized as ideal points in a policy space. The rules, which the institutional setting provides, are similarly treated as exogenously provided. The rules determine the sequence of moves, permissible strategies of the players, and, along with the preferences, who wins.

The spatial theory of voting was introduced as a way to explain voters' strategies and election outcomes when voters and candidates (or parties) can be placed in a policy space (Black 1958; Davis and Hinich 1966; Davis et al. 1970; Downs 1957; Hinich and Enelow 1984). While it took some time, spatial theory began to influence the theory and methods of research on congressional politics (Krehbiel 1988). The most basic ingredient of spatial theories is the policy preference (often called an ideal point): For a given issue, a legislator is assumed to have an ideal outcome and, for any direction, prefers outcomes closer to her ideal point than outcomes farther away (single-peaked preferences). With a given set of preferences and rules, the theorist deduces the strategies (behavior) that legislators will pursue and the resulting outcome. Theories differ in their treatment of legislators' preferences, the rules governing the sequence of decision making and permissible alternatives, and the nature of information available to legislators.

Spatial theories' focus on legislators' strategies and outcomes had a natural appeal to congressional scholars. Previous work left a question unanswered. If forces internal and external to Congress determined legislators' policy preferences, we still needed to explain how those preferences translated into voting behavior and specific legislative outcomes. Spatial theory provided tools for addressing the issue.

Arriving nearly simultaneously with the new spatial applications in legislative politics in the 1970s and 1980s were new methods for characterizing legislators' policy positions. In fact, as spatial theorists' concepts began to reorient thinking about floor voting, methodologists began to think of data reduction and dimensional analysis techniques as approaches to measuring ideal point or preference locations. That is, the observed voting *behavior* came to be viewed as an approach to measuring *preferences*. Political scientists Keith Poole and Howard Rosenthal devised the NOMINATE dimensional unfolding technique based on a spatial (Euclidean) utility function – that is, on a conception of the voting decision suggested by spatial theory (Poole 1988; Poole and Rosenthal 1985, 1991, 1996).[6] The general idea is to assume that legislators operate in a policy space and cast "yea" and "nay" votes on motions on the basis of the alternative closest to their ideal points. Over a large number of votes, the method identifies the spatial location of legislators that best fit their votes. Each legislator's spatial location is identified by a scale score on each dimension. In their analysis of all Congresses through 1985, Poole and Rosenthal found that a single dimension, on which legislators appeared to be aligned in a manner consistent with liberal and conservative labels in everyday usage, accounted for most of the observed behavior. A second dimension was significant in a few periods, but each of the additional dimensions

---

[6] NOMINATE is an awkward abbreviation for *nominal* three-step estimation.

that could be uncovered never accounted for much more than a trivial amount of the variation in behavior.

The marriage of new theoretical concepts and a method of roll-call analysis based on them redirected analysts of congressional voting from the study of party and constituency influences to party and ideology.[7] Personal ideology as a force in voting choices was an interest of political scientists for some time (MacRae 1958). For Poole and his colleagues, ideology was equated, at least at first, with the underlying preferences said to be estimated by NOMINATE methods (Poole and Daniels 1985). The basic premise seemed to make sense: If ideology is a basic frame of reference about politics that shapes attitudes about everyday issues, then a recurring, coherent pattern of behavior uncovered from an analysis of the entire roll-call record would be strong evidence that an ideology exists and can define legislators' relative locations on an ideological continuum. Consequently, many scholars used NOMINATE scores to represent preferences or ideology in analyses intended to show the effects of ideology, party, and other factors in decision making.

In the eyes of many of their readers, the most noteworthy finding of the Poole–Rosenthal studies was the ability of a single dimension to account for a very large part of the voting behavior in the House and Senate. This observation seemed inconsistent with the thrust of previous research, particularly the Clausen studies, that emphasized multidimensionality and variation in the political forces at work across the issues addressed by Congress. The Poole–Rosenthal finding suggested that legislators' attitudes or the basic forces in American politics aligned themselves from liberal to conservative on a single dimension. If so, then the kind of spatial theory required to explain congressional voting behavior and outcomes was fairly simple. The complexities of multidimensional decision making – bargaining across dimensions, instability in outcomes, and so on – were not an issue.

Challenges to the Poole–Rosenthal argument came quickly. Some scholars are skeptical about the importance of the first NOMINATE dimension (Koford 1989; Poole et al. 1991; Wilcox and Clausen 1991).

---

[7] Scholars continued to take an interest in constituency influences, of course, but by 1990 the balance of scholarship shifted to the issue of whether party effects are significant once ideology or policy preferences are controlled.

The details of this important debate are beyond the scope of this essay, but some observations about the debate are required. Wilcox and Clausen are correct that the Poole–Rosenthal technique, which is based on a spatial utility model with orthogonal (uncorrelated) dimensions, (a) cannot test Clausen's theory that legislators perceive distinct policy domains and (b) does not allow for correlated dimensions that might show different relationships with party, constituency, and other political forces. Koford is correct that the NOMINATE technique extracts a single dimension that explains the majority of variance even when the ideal points are arrayed perfectly in two dimensions. Unavoidably, this gives the impression that the political world of legislators operates in one dimension when the situation may be more complex.

The fair conclusion is that a liberal–conservative dimension is commonly present in the policy space and that the NOMINATE first dimension provides an appropriate measure of liberal–conservative alignments, but, as Congress moves from issue to issue, other dimensions are frequently present but are rarely statistically significant. Thus, in using NOMINATE's first dimensionfirst-dimension scores to the exclusion of other, possibly correlated, dimensions, studies are capturing the liberal–conservative locations of legislators. Studies are probably inappropriately setting aside divisions among legislators that may be at work in many legislative battles and research points in that direction (Hurwitz et al. 2001). In fact, when final passage and conference report votes related in individual bills are examined, only a minority can be safely claimed to fall on NOMINATE's first dimension (Vander Wielen 2006).

Other political scientists were quick to point out that a problem with the NOMINATE, like interest group ratings based on roll-call votes, is in its application (Jackson and Kingdon 1992). Some analysts want to do more than merely demonstrate the existence of patterned behavior that mirrors common observations about ideological alignments in Congress; they want to evaluate the relative importance of ideology, party, and other factors in legislators' decision making. However, the location of legislators arrayed on the basis of roll-call votes, even as extracted in NOMINATE's first dimension, may reflect the full array of forces outlined by Clausen, Kingdon, and others. That is, scores on the first dimension are affected by more than ideology. Moreover, if the variable to be explained is based on roll-call votes, then including NOMINATE or some other "ideology" measure based on votes as an explanatory variable creates a dependency between the explained and explanatory variables that is likely to produce misleading results.

Poole and Rosenthal developed a version of NOMINATE that takes into account a legislators' votes over several Congresses and allows a legislator's score to vary in a linear (one-way) direction (Poole and Rosenthal 1991). This "dynamic" method was labeled D-NOMINATE and is widely used. Because it provides only for a linear, averaged change in legislators' scores, D-NOMINATE has not proven to be a useful tool for understanding change in legislators' voting patterns (Roberts and Smith 2003).[8]

Nevertheless, NOMINATE proved useful. If it is only a theoretically grounded data reduction method that is readily applied to the masses of roll-call data, it is a major contribution. The first dimension of D-NOMINATE provides a summary of legislators' observed policy positions on a liberal–conservative scale. It is probably the most frequently present dimension in congressional decision making, but, for many issues, it probably is not the only important dimension. Legislators' observed policy positions on the first dimension are likely to be the product of a variety of political forces at work, including partisan forces, inside and outside of Congress.

The question remaining is whether D-NOMINATE proved to be a useful baseline for evaluating party effects. It has been used for that purpose and the studies that do so are the subject of the rest of this chapter.

THE MISGUIDED KREHBIEL CHALLENGE

Keith Krehbiel's article "Where's the Party?" is the most frequently cited application of the spatial model to the evaluation of party effects (Krehbiel 1993). The argument is similar, although not identical, to the argument made in his previous book (Krehbiel 1991).[9] Krehbiel

---

[8] An ideal point estimation procedure that allows nonlinear change in estimated ideal points is described in Martin and Quinn (2002).

[9] The theory in Krehbiel (1991) is different from that in Krehbiel (1993) in that in the former, legislators are uncertain about how their policy choices are connected with policy outcomes. This gap motivates the creation of standing committees and motivates

asserts a baseline against which claims about party effects should be judged. The article stimulated a variety of responses, but Krehbiel's original argument has not been addressed directly. Its importance as a point of departure for the second stage of voting studies requires that I give close attention to the theoretical and methodological claims of the article.

Krehbiel's primary claim is that "significant party behaviour is behaviour that is consistent with known party policy objectives but that is *independent* of personal preferences" (Krehbiel 1993). "Personal preferences" are equated with ideal points but are not given further definition. Methodologically, Krehbiel asserts that a "partisan" process of standing committee assignments is one for which either (a) majority-party status increases a legislator's probability of obtaining a given committee seat, independent of preferences, or (b) the parties respond to legislators' preferences differently (one party appoints high demanders and the other low demanders). Similarly, a partisan process of conference committee appointments is one in which majority-party status increases a legislator's probability of obtaining a conference appointment. Empirically, Krehbiel measures preferences by using interest group ratings that appear related to each committee's jurisdiction. For conference appointments, Krehbiel controls for committee membership, committee seniority, and House seniority in addition to "preferences."

The Krehbiel challenge, while stated strongly, is weak on theoretical and methodological grounds. Underlying the argument is a spatial theory for which preference is a native concept and is treated as exogenous (i.e., not explained within the theory). In spatial theory, preferences are "opinions about which policies should be adopted" (Krehbiel 1988). The factors that influence those opinions – constituency interests, lobbyists, presidential pressure, personal ideology, and even party leaders and other fellow partisans – might be interesting but are not within the scope of the theory. Thus, if we were to accept the spirit of

Krehbiel's analysis of committee membership. Furthermore, Krehbiel (1991) requires the existence of a median legislator and, therefore, a unidimensional policy space. It is the median whose interests institutional arrangements are theorized to serve – labeled "remote majoritarianism." Krehbiel (1993) allows the dimension to vary from committee to committee and makes no reference to the need for a unidimensional model with a single median legislator.

spatial theory, party considerations may influence preferences but party and preference cannot be treated as concomitant forces on voting. To pit party and preference effects against each other without additional explanation of the meaning of preferences yields a confusing formulation at best.[10]

To make any sense, Krehbiel must mean that, as a theoretical matter, preferences are constituted independently of party influences. If not, preferences cannot serve as the baseline against which party effects are measured. As others have noted, it is not persuasive to argue that preferences are constituted independently of party influences. Rohde, for example, argues that

Krehbiel's exogeneity assumption requires us to accept all three of the following propositions. If the leadership of the House Democratic party supports a bill and if a Democratic member wants to serve on the Rules Committee, the member's inclination to support the bill will not be affected by a promise of appointment to the Rules Committee. If the Democratic members strongly favor the bill and a committee chair is inclined to vote against it, the chair's floor vote will not be affected by an organized threat in caucus to remove him or her from the chair. If a member mildly opposes the same bill but strongly favors another bill which, the leadership informs her, will come to the floor by the end of the session if she votes for the first bill, her preferences will not be affected. (Rohde 1994)

Krehbiel must confess, "I do not dispute claims that parties play roles in the formation of preferences." Oddly, he goes on:

I question whether these claims in the present legislative formulations are amenable to the extracting and testing of predictions. Granted, we can imagine a theory in which legislative parties, in some sense, precede preferences. But exactly what are this theory's refutable implications, and how can we test them? Lacking a clear answer to the question of whether party precedes preference or vice versa, the research strategy here has been relatively agnostic. (Krehbiel 1993)

The agnosticism – really, confusion – appears to be due to a lack of conceptual clarity about preferences. One possibility is that preferences are the opinions held at the moment of decision, as is implied by

---

[10] Krehbiel refers to "personal preferences" as if they are unaffected by partisan influences, but he does not explain what forces might be incorporated in the theoretical definition of preferences.

spatial theory, in which case preferences surely can be influenced by partisan forces and the treatment of party and preferences as wholly independent forces is meaningless. A second possibility is that preferences are deeply held or long-standing opinions about policy that legislators bring with them into Congress and that are, in principle, only one of several possible sets of forces and calculations that might influence roll-call voting and other legislative behavior. Partisan forces are among those other forces. This rendition puts preferences in the category of ideology, which, I have noted, was a concern of political scientists for many years. Preferences, as long-term opinions or attitudes, would not be subject to partisan forces internal to the Congress, but may be weighed against party demands. They also may be weighed against other forces that must be modeled to evaluate the effects of either preferences or partisan forces. In any event, the meaning Krehbiel intends to assign to preferences is not self-evident and goes unexplained.

Krehbiel is not explicit about the arrangement of preferences on a single dimension, but his theoretical discussion and empirical applications are unidimensional, a practice that he continues in other work (Krehbiel 1991, 1998). The consequence of this theoretical move is to rule out important party strategies – controlling the issues and policy alternatives over which coalitions form on the floor and offering side payments to win support. A considerable literature on the importance of setting the agenda through the manipulation of House special rules pre-dated Krehbiel's challenge (Bach and Smith 1988; Rohde 1991; Sinclair 1983, 1989; Smith 1989), and yet this central feature of accounts about the resurgence of party are ignored (Sinclair 2002). Moreover, it is easy to see how offering side payments, such as earmarks or other distributive policy considerations, each of which may be viewed as a (small) separate dimension, might help leaders win support, yielding coalitions that are composed of legislators with non-consecutive preferences on any one dimension (Jackson and Moselle 2002).

The meaning of preferences and the treatment of dimensionality matter for methodological reasons. As I have noted in this chapter and the previous one, scholars have long worried about an adequate operationalization of a full model of the roll-call voting decision (Greenstein and Jackson 1963; Jackson and Kingdon 1992). The challenge, as these scholars have viewed it, is to identify and measure the full range of significant forces on legislators' choices so that the relative effects of each force, including party influences, are estimated properly. To reduce the theoretical problem, as Krehbiel does, to party and preferences after years of more sophisticated argument about ideology, constituency, presidential, and other influences on legislative decisions is a backward step in the science of legislative behavior.

On the empirical side, Krehbiel's 1993 paper sidesteps the complications of estimating party effects for legislators in a properly specified multivariate model by dropping further discussion of individual behavior. Instead, he addresses two forms of collective behavior, appointments to standing and conference committees, that are only indirectly related to individual behavior and policy choices. This is noteworthy because the discussion of "significant party behavior" (Section 1 of the paper) concerns individual behavior exclusively and the standard that we are asked to follow concerns personal preferences. The empirical analysis, while related to party and personal preference, concerns the choices of *party and committee leaders* about who to appoint to committees, not rank-and-file legislators' policy choices. Moreover, for both standing committee and conference committee appointments, he amalgamates two sets of decisions, majority and minority party decisions, into one analysis. The analysis is, at best, indirectly relevant to demonstrating the importance of party and preferences in policy choices that appear to have motivated his theoretical discussion.

The specific form of the "party" hypotheses warrants scrutiny. The primary hypothesis is that majority-party status increases a legislator's probability of receiving a given committee appointment. Given that the parties are intentionally allocated seats on the examined standing committees and conference committees in proportion to party size in the House, it should be no surprise that a dummy variable for party (1 = majority; 0 = minority) has a near zero statistical effect on the probability of assignment in most cases. That is, in a process deliberately structured by party so that proportionate representation is achieved (usually with rounding error working to the majority party's advantage), the expectation is a zero effect for the party variable. To observe a positive effect for majority status, the majority would have to reserve a larger than proportionate share of seats on a committee. For some committees (Appropriations, Budget, Rules, and Ways and Means), the majority party does so, but it does not do so for the committees that Krehbiel chooses to examine (Ray and Smith 1983).

Does the majority party's decision to structure party ratios as it does mean that there is no party effect in committee assignments? Does it mean that the majority party is conceding to the chamber median or simply indifferent about committee composition and so is willing to give away a "fair share" of seats to the minority party? No and no. The majority party only needs a majority of votes on the committees whose policy choices affect the party's interests. For the committees that matter most to the majority party, the majority party leaders reserve a disproportionately large number of seats for their party. These "exclusive" committees are excluded from Krehbiel's analysis. Krehbiel cares about explaining variation around the mean; parties worry about controlling majorities. Those (largely proportionate) majorities give the majority party a monopoly over committee and subcommittee chairmanships, control of committee agendas, and two-thirds or more of committee staff.

Finally, Krehbiel makes a strange move in characterizing the dimensionality of the policy space in his applications (Krehbiel 1991). Each committee is assumed to have jurisdiction over a single policy dimension that can be measured by a related interest group rating scale. Collectively, there are multiple, separate dimensions that must be assumed to never be at issue in the same legislative battle. Apparently, the larger policy space in which Congress operates is multidimensional, but no standing or conference committee suffers the complexities and possibilities of a multidimensional space. This is not credible.

SECOND-STAGE STUDIES OF PARTY EFFECTS

Krehbiel bequeathed an ambiguous standard for evaluating party effects and an unconvincing illustration of its importance. Nevertheless, a small industry emerged to demonstrate party effects in congressional roll-call voting controlling for "preferences." Most of the subsequent studies also relied on the spatial model but were no more clear than Krehbiel about the nature of preferences or party influence. This literature is large and reflects great ingenuity. Between 1993 and 2006,

I count about 90 articles, book chapters, and books that address party effects. Wisely, the authors of these studies have ignored Krehbiel's analysis of the allocation of committee assignments between the parties, but the literature does address a wide range of subjects. I can only discuss a sample of these studies.

The Preferences and Parties Series

The Krehbiel argument was the explicit foundation for a set of studies of floor voting in which the preferences versus party contest was made the central issue. Like Krehbiel, the authors of these studies adopted the spatial model as the baseline for evaluating party effects. As a consequence, they share some of the weaknesses of Krehbiel's argument.

Snyder and Groseclose initiated this series of papers by proposing a way to estimate legislators' preferences from the roll-call voting record without the contamination of party effects (Snyder and Groseclose 2000). The argument is that party influence (direct influence) will be exerted on close votes only where the outcome is in doubt. Party-free estimates of preferences can be obtained by dropping the close votes and estimating preferences on the lopsided votes (greater than a 65–35 split, in this case, with comparable splits used for votes on which a supermajority is required). Snyder and Groseclose improve on Krehbiel's approach by allowing multiple dimensions (and scores) to represent preferences. The party-free measure then serves as the baseline for estimating party effects on the close votes. Most of the post–Civil War Congresses were examined, although a significant number of Congresses were dropped for a variety of reasons – a small number of lopsided votes, a very high correlation between party and preferences, which prevents estimates of their independent effects, or a very small minority party. In the average Congress for the House, 54 percent of the close votes showed a statistically significant party effect (with party coded as Democrat vs. Republican) controlling for preferences. Significant party effects are observed most frequently for priorities of the majority party leadership, procedural motions, and economic and budgetary measures. Overall, party effects are about the same for two houses of Congress.

Direct party influence, Snyder and Groseclose suggest, can be calculated by determining the proportion of total party differences (Rice's index based on the percent voting yea in each party) that is due to the estimated party effect. The party effect ranges from about one-fifth to about three-fifths of party differences. The effect is larger in the late nineteenth and early twentieth centuries than in the mid– to late twentieth century and then intensifies in the 1990s.

The Snyder–Groseclose technique of estimating preferences was challenged by McCarty and colleagues on the grounds that the technique exaggerates party effects (McCarty et al. 2001). The critique is based on the observation that dropping close votes before estimating preferences makes it unlikely that legislators in the moderate range of the policy spectrum can be differentiated. If moderate legislators are incorrectly estimated to have similar or identical preferences when they are different, then behavioral differences that are due to differences in preferences will be attributed to the correlated differences in party affiliation. Preference effects will be underestimated and party effects will be overestimated. McCarty and colleagues claim to have demonstrated the exaggerated party effect by examining the correlation of (a) the ranking of legislators based on all votes and (b) the ranking based on close votes for the same single dimension. For moderate legislators, the correlation is strong, which suggests that dropping close votes, where party effects were hypothesized to be strong, makes little difference and preference-based voting predominates even on the close votes for which Snyder and Groseclose hypothesize that party effects are most pronounced.

McCarty and colleagues then propose another test of party effects. A little background is necessary. In applications of spatial theory, a *cutpoint* is the location on a dimension that best divides the yea and nay votes. Put differently, it is the location that minimizes the errors in predicting which legislators vote yea and which legislators vote nay, as is illustrated in Figure 4.2. If legislators are voting according to their preferences, they vote for the closest of two proposals, creating a cutpoint that bisects the line segment between the two proposals.

The McCarty team postulates that party influence affects the location of ideal points. Relative to where they would be otherwise, Democrats' ideal points are pushed to the left and Republicans' ideal points are pushed to the right. In practice, a single cutpoint for all

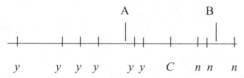

FIGURE 4.1. Legislators arranged on a left-right dimension, hypothetical yea and nay votes (y and n) on amendment (A) proposed to a bill (B), with cutpoint (C).

legislators produces some errors in prediction. Some of these errors may be due to the success of parties in attracting the votes of partisans who, on the basis of their overall voting record, would be expected to vote with the opposition. If this party influence is present, identifying a cutpoint separately for each party's legislators should produce fewer total errors. The McCarty team claims that the two-cutpoint analysis makes only a very small improvement over the single-cutpoint approach – the equivalent of a shift across somewhat more than 10 percent of the House membership.

Snyder and Groseclose refused to accept the McCarty team's broadside on their analysis (Snyder and Groseclose 2001). Their response was that a significant number of errors occur in the estimation of a unidimensional spatial model. A significant number of legislators who should be on the winning side of some votes are, in practice, on the losing side. Errors generate variation in estimated preferences among moderate legislators, as we might expect because they are the likely targets of party influence. And, because the Snyder–Groseclose approach sets separate bounds for defining close votes on motions requiring supermajorities to pass (suspension of the rules, veto overrides), the moderate legislators were split on many votes and could be differentiated.

More important, Snyder and Groseclose introduced new data on preferences derived from candidates' responses to a survey administered by Project Vote Smart to inform voters about candidates' policy positions (Figure 4.2). The results, which were reported elsewhere in greater detail (Ansolabehere et al. 2001), provide a more direct measure of preferences, which can be compared with voting behavior. Scatterplots of the scaled survey responses (labeled NPAT) and two sets of voting scales, one for all votes and one for lopsided votes, are shown in the figure below, which is taken from the Snyder–Groseclose response.

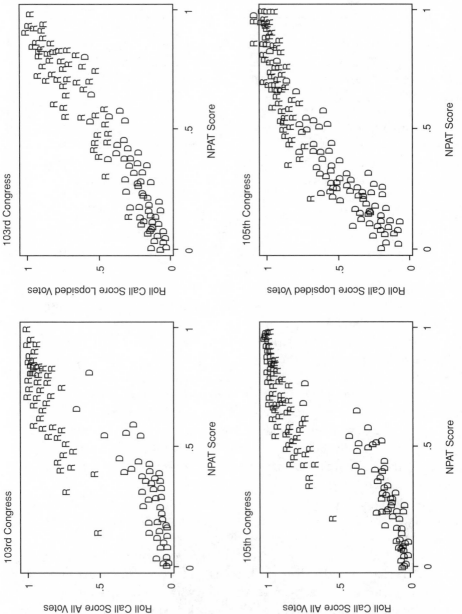

FIGURE 4.2. Ideal point estimates using NPAT, all roll calls, and lopsided roll calls. *Source:* Snyder and Groseclose (2001;

In contrast, the scales for lopsided votes show a much longer linear relationship with the survey scales, leaving us with the inference that party effects are significant in scales that include all votes. Not surprisingly, the party effect, controlling for either the survey scale or the lopsided votes scale estimates of preferences, is significant in the three Congresses in the 1990s for which the survey data were available at that time.

Last in this series of papers is the argument by Cox and Poole that confronts errors of interpretation in previous work and reports that significant party effects are incorporated in NOMINATE-based scores (Cox and Poole 2002). The argument is that estimates of ideal points from all roll-call votes in a Congress reflect average party effects across the votes for that Congress. No party effect would produce a constant zero estimate of the party effect for all votes. The NOMINATE procedure yields estimated ideal points and cutpoints, which generate a predicted Rice index of party difference for an average vote. For any single vote, a party difference that is either greater than the mean or lesser than is expected on the average demonstrates that variation in party effects occur and, therefore, that a party effect exists. Cox and Poole find variation in Rice scores that (very loosely) relate to expected patterns in party influence, and observe stronger party effects for votes on procedural, organizational, and priority matters. These stronger effects are reported as confirming the view that congressional parties are, at the bottom, procedural cartels to which legislators give allegiance (see Chapter 6).

Comments on the Party and Preferences Series

I cannot argue that the ingenuity and computational technology put into the party-and-preferences series represent a substantial improvement over studies like Clausen's, published a scholarly generation earlier. The new arguments reflect a more fully developed model of individual decision making and benefit from the computational power that makes it possible to estimate models repetitively over all Congresses. Nevertheless, these studies reflect several weaknesses that earlier studies at least attempted to address. I divide my observations into three parts related to preferences, party, and the vote.

The bottom line about preferences is that they come from some-where, and that "somewhere" is masked in empirical analysis of the party and preferences series. Preferences become a substitute for all of the nonparty influences that should be incorporated into the multivari-ate analysis required to evaluate claims about party influence. Kingdon, Clausen, and others warn us that party is correlated with many of the forces that impinge on legislators. There is no doubt party is correlated with preferences, however conceived, but it is likely to be correlated with many other features of the congressional environment that may influence floor voting. Constituency preferences, the strain of lobbying pressures, administration effort, and other forces are likely to be at work. Only if we assume that these factors have constant or random influence relative to party – and so do not produce any systematic vari-ation across votes and legislators – can we safely assume that they do not account for behavior that we might incorrectly attribute to party. This is a truly heroic assumption.

The implications of this theoretical misstep and methodological sin are readily apparent for both the Snyder–Groseclose and the Cox–Poole studies. In the original Snyder–Groseclose study, the case is made that party influence is more likely to be at work for close votes than lop-sided votes. My working hypothesis would be that all political forces are more actively engaged on close votes than lopsided votes so that cal-culating "preferences" on lopsided votes eliminates at least the short-term influence of many political actors from the resulting rankings. Consequently, the preferences, so measured, do not control for all of the important nonparty, short-term forces that may be correlated with party. And the estimated party effect captures the effects of all of the forces that are correlated with it. In the Cox–Poole study, the ques-tion is whether the Rice party differences scores on individual votes are different than what is expected on average for a given Congress on the basis of the estimated ideal point and cutting lines. The implicit, but unjustified, assumption is all nonparty forces are constant or at least vary randomly relative to party influence. The remarkably explicit Cox–Poole argument that "party pressure" from leaders produces the observed variation in the Rice index is not credible. In both studies, explicit and specific claims about total party effects are made, but these claims are deceptive.

The conceptualization of party influence does not fair much better in the party and preference series. Direct party influence, as I defined it in Chapter 3, is the somewhat ambiguously specified subject of papers in this series. If we take seriously the phrasing used in these studies, then we are asked to believe that "party pressure" and "party discipline" are being measured. Missing is a theory of when and where direct party influence will be applied and when, in the face of competing forces (not just from the other party in the chamber), party influence wins. To be sure, after specifying a preference-party test and demonstrating it, these studies show some predicted variation in party effects over types of votes and issue domains, but the studies do not justify the inference that the parties influence the behavior of all legislators.

A theory of party effects matters. If we think that party pressure tends to be targeted at only a few legislators in any given legislative battle as the logic of the spatial model implies, it is unlikely to be observed as statistically significant effects in estimates based on the behavior of all legislators or analysis of group-level scores. My guess is that, as a general rule, party leaders do not care about generating statistically significant influence; they would rather win legislative battles. Moreover, if the unidimensional spatial model (plus party) captures legislative politics, then party pressure would be directed repeatedly at the same legislators whose support for party positions on motions for which their votes are pivotal would alter their estimated ideal points. If so, the party effect would not be visible. If, to the contrary, the targeted group of legislators is quite large and varied – say, 10 percent or more of a party on a regular basis – then it seems likely that the underlying spatial account or the unidimensional characterization of the policy space is inadequate.

If party pressure is truly targeted at a few legislators, then how do we account for the party effects that *are* found? I have reported my hunches. There are other forms of direct and indirect influence and there are many nonparty actors attempting to influence legislators whose influence, collectively, condition voting in ways that correlate with party.

The Cox–Poole formulation of ideal points as a summary measure of the political forces at work in legislators' voting decisions brings us almost back to Clausen's conception of legislators' policy positions.

Rather than juxtaposing preferences and party effects, we return to sorting the party effects from the net effects of other influences on legislators' policy positions. This is an improvement over the other efforts in the preferences and parties series. Still, the term *ideal points* remains in use, a term that elsewhere is used interchangeably with *preferences*. But the fundamental conceptual flaw remains and is reflected in the Cox–Poole conclusion:

> The methodological issue is quite general: how best to detect the presence of party pressure in legislative voting analyses, given only members' recorded votes on each roll call? The trick is to identify systematic departures from the voting behavior one would expect on the basis of members' estimated ideal points alone, while recognizing that those ideal point estimates may already reflect party pressure. (Cox and Poole, 2002, 488)

This remains a misguided research design. They cannot – in fact, no one can – detect party pressure given only members' recorded votes, trick or no trick.

The final Cox–Poole claim that stronger-than-average party effects on procedural and organizational votes supports the cartel theory requires care in interpretation. The argument that "party pressure" is greater on procedural and organizational votes may be an overly simplistic characterization of the relationship between legislators and their parties. It remains unclear that pressure is applied widely enough to affect the Rice index scores in a systematic way. If, instead, legislators recognize the importance of such votes for the party and appreciate the value of their parties as procedural cartels, they would voluntarily support the party position. Pressure would not be required. Moreover, it is not clear why the argument applies to minority legislators whose party cannot be expected to win procedural votes even if the cartel theory is correct. To repeat, these studies lack a meaningful theory of legislative parties and use terms like *pressure* far too loosely.

A final observation: Even if the preferences versus party debate is misconceived, I have great sympathy for the party and preferences series of papers. Among the most deserving research interests in the study of Congress are long-term trends in party influence and the forces that drive them. As the authors of these papers are fully aware, the absence of appropriate data does not allow us to estimate the effects of the multiple forces at work over the many decades for which we seek to characterize congressional policy making. Although we know better, we hope that many of the forces that might alter partisan voting alignments in Congress are either constant or random over time, allowing us to attribute change in partisan alignments over time to change in associated partisan processes. The subject is important so we do the best we can. We go wrong when we make claims about the existence and size of party effects and fail to note essential qualifications about the limits of the analysis.

Alternative Approaches to the Party vs. Preferences Debate

Examining the totality of the massive roll-call voting record of Congress since the Civil War is not the only way to identify party effects. Other analytical and empirical approaches take the Krehbiel challenge seriously but do a better job of establishing the presence of party effects and, in some cases, estimating the strength of those effects. By giving attention to situations in which specific actions by leaders and individual legislators can be associated with partisan behavior, the findings of these studies are, on the whole, more persuasive than the general voting studies reported in the previous subsection. In most cases, the research design involves a natural experiment that sheds light on partisan forces.[11] Regrettably, while they are more persuasive with respect to establishing party effects, the studies with alternative approaches are placed in less visible publications and receive less attention than the general voting studies.

In first place among the alternative approaches are two studies of voting on House special rules and final passage motions (Sinclair 2002; Young and Wilkins 2005). In both studies, the argument is that House majority party leaders must attract the support of legislators who seek to balance sometimes competing electoral and policy goals. Leaders do so, in part, by designing special rules for the floor consideration of major bills that package provisions, exclude policy alternatives, and provide political cover for party colleagues. These tactics help to attract

---

[11] The most common natural experiment in research on Congress involves a comparison of legislators before and after a seat in the House or Senate has changed. This comparison has been used to examine incumbency, constituency, and party effects. A good entry point to relevant literature is Brady and Sinclair (1984).

votes for the leadership position from legislators who otherwise would be pressured by other forces.

The empirical question is whether the pattern of voting on the special rule and on the bill reflects party considerations. If all legislators vote on the rule according to their preferences about the bill, the rule and bill votes would be identical. In practice, the two votes are far from identical. Commonly, some legislators, particularly majority party legislators, vote for the rule and against the bill. They either hoped for changes in the bill that did not materialize or, it is reasoned, cast a "procedural vote" as their leadership requested. If the rule did not allow amendments and the opposing legislators still voted for the rule, they were casting a partisan procedural vote, too. Thus, the more restrictive the rule, the more partisan procedural votes are likely to be cast.[12] In fact, there are many majority party legislators who vote for the rule and against the bill, particularly for closed rules. Moreover, among those who voted for the rule and against the bill, being a member of the majority party greatly increases the probability of voting for the rule, controlling for NOMINATE scores. The conclusion: Majority party legislators allow legislation to proceed that they do not favor on final passage.

Several scholars have taken advantage of an uncommon occurrence – a legislator switching parties and remaining in Congress – to observe the partisan effect on floor behavior. McCarty and colleagues tucked into their article of the two-cutpoint analysis a report on changes in estimated ideal points for the 19 legislators who switched parties between 1947 and 1998. On average, the party switchers leaped over 25 percent of their colleagues in their relative rank on the liberal–conservative dimension, suggesting a sizable party effect. Other studies, based on longer time series or more recent cases, report finding similar changes (Clinton et al. 2004; Hager and Talbert 2000; Nokken 2000; Nokken and Poole 2004). Only one study is reasonably comprehensive

---

[12] On the other side, it is common for some legislators, particularly minority party legislators, to vote against the rule and for the bill even when the bill is not changed much between the two votes. Such legislators could not have voted on the rule hoping to kill the bill, although they may have preferred more opportunities to amend it than was allowed in the rule. Thus, contrary to Sinclair's argument about minority legislators, there is nothing necessarily inconsistent with preference-motivated votes against the rule and for the bill.

and it demonstrates that significant changes in behavior among party switchers tends to occur when the parties are polarized (Nokken and Poole 2004). Plainly, party switching shows some form of party effects, even substantial party effects, indicating that party influence or other factors associated with party affiliation, such as the composition of the primary electorate in the home district, are at work.

Also worthy of special notice are studies that attempt to see the application of direct influence as party leaders do. Two studies examine the whip process. In the House, the parties' whip systems are used to identify legislators' intentions to support or oppose party positions, which assists leaders in their efforts to target direct influence. In a study of the Democrats' whip counts for 16 bills in 1971 and 1972, two-thirds of the legislators who switched positions between the whip count and floor vote did so in favor of the party (Burden and Frisby 2004). Moreover, more detailed study of leaders' influence efforts on one of those bills shows that leaders target just a handful of legislators whose votes are most readily acquired – those reporting uncertainty about their intended vote (Burden and Frisby 2004; Dodd 1978; Dodd and Sullivan 1981).

Even more useful is a study by Behringer and Evans in which the whip polls of the two House parties for the same bills in the 1977–1980 period were examined (Behringer and Evans 2006). Particularly noteworthy is that on 13 (59.1 percent) of the 22 items on which the parties had comparable polls the minority party position won. On 20 of the bills, the majority leadership's poll showed that the party was short of a floor majority. Moreover, these jointly polled bills on which the outcome was in doubt were plainly important to the majority party leadership. Thus, the majority leadership was *simultaneously* seeking to schedule legislation for floor action and looking for additional votes and was not always successful. The whip polls of the period allowed the investigators to identify undecided legislators in both parties and observe their subsequent behavior. Leaders won the support of a majority of undecided legislators within their parties. Controlling for NOMINATE scores, the party effect on eventual voting behavior was statistically significant and substantively strong for undecided legislators.

The findings of the whip studies are important. The observation that there are a substantial number of undecided legislators in important legislative battles calls into question the assumption that ideal points based on the total roll-call record account for the policy positions in those battles. As a consequence, it undermines the assumption of some studies that a chamber median exists, is always known, and drives party strategies. And the observation suggests that party leaders must possess, or must acquire, more detailed information about their colleagues' political motivations, diverse issue concerns, and susceptibility to influence than the simple versions of the spatial model imply.

Closely associated with the conduct of whip polls is the practice of legislators promising their votes to leaders if their votes are needed to win. This is a situation that is sometimes reported in journalistic accounts and can be found in notations on party whips records.[13] King and Zeckhauser hypothesize that this practice, which clearly shows a partisan process, should produce two kinds of outcomes for the majority party – narrow victories and substantial losses. On examining the "key" votes identified by Congressional Quarterly, that is what the investigators find (King and Zeckhauser 2003).

CONCLUSION

The evidence that congressional parties exert direct influence on legislators is substantial. The half-century struggle to estimate the effects of party independent of other forces is not over, but the circumstantial evidence that direct party influence is significant is beginning to appear overwhelming. The most impressive evidence comes from the studies in which investigators use related votes (votes on special rules and final passage) or contrast whip counts with subsequent behavior. These studies feature a specific form of party influence and a closer match of party action (selection of special rules, whip polls) to legislators' behavior. They also go beyond the roll-call voting record to creatively exploit the documentary record of congressional policy making.

The spatial model has clarified some of the important issues in estimating the direct influence of party. Unfortunately, the original challenge laid down by Krehbiel was poorly conceived. Subsequent efforts to control for legislators' preferences in estimating party effects are

---

[13] Personal correspondence with Professor C. Lawrence Evans, who has inspected many years of whip poll records and related documents.

plagued with conceptual and methodological problems. The relationship between preferences and nonparty forces is never clarified, the nature of the party influence being measured is hardly discussed, and the claims about total party influence are not credible.

In the end, a theory of party is required to search for party effects. Even when the search focuses on direct effects, as the studies reviewed in this chapter do, we have to know how we might expect that influence to be exercised. Will it focus on a few pivotal legislators? Will it shift all fellow partisans' scores to the left or right? Will one party's influence reach into the other party to acquire votes? Will it be used to reinforce the correlated influence of the president? For the most part, the political science of direct influence is silent on these questions. There is work to be done.

5

Recent Theories of Party Influence: Cartel and Conditional Party Government Theory

Observant political scientists look for patterns and trends in the contemporary Congress and try to identify the generalizations that explain them. During the time I have followed congressional politics closely, we have witnessed two waves of change in the political of the House of Representatives that motivated explanatory efforts. In the first wave, stretching from the mid-1960s to the mid-1970s, the committee-oriented, chairman-dominated politics of the mid–twentieth century was challenged by liberal Democrats, who required chairs to stand for election in the party caucus, forced the creation of subcommittees with real policy-making capability, and enhanced the influence of the Speaker over the referral of legislation to committee and over the floor agenda. Hyperdecentralization was the theme of writing about the effects of the first reform wave. In the second wave, from the late 1970s to the present, House party leadership asserted even more control over the agenda and often directed the details of the policy-making process in the House. Centralization was the theme of political scientists writing about the postreform wave.

Many political scientists contributed to our understanding of the reform and postreform eras. Dodd and Oppenheimer's 1977 edited volume, *Congress Reconsidered*, did more than any other book to review and interpret the reform era and its consequences (Dodd and Oppenheimer 1977). A key theme of the essays in the book was that weakening institutional capacity of a more decentralized Congress in the face of many challenges – the energy crises, environmental challenges, and so on – that required large, integrated, coherent legislation that only effective central coordination by party leaders could provide. Dodd argued that the 1970s were a part of a long-term cycle in which legislators sought to improve their individual power at the expense of the institution (Dodd 1977)

One political scientist more than any other is responsible for characterizing House decision making in the postreform era. In 1981, following her service on the staff of Majority Leader James Wright (D-TX) as a Congressional Fellow of the American Political Science Association, Barbara Sinclair began to write about developments in majority party leadership that ran counter to the trends often emphasized in the first wave of accounts of the reform era (Sinclair 1981a, 1981b, 1983, 1994, 1995b, 2000). Sinclair observed that new issues challenged the old committee system, deference to senior committee and party leaders evaporated, rank-and-file legislators demanded more involvement in decision making on major issues, an assertive membership exploited the advent of recorded voting in the Committee of the Whole by offering more floor amendments, and leaders operated in an environment of much greater uncertainty about what would happen and when. She reported that the Democratic leadership responded to the new challenges by expanding the whip organization efforts and naming numerous task forces, rewarding loyalists with coveted committee assignments, manipulating bill referral to party advantage, and structuring the floor agenda to party advantage through control of the Rules Committee. Almost inadvertently, Sinclair labeled this the postreform House, one in which the power of committee chairs was weak, the majority party caucus was strong, and the majority leadership assumed a more central place in House policy making (Sinclair 1981b).

Thanks to the work of Sinclair and others, parties regained a central role in the study of Congress. In this chapter, I outline and evaluate two theories of congressional parties, conditional party government and cartel theory, that emerged in the late 1990s that reflect this new focus on parties. As I will note, both were built on the work of scholars of the 1980s and early 1990s who identified ways in which parties were influencing legislators and legislative outcomes. My conclusion about these theories is that they are incomplete but compatible.

The most glaring deficiency in accounts of both theories is the lack of attention given to the Senate. As I argue, this matters. My conclusion about the evidence for the two theories is that their proponents have been less persuasive than they need to be. The discussion establishes some testable propositions that are explored with new evidence in Chapter 7.

CONDITIONAL PARTY GOVERNMENT

Preliminary Developments

In the 1980s, majority party leadership appeared to become more important. Both more pro-active efforts to influence legislators and more creative use of special rules to structure floor action on major bills received the attention of outside observers. Plain to all observers was that the composition of the Democratic party in Congress was changing. Republicans began to win seats in the Democratic stronghold of the South in the 1970s and continued to be successful in that region in the 1980s (Abramowitz 1980, 1994; Cohen 1981; Rohde 1992). As the Republicans replaced conservative southern Democrats, the Democrats became more uniformly liberal and the Republicans become even more conservative, producing more polarized parties in the House and Senate.

These developments internal and external to Congress seemed to be related to each other – just as a parallel literature was suggesting for previous eras. I noted in Chapter 2 that Cooper and Brady argued that the degree of homogeneity in the electoral coalition determines the legislative party's cohesiveness or strength, an argument that Brady made a general argument for congressional policy making and extended to the Senate in a series of articles published in the 1970s and 1980s (Brady 1985, 1988; Brady et al. 1989; Cooper and Brady 1981; Cooper et al. 1977). By the time the developments in the House of the 1980s were digested, the connection between the homogeneity of parties' electoral coalitions and congressional voting patterns was established.

A more difficult question is whether congressional party leadership behaved any differently, and with stronger effects, when the electoral and congressional parties were polarized. After reviewing the basic strategies of House Democratic leadership at the start of the 1980s, Sinclair observed:

The majority party leadership does not have now and never has had the resources necessary to lead successfully an utterly fragmented party. Without agreement among a substantial portion of the Democratic membership on at least some basic tenets, the most skillful leadership is doomed to failure. (Sinclair 1981a)

Sinclair's observation echoed the Cooper and Brady view that leadership strategies, relative to the underlying degree of agreement within the party, have a marginal effect on legislative outcomes. Innovation in party efforts represented a "coping strategy" that hardly suggested that leaders were becoming more powerful at the start of the 1980s (Bach and Smith 1988; Smith 1985).

The experience of the 1980s produced a change in emphasis. In the late 1980s, congressional parties were more polarized and majority party leaders – Speakers Thomas P. "Tip" O'Neill, James Wright, and Thomas Foley – appeared to be wielding more influence. The fear of a dysfunctional, decentralized policy-making process in the House had faded. Sinclair, writing in 1989, observed that "House Democrats are more cohesive in their voting behavior than they have been in decades," contributing to "strong, policy-oriented leadership" (Sinclair 1989). Writing in 1990 about the influence of standing committees, Smith and Deering hypothesized that

the alignment of members on important issues shapes the role of committees as well. The alignment of members, of course, is primarily a function of constituency preferences, although forces internal to Congress – the persuasiveness of a party leader, for example – can make a difference at times. But whatever the cause, if the majority party is highly cohesive on the issues and most issues are salient, it will be in a position to impose policy decisions by virtue of having enough votes to win, and a system of party-dominated committees will develop . . . [The] development of stronger parties and weaker committees is exactly what came to pass in Congress during the 1980s". (Smith and Deering 1990)

Finally, in 1991, Rohde summarized the lessons of the 1980s by going a step farther: "Parties are consequential in shaping members' preferences, the character of the issues on the agenda, the nature of the legislative alternatives, and ultimate political outcomes, and they will remain important as long as the underlying forces that created this partisan resurgence persist" (Rohde 1991) This argument was labeled "conditional party government" by Rohde. The label stuck.

By the time Republicans gained a House majority in 1994 and Newt Gingrich was elected Speaker, political scientists were primed to connect Speaker Gingrich's influence to the polarization of the parties – particularly, the cohesiveness of the House Republicans – and to attribute some of the subsequent Republican success to Gingrich's remarkable assertion of control over committee chairs and their agendas. That is, the underlying homogeneity of policy views in the majority party was the most important force at work, but the influence that Gingrich exercised over committees and individual legislators made an additional contribution to the expeditious passage of the Republican program. Several of the essays in the 1997 edition of *Congress Reconsidered* explored the theme of how the new party and committee strategies and practices altered the policy-making process, enhanced the capability of the majority party leadership, and rushed a considerable volume of legislation through the House (Dodd and Oppenheimer 1997).

Theoretical Arguments

With the new House majority party in place, Aldrich and Rohde picked up on the theme emerging in the late 1980s to extend the application of the conditional party government (CPG) thesis and transformed the discussion into an explicit contest of theories. The first post-1994 expositions on CPG were staged as responses to Krehbiel's challenge (Krehbiel 1993) and later the attention shifted to an alternative theory of congressional parties, cartel theory. From these various accounts of CPG, several theoretical claims and empirical propositions were offered (Aldrich 1995; Aldrich et al. 2002; Aldrich and Rohde 1995, 1997, 2000a, 2000b, 2004).[1]

---

[1] CPG has not yet been given a single authoritative treatment by Aldrich and Rohde. In each presentation, a nuance or two is added to the argument. In one account (Aldrich and Rohde 2000b), the authors cite Rohde (1991) as the initial account and Aldrich (1995) as amplifying and formalizing the theory. No spatial or game theoretic treatment is provided in the Aldrich publications. In another account of the same year (Aldrich and Rohde 2000a), a conference paper is cited as the source for the theory (Aldrich and Rohde 1995). The conference paper was the basis for a published paper (Aldrich and Rohde 1997), but the spatial theory in the original paper was dropped from the published version. Lacking a single source, I reconstruct the frequently repeated elements of the argument in this section.

The following theoretical and empirical claims are associated with the CPG argument:

Policy space
- The policy space in which legislation is considered often is not unidimensional; on many bills, many possible majorities could be constructed to pass or oppose legislation.
- Only issues that divide the electorate and candidates on partisan lines motivate legislators to increase the power of party organs within Congress.
- Party-led agenda setting will favor a selection of issues that have partisan cleavages.

Legislators' Goals and Delegation of Power to Party
- A legislator is willing to delegate power to central party leaders in proportion to the frequency with which that power will be used in his or her interest.
- Legislators have multiple motivations (reelection, policy, power) that can conflict at times.
- Fellow partisans' willingness to delegate power to central party leaders increases as the homogeneity of their policy preferences (intraparty cohesiveness) increases.
- Fellow partisans' willingness to delegate power to central party leaders increases as their policy preferences become more differentiated from legislators in the opposing party (interparty distance).
- Fellow partisans' willingness to delegate power to central party leaders increases as the policy preferences of legislators become more polarized by party.

Party Influence and Legislative Outcomes
- Even if a floor majority exists, collective action problems stand in the way of mobilizing it.
- Parties, because of their organization, are advantaged in the process of building floor majorities.
- Party organization and leadership is at least a partial solution to the collective action problems associated with building floor majorities.
- As more power is delegated to partisan institutions, party institutions are better able to overcome collective action problems and realize collective interests.

- When the parties are polarized and partisans delegate power to partisan institutions, the majority party, by virtue of being in the majority, can increase the power of its party organs more than the minority party can.
- When the parties are polarized, the enhanced power of the majority party leadership will move outcomes toward the center of the majority party and away from the center of the whole chamber, as would be expected from the preferences of legislators alone.

The bottom line is the last proposition – party influence varies with party polarization. The argument should not be confused with the argument of Cooper and Brady (1981). The Cooper–Brady claim is that the influence of party leaders is never particularly strong; rather, party success is determined almost entirely by the alignment of policy preferences that legislators bring with them into office. The CPG argument is that the alignment of policy preferences – the degree of party polarization – determines the extent to which party leaders can influence legislators to move in the party's direction beyond the preferences they bring with them into office. Therefore, the majority party experiences increasing returns on polarization. With polarized parties, the majority party wins more than it should from the imported preferences alone.

Observations about CPG Theory

The CPG arguments bring together a remarkably wide range of empirical claims into a fairly coherent story about variation in party influence in Congress. The account integrates the Cooper–Brady line of argument on electoral coalitions and congressional party alignments, collective action arguments, and arguments about the bases of party influence within Congress. Broadly speaking, it appears to be confirmed by the aggressiveness of party leaders in recent years. Still, CPG, as presented to date, has ambiguities.

The presentations of CPG argument focus on variation in party influence rather than on the motivations of legislators for joining and maintaining congressional parties. Consequently, there is no discussion of the baseline level of direct or indirect influence, if any, that is exercised by parties by virtue of their existence (for multiple reasons) and there is no hint at the range in party influence that we might expect. The credible but implicit argument is that party influence is substantial when parties are polarized, but the investment in party mechanisms may yield party influence at other times. Just how much influence is due to a commitment to enhancing the party's reputation, getting colleagues reelected, and other possible interests? The CPG thesis is silent on this.

CPG theorists appear to share my point of view about the multiple motivations of legislators. These motivations create certain strategic problems for party leaders (as addressed by Bach and Smith 1988; Gamm and Smith 2002; Sinclair 1983, 1995b) and allow for multiple ways to appeal to legislators, as I have outlined in previous chapters. Nevertheless, the primary party effect that CPG theorists are concerned about is the shift in policy from the chamber median toward the majority party median. Another possible set of goals, getting colleagues reelected and gaining or maintaining majority party status, is not given serious treatment. As a result, the strategic tradeoffs between policy objectives and majority party status that motivate leadership and themselves constitute collective action problems for the party, are not addressed. There may be times when shifting legislative outcomes away from the chamber median toward the party median is less important than competing electoral objectives.

Still, we certainly should expect to find policy effects even if some situations require that party leaders take into account nonpolicy considerations. The question is, How do we characterize the expected policy effects? I phrased the relevant proposition as follows: When the parties are polarized, the enhanced power of the majority party leadership will move outcomes toward the center of the majority party and away from the center of the whole chamber, as would be expected from the preferences of legislators alone. This is taken from Aldrich and Rohde (1997), where the somewhat ambiguous term *center* is used, presumably to avoid the implication that the policy space is unidimensional, which would be contrary to the Rohde (1994) critique of Krehbiel's spatial theory. In contrast, in Aldrich and Rohde (2000b) and elsewhere (Aldrich et al. 2002), the majority *median* and chamber *median* are used in the description of the same principle, which implies a unidimensional space. Yet, in the same paper it is emphasized that parties take an interest in some issues, perhaps multiple issues, but not others, which implies a multidimensional space. Thus, CPG accounts do not provide clear guidance about the dimensionality of the policy space and remain imprecise about the medians, if they exist, that are to be compared.

The dual components of party polarization – intraparty cohesiveness and interparty distance – are given treatment in the theoretical expositions of CPG, but only intraparty cohesiveness is regularly discussed in applications of the theory. In fact, the role of interparty distance is unclear, at least as a theoretical matter. We can imagine that the median policy preferences of two parties could drift apart while the parties' internal cohesiveness does not change. For most legislators, such a drift would make a win for the other side more costly, so perhaps a greater investment in the party would be justified, as Aldrich and Rohde argue. Nevertheless, it remains unclear why a majority party would not exploit its advantages to maximize its policy gains even if the parties were not far apart and the policy gains over a chamber median outcome were not large. The total policy gain could not be large because the distance between the chamber and majority party medians would not be large, but, relative to the possible gain, the realized gain could be substantial. I would expect that most majority party members would insist on exploiting their advantages to realize the possible gains. We must introduce other considerations – transaction and opportunity costs, for example – to conclude otherwise. And if those considerations vary systematically, we should incorporate them in our theory of party.

An unanswered question is whether intraparty cohesiveness and interparty distance exhaust the major features of election outcomes that are relevant to party strategies and influence. For example, CPG assumes that majority status matters but otherwise is silent on the question of whether the size of the two parties makes a difference. A case can be made that party size conditions the exercise of party influence and, therefore, conditions the strength of party effects that are measured. As studies of the development of parliamentary rules argue, relative party strength, taken as the product of party size and party cohesiveness, appears to be related to the suppression and creation of minority rights (Binder 1996, 1997; Dion 1997). This makes sense. A large majority party can accomplish its objectives even if it loses the votes of many fellow partisans, but a small majority party, even if it is fairly cohesive, may need to exercise care in setting the agenda, exercise influence over legislators at critical moments, and exercise exceptionally good judgment in weighing its policy and electoral interests. For the minority party, larger size improves the chances of winning and is likely to affect its leaders' strategies. Put differently, holding party cohesiveness constant, an increment of party influence is of greater value to the smaller majority party and to the larger minority party. Thus, I would hypothesize that greater party influence will be observed as the party strength of the two parties approaches parity, controlling for polarization.

If Aldrich and Rohde are correct that legislators have interests beyond policy outcomes, such as electoral and power interests, legislators and their parties should be concerned about party size. Any political interest that is served by being in the majority party status will motivate an interest in increasing and maintaining majority party size. Majority party status affects both legislators' personal power and their fundraising capacity. Party size surely is related to the vulnerability of the majority party at the polls and therefore is likely to shape party leaders' strategies in important ways.

Additional Observations About the Evidence

We must look for three kinds of evidence to confirm the CPG theory. The first is that party polarization varies in a manner that could plausibly be related to changes in party mechanisms within the House and Senate. The evidence from Aldrich and Rohde is mixed. The second kind of evidence would support the argument that party mechanisms are delegated more resources when the parties are polarized than at other times and that these resources are deployed to influence legislators' behavior. The evidence is strong. The third kind would show that party influence (measured as a shift on policy outcomes away from the chamber median and toward the majority party median) is greater when the parties are polarized than at other times. The evidence is weak.

Aldrich, Berger, and Rohde (2002) calculate polarization by mathematically combining measures of four features of the distribution of legislators' policy positions – the difference in the parties' median D-NOMINATE scores, the ratio of the majority party's standard

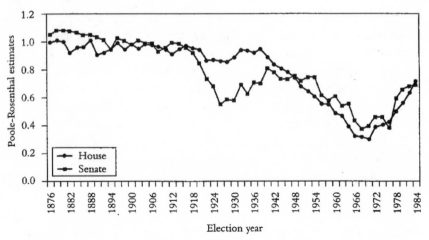

FIGURE 5.1. Aldrich–Berger–Rohde measure of party polarizaton in the House and Senate, 1876–1984. *Source:* Aldrich, Berger, and Rohde (2002), Figure 2.5.

deviation in D-NOMINATE scores to that of the full House, the correlation between D-NOMINATE scores and party, and proportion of D-NOMINATE scores of the two parties that overlap (Aldrich et al. 2002). The factor scores of the four variables are used as a measure of polarization across the Congresses for the 1876–1984 period. The result, shown in Figure 5.1, do not extend to the developments in the late 1980s and 1990s.

The measure of polarization shows a low level of party polarization in the 1950s and 1960s. Relatively stable levels of polarization characterized the late nineteenth and early twentieth centuries, with the exception of the Senate in the 1920s and 1930s. Thus, by the measure proposed by Aldrich and Rohde, majority parties should have improved the influence of party leaders in the 1980s when party polarization returned. This observation is consistent with the developments in the House that have been noted in this chapter.

The long period of highly polarized House parties in the beginning of the series poses a more serious interpretive problem. The central CPG propositions suggest that the 50-year period – 70 years for the House – following Reconstruction should have been characterized by polarized electoral coalitions and uniformly strong party mechanisms and party effects. Hardly any scholar would characterize the House or Senate in that way. It is inconsistent with the arguments of Cooper,

Brady, and their colleagues cited in the previous section, who observe the relationship between electoral coalition polarization and strong party leadership at the turn of the twentieth century and the subsequent demise of that centralized process after the first decade of the twentieth century. Aldrich et al. offered no explanation for this, except to question their measure of party polarization. We are left with either an unsatisfactory measure of party polarization or a theory in need of elaboration. Thus, the plausibility of the thesis that polarization drives the waxing and waning of party influence remains an open question.

Aldrich and Rohde devote considerable space to the elaboration and centralization of resources in the hands of majority party leaders in the period since the late 1980s. As I have suggested, the evidence from these authors and others is strong. The tightening of the Speaker's grip over the policy-making process of the House following the 1994 elections fits the expected pattern of strengthened party mechanisms when the parties are polarized.

Less well explained by CPG arguments are the developments in the House of the 1970s and early 1980s and, generally, the Senate. Beginning with the revitalization of the Democratic caucus in 1969 and continuing through the mid-1970s, Democrats strengthened the hand of the Speaker in committee assignments, bill referral, and Rules Committee deliberations. They also forced committee chairs to stand for election in the caucus, and forced the decentralization of power within standing committees. These reforms were not fully exploited by Speakers Carl Albert and Thomas O'Neill, both of whom were raised in the old school, but O'Neill eventually used assignments to reward loyalists, used the bill referral process to package legislation in the interests of the party, and initiated a new era in the creative construction of special rules from the Rules Committee. All of this started at the all-time low in the party polarization index of Aldrich et al. and continued more than a decade while polarization remained low.

A way to square the reform era with CPG is to observe that the reforms were intended to weaken the power of full committee chairs and to empower rank-and-file Democrats more than to empower the central leadership (Smith 1985, 1989). Indeed, as I have noted, the decentralizing effects of the reforms were the more prominent immediate consequence. Nevertheless, stronger leadership in Speaker O'Neill emerged before the sharp increase in party polarization in the late 1980s as a product of demands from the liberal wing of his party (Smith 1989).

Direct evidence on the relationship between party polarization and party influence is still missing. There are piles of anecdotal evidence of party influence and a considerable body of fairly strong circumstantial evidence from systematic studies, as I noted in earlier chapters. Moreover, Aldrich and Rohde make the reasonable argument that the extensive efforts devoted to empowering leaders and the leaders' extraordinary labors would not have occurred without the legislators expecting an effect on outcomes. Nonetheless, the essential task to demonstrate that party influences the location of policy outcomes remains incomplete.

Aldrich and Rohde make their strongest case for outcome effects in their study of the House Appropriations Committee (Aldrich and Rohde 2000b). Their research design is a limited one. The qualitative and quantitative evidence spans the years in which the House moved from low polarization back toward the long-term norm in party polarization, at least according to the measure reported in Figure 5.1, and focuses on appropriations action in four recent Congress – the 96th (1979–1980), 100th (1987–1988), 103d (1993–1994), and 104th (1995–1996). The 104th Congress is the first Republican House since 1954 and so involves a new majority party, one that had been a frustrated minority for two generations.

Here again, the evidence of heightened party supervision and intrusion into appropriations decision making and sharper partisan lines in committee and floor voting on appropriations matters in the Republican Congress is noncontrovertible. Partisans both before and after the 1994 elections claimed that committee processes and special rules were being used to bias outcomes. The question is whether policy outcomes were pushed to the right of the new (at least hypothetical) chamber median created by the 1994 elections. If the majority party Republicans were cohesive and the chamber median was within the range of Republican preferences, establishing that policy moved farther than the new chamber median is not easy.

The key observation of Aldrich and Rohde is that legislators and journalists close to the scene argue that party strategies affected outcomes. With respect to special rules designed by the party and committee leadership, legislators objected to provisions that protected legislative provisions and banned floor amendments. Leaders cajoled and bargained with colleagues to win support. In one instance, a vote on an amendment was reversed when the leadership called for a second vote when a few opposing legislators were absent.

Still missing is clear evidence that appropriations outcomes, which Aldrich and Rohde argue were vital to the Republican revolution, were to the right of the chamber median. Aldrich and Rohde might ask, Why did the Republicans tolerate and even encourage the development of strong, centralized leadership if not to influence the outcome? They might be right in inferring that Republicans intended to push policy outcomes to the center of their party, more to the right than the chamber median. In fact, they insist that they identified "a dozen or more" instances of nonmedian outcomes in appropriations in 1995–1996. But it also is plausible that Republicans were aware of biases among committee members that had to be changed or kept in check in order to achieve policy outcomes at the chamber median. Elements of the Aldrich–Rohde account support this view.

Moreover, it is possible that the best that the majority party leadership can do, or even hope for, is to neutralize opposing forces in the legislative tug-of-war (Evans and Oleszek 1999). Legislative battles on important legislation, I emphasized in Chapter 4, usually involve the administration and many other actors with potential influence. No identification of the relative locations of the chamber median, party median, and outcomes is provided in any of the Aldrich–Rohde analysis to date.

The Aldrich–Rohde evidence for CPG is mixed. The long-term relationship between party polarization and party influence is yet to be established, although the record for the last decades of the twentieth century, which originally motivated the theory, are consistent with the theory. The Brady studies cited above provide more persuasive evidence. Associated with stronger leadership are real efforts to exercise direct and indirect influence and, as Aldrich and Rohde argue, it is reasonable to infer that such efforts would not be pursued unless their potential effect was meaningful to legislators. Less effectively argued is the claim that such efforts move outcomes away from the chamber median and toward the majority party median. That there was even greater movement in the 1990s than there was previously is an argument that is barely attempted.

LEGISLATIVE PARTIES AS PROCEDURAL CARTELS

The creative use of special rules by the House Democratic leadership in the 1980s stimulated scholars to renew their attention to control over the floor agenda as a source of party influence (Bach and Smith 1988; Dion and Huber 1996, 1997; Fox and Clapp 1970a, 1970b; Krehbiel 1997a, 1997b; Marshall 2002; Robinson 1959, 1961; Sinclair 1983, 1995a; Smith 1989). That observation, combined with the long-standing recognition that party loyalty was high on procedural and organizational votes (Froman and Ripley 1965) and the theoretical recognition of the importance of rules and agenda setting (Shepsle and Weingast 1984a, 1984b), led political scientists to assert that control over special rules was the most important source of majority leadership power in the House of Representatives. A few studies considered the use of unanimous consent agreements in the Senate (Roberts and Smith forthcoming; Smith 2005; Smith and Flathman 1989), but the House retained the focus of scholarly attention.

Step by step, Cox and McCubbins have taken the agenda-setting theme and molded it into a general theory of legislative parties (Cox 2001; Cox and McCubbins 1993, 1997, 2002). The theory is labeled "cartel theory" to reflect the view that partisans organize as a cartel to control those features of Congress that influence their common interests. Specifically, parties are procedural cartels that seek to control the legislative agenda. The full statement of cartel theory is available in *Setting the Agenda* (Cox and McCubbins 2005), so I take it as the intended authoritative account of the perspective.

The following theoretical and empirical claims are associated with the cartel argument:

Legislators' Motivations and the Party Record
- Legislators are motivated by their interest in reelection, good public policy, and majority status.
- The congressional party record has a measurable effect on its members' reelection prospects.
- The party record is a public good that tends to be maintained and enhanced inefficiently.
- Party leadership and organization are created to improve the efficiency with which the party record is maintained and enhanced.

- Legislative parties are cartels that seek to control those factors that influence the party record.
- Legislative success on issues on which most fellow partisans are likeminded enhances the party record; avoiding legislative issues on which fellow partisans are divided preserves the party record.

Agenda Control and Roll Rates

- Controlling the agenda of issues that receive a floor vote is the most important means for controlling factors that influence the party record.
- The majority party will bring to the floor only legislation that is supported by the party and will pass – that is, is supported by the party and chamber medians. Otherwise, the party exercises negative agenda control.
- The roll rate for the majority party will be zero.
- The roll rate of the minority party will be higher than for the majority party and in proportion to the distance between the medians of the two parties.

Parties and Standing Committees

- When there is little legislation that is supported by the party and will pass – that is, is supported by the party and chamber medians – the majority party will create standing committees that are capable of blocking legislation.
- When there is much legislation that is supported by the party and will pass – that is, is supported by the party and chamber medians – the majority party will not allow standing committees to block legislation.

Party Polarization and Positive Influence

- Party polarization will expand the agenda of the majority party – that is, polarization enhances positive agenda control.
- Party polarization is unrelated to the majority party roll rate but will increase the minority party roll rate.
- Positive direct party influence exists but has a marginal effect on outcomes.

Cox and McCubbins argue that negative agenda power is the foundation of the power of majority parties in Congress. The majority leadership oversees a procedural cartel of fellow partisans who agree not to bring legislation to the floor unless the leadership can win.

Operationally, the strategic premise of party leadership is to send legislation to the floor only when the party's median and the chamber median favor the legislation. In a unidimensional world, the only one in which medians are sure to exist and the only one that can be operative under the strategic premise, agreement between the majority party and chamber medians guarantees passage of the bill and yields a zero rate of defeat (a zero "roll rate") for the majority party. No positive influence, direct or indirect, is required because the leadership merely gauges legislators' preferences – which, in a liberal–conservative world, are largely fixed at the start of each Congress – and acts accordingly. In practice, Cox and McCubbins (2005) allow, leaders exercise a little positive influence. They argue that positive influence operates "on the margin" to round up the last few votes required to adopt a special rule or pass a bill. This marginal effect may expand the number of bills that can be passed.

Observations About Cartel Theory

The genius of the 1993 Cox–McCubbins treatment of cartel theory is that it takes the electoral motivation and parlays it into a theory that asserts a substantial baseline level of influence for legislative parties. This initial version of cartel theory stands in sharp contrast with Mayhew's argument about the implications of assuming that legislators are single-minded seekers of reelection. Mayhew contends that the electoral motivation for legislators running for reelection in many disparate districts and states leads to the creation of weak, service-oriented parties that are created to address the nonpartisan collective action problems of keeping legislation flowing through Congress (Mayhew 1974). In contrast, Cox and McCubbins offer a perspective that emphasizes a partisan motivation for creating parties with an impact on policy outcomes. The key insight is that Mayhew's emphasis on the weakness of the direct influence of parties ignores the potential importance of parties' indirect influence through control of the agenda.

Cartel theory has a core causal sequence – legislators' goals produce collective concern for the party record, which in turn leads party leaders to emphasize setting the agenda (negative agenda control) over other strategies and to adopt a strategic premise (move legislation only when you can win) in setting the agenda. A series of questions can be asked about these claims. Does concern about the party record follow from legislators' goals? Does an emphasis on negative agenda control follow from concern about the party record? Does the strategic premise of negative agenda control follow from the characterization of legislators' goals, the party record, and policy space? My assessment of these features of cartel theory calls into question core interpretations of party politics offered by Cox and McCubbins.

Does Concern About the Party Record Follow From Legislators' Goals?

I find the argument persuasive, but it is worth noting its differences from another prominent perspective on legislators' goals and strategies. Mayhew, who posits that legislators are single-minded seekers of reelection, would say no. Mayhew argued that legislators do not care about winning legislative battles. Instead, they emphasize taking positions and advertising those positions. If they care about policy, it is particularistic policy that benefits their local districts and states for which they can take personal credit. Mayhew observes that no legislator loses reelection for taking the popular position but not winning the legislative battle.

Cox and McCubbins do not address the Mayhew formulation. In their 1993 exposition of cartel theory, they showed some sympathy for the Mayhew formulation but moved beyond it (Cox and McCubbins 1993). The sympathy is demonstrated by the effort devoted to showing the connection between legislators' electoral interests and the party record without so much as a sentence about how other goals (say, good public policy or personal power) are related to the party record. They move beyond Mayhew by conducting an empirical investigation of the relationship between party affiliation and legislators' reelection prospects. The finding is that a nationwide party effect, or party trend, is detectable in statistical estimates of the determinants of congressional election outcomes. The direct evidence for a relationship between the *party record* and reelection prospects is not demonstrated, but the systematic relationship between national party trends and incumbents' vote-getting ability is strong circumstantial evidence. Nevertheless, Cox and McCubbins emphasized, party influence is limited to those issues that are deemed relevant to the party record.

The importance of the 1993 formulation was that there is a non-policy (nonspatial) motivation for creating legislative parties. This provides an answer to the question, Why would the chamber median allow the adoption of rules that give agenda control to the majority party median? If the chamber median is a single-minded seeker of his or her ideal point, then there is a paradox. But if the chamber median also has a stake in his or her party's reputation, he or she may be willing to sacrifice something on the policy side to gain something on the electoral side and the paradox evaporates. Party influence, then, is a somewhat ambiguous concept – legislators bend their behavior in the direction of the party from where it would be on the basis of all non-party forces; however, the electorate considers their partisan affiliation and legislators must consider the party reputation in their own interest.

That approach addresses the obvious criticism of the cartel argument: In fact, no House majority party leader, no majority party committee, and no standing committee has monopoly agenda-setting power under the rules of the House. In principle, under the rules, a majority can sign a discharge petition to force a bill, or a resolution embodying a special rule, to the floor (Krehbiel 1995, 2005). So the question arises, Why would a majority party member on the opposite side of the status quo from the rest of his party refuse to sign a discharge petition that would bring a bill to the floor that he favors? In their formal model, Cox and McCubbins treat this by assumption – that is, agenda setters are assumed to exist (Cox and McCubbins 2005, 39). But in the original treatment of cartel theory the question is answered: A legislator's reelection prospects depend on more than the position they take on issues. Legislators sacrifice policy positions at times in order to improve their net prospects for reelection.

The emphasis of the 2005 treatment of the goals is explicitly non-Mayhewian. Legislators are said to have multiple goals (reelection, policy, majority party status) and the possibility of fellow partisans having heterogeneous policy preferences is a central theme. Because legislators are stuck with their party labels for the most part, they are stuck with their party reputation at election time, too. It is in their collective interest to do something about it. Unfortunately, while elaborating on the list of goals in the 2005 version, Cox and McCubbins provide no discussion of legislators' goals and the party reputation. I surmise that if reelection is sufficient to motivate legislators' interest in the party reputation, as the 1993 treatment implies, then it seems likely that shared policy views and majority party status are likely to introduce both more motivation and additional complications. For example, majority party status creates additional incentive to help the party create a favorable reputation in the electorates of fellow partisans.

The complications of multiple goals involve the tradeoffs that are sometimes required of legislators and parties, as I emphasized in Chapter 2. If the policy interests among fellow partisans are not compatible, then election of fellow partisans, essential to majority party status, may harm prospects for achieving personal policy goals and support for efforts to enhance the party reputation may be counterproductive. Similarly, the personal goal of majority party status implies additional tradeoffs, such as a willingness to take personal electoral risks in order to enhance the electoral prospects of party colleagues. On the other hand, as Mayhew implies, legislators may prefer to sacrifice their colleagues for themselves. To be sure, introducing additional goals is realistic, but it yields uncertainties that Cox and McCubbins ignore.

Does an Emphasis on Negative Agenda Control Follow From Concern About the Party Record?

The second question concerns the view that positive influence is not as fundamental to legislative parties as negative agenda control. The 2005 book represents a large shift in emphasis from the 1993 book, which emphasizes direct influence. Consequently, Cox and McCubbins must be read very carefully to catch their rationale for legislators' concern about the party record leading to an emphasis on negative agenda control.

Negative agenda control, Cox and McCubbins argue, is used to keep bills off the floor. The circumstances that lead the party to keep a bill off the floor are described in various ways –

- Leaders "always obey the 'first commandment of party leadership' – Thou shall not aid bills that will split thy party – and to sometimes obey the second commandment – Thou shalt aid bills that most in thy party like." (24)
- "... the majority party routinely uses its near-monopoly of formal agenda power in order to keep bills off the floor agenda that would, if passed, displease majorities of its membership." (37)

- "A majority of the majority party will vote against putting a particular dimension...on the floor agenda...if and only if the status quo...is closer to the majority party median...than is the floor median." (44)

The first statement is ambiguous: it suggests that any "split" in the party will deter party action and yet satisfying "most" partisans is enough. The second statement is specific and, I assume, provides the intended guidance: a simple majority of the party determines how the party will act. The last statement means that the majority party median (and therefore a majority of the majority party) will avoid floor action that will make him worse off. Negative agenda control is acquired because, critically, even the minority of the majority party on a given bill is expected to support the party median's position on procedural votes. The party minority is willing to do so because they value the nonpolicy benefits of having their party avoid losses on the floor (Cox and McCubbins 2005).

What is the connection between the party reputation and having the majority of the majority party avoid floor losses? Actually, Cox and McCubbins seem to lose sight of this question. The closest direct answers to this question are two statements:

- "The policies with which a particular party and its leaders are associated – both those it promotes and those it opposes – can significantly affect the party's reputation." (21–22)
- "The value of a party's brand name depends on its legislative record of accomplishment. Thus, a key problem for majority parties is to manage the legislative process, in order to secure the best possible record, hence contributing to the best possible reputation." (32)

Ambiguity reins. Plainly, being "associated" with popular causes, as Mayhew emphasizes, establishing a "legislative record of accomplishment," as Cox and McCubbins emphasize, and avoiding floor losses are not identical recipes for a favorable party record. Mayhew would argue that no legislator (or party, he surely would argue) has been defeated at the polls for doing its best to pass popular legislation but failing. In fact, it could be argued, pressing the issue to force opponents on the record is a common strategy and may be the minority party's most common strategy. Conversely, it is hard to imagine a small or incohesive majority party maintaining or improving its reputation by doing nothing for fear of losing on the floor. Effort and accountability are expected. Thus, there remains a gap in the causal argument. A favorable record of accomplishment surely is important to the majority party, but it is hardly the only way to establish a favorable party record. If it is not, then the majority party may be willing to lose a legislative battle in order to realize a net gain in party reputation and public support. Avoiding losses on the floor is not a necessary or a sufficient strategy for enhancing the party reputation.

It makes eminent sense to claim that a majority of the majority party seeks to avoid floor outcomes that make it worse off than the status quo. We must attach an "all things being equal" proviso to the claim however, because the real world presents more complicated scenarios. For example, it is not clear why it harms the party interest to forward to the floor a bill that is popular with the public but cannot muster the required floor majority. Perhaps it can be argued that the bill can be amended and then passed on the floor so as to make the majority party median worse off than the status quo, which is an outcome that outweighs the benefit of championing the popular bill and putting the opposition on the record against it. Cox and McCubbins eschew the balancing of electoral and policy interests that this argument entails. Moreover, in many circumstances a special rule that restricts amendments could prevent the unpopular or undesired changes and still produce a bill that can be passed. Cox and McCubbins (2005, 39) hint that restrictions on amendments through special rules have no effect on their "main prediction" of a zero majority party roll rate and so deserves little further discussion. This is a simplistic conception of party calculations.

As I see it, then, the multiple goals of legislators that Cox and McCubbins assume do not inform their subsequent analysis. The majority party is reduced to a machine that passes legislation supported by a majority of its members when a chamber majority can be mustered, but it seems to do little else. It remains mum when it cannot succeed on the floor and it remains inert in devising strategies that may facilitate tradeoffs in building a record of legislative accomplishment.

The flip side of the party control coin is positive party influence, a subject relegated to the next-to-last chapter of the 2005 book. Much of the Cox and McCubbins discussion of positive influence is limited to "proposal power," a pseudonym for positive agenda power, which

I take as a just one form (upper right cell in Table 3-1) of positive influence. Proposal power is the ability to bring a bill to the floor that will pass, even one that is opposed by most legislators. The discussion implies that majority party leaders' proposal power varies as the party's homogeneity varies – more like-minded legislators will trust leaders' exercise of proposal power as the party becomes more homogeneous.

The treatment of positive influence fails to address the necessarily integrated use of its two forms – direct influence on legislators' votes and indirect agenda-setting strategies. In the chapter entitled "Positive Agenda Power," the theoretical discussion concerns agenda control, and the discussion of the chief alternative theory, CPG, focuses on positive agenda power. The chapter's argument is that negative agenda powers are everpresent while positive agenda powers are added and retracted in response to the changes in the homogeneity of policy views among members of the majority party. When members of the majority party are homogeneous in their policy views, the majority leadership acquires strengthened positive agenda powers. This is confirmed, it is claimed, by evidence that changes in majority party homogeneity are associated with the size of the majority party's agenda and the minority party roll rate.

The complication is that the observed patterns in the size of the majority party's agenda and the minority party roll rates also can be caused by variation in the direct influence. The strength of positive agenda control may play no role. Direct influence over marginal legislators may allow the majority leadership to bring additional bills to the floor and get them passed, thus expanding their agenda and increasing the relative number of defeats for the minority party even without strengthening leaders' tools for positive agenda control. Consequently, the evidence on the size of the majority party's agenda and the minority party roll rate supports an argument for positive influence, just as CPG provides, but does not allow an inference that the source of the positive influence is agenda power rather than direct leverage with legislators. It does not support a distinctively agenda-based theory of positive influence.

In a subsequent section, Cox and McCubbins praise studies that provide evidence of direct influence, but, strangely, the findings of these studies are not connected with the story about the size of the majority party agenda and the minority roll rates. In fact, despite the emphasis on direct influence in presentations of the CPG thesis (Aldrich 1995; Aldrich et al. 2002; Rohde 1991), no sketch of a theory of conditionality of direct influence is offered, in contrast to the lucid theory about the conditionality of agenda setting (Cox and McCubbins 2005, 215–18).

The argument about the conditionality of positive agenda power has an additional weakness. Implicit in the Cox and McCubbins discussion of the "mix of agenda powers" is that resources essential to negative and positive powers are distinguishable. Frequently that is not true (see Chapter 3). For example, the Speaker's control of the House Rules Committee grants both negative and positive influence to the Speaker. On the negative side, the Rules committee, under direction from the Speaker, can deny a special rule to a bill or fail to allow an amendment to receive a vote on the floor. On the positive side, the Rules Committee can protect an amendment from a separate floor vote or even provide that an amendment is considered adopted upon adoption of a multifaceted special rule providing for consideration of a bill.[2] Similarly, the Speaker's powers as presiding officer to recognize members to speak or make motions, make parliamentary rulings, and so on can be used to block or promote legislation. The fact that the mechanisms of agenda control by party leaders often create both negative and positive possibilities casts some doubt on the claim that only positive agenda powers, rather than the strength of agenda powers generally as suggested in CPG accounts, is adjusted according to the degree of homogeneity in the party.

An additional observation about positive influence is required. It bears notice that Cox and McCubbins, implicitly, give far greater emphasis to the direct influence of presidents than of congressional parties. Citing Kernell on the way in which presidents seek to mobilize public support for their programs (Kernell 1986, 1997), Cox and McCubbins argue that presidents, particularly under divided party control of the White House and House, can generate public pressure on Congress to act on their legislative agenda. They find somewhat higher House majority party roll rates under divided party control of the House and White House (and Senate, although the Senate's role is not

---

[2] We would not expect an elected leader like the Speaker to force the Rules Committee to pave the way for floor passage of a bill opposed by most majority party members, but there is little doubt that the Speaker's influence over the Rules Committee has the potential for both negative and positive uses.

explained). Thus, we are asked to be persuaded that the president exercises positive influence on the House agenda, but, without seeing any evidence, that the House majority party exercises insignificant positive influence on the majority party roll rate.

Does the Strategic Premise of Negative Agenda Control Follow From the Characterization of Legislators' Goals, the Party Record, and Policy Space?

I already have questioned the logical relationship between legislators' (and party) goals and the narrow strategic premise that the majority party does not bring legislation to the floor unless it can win. Additional observations are in order.

As for CPG, the size of the two parties appears to be a missing ingredient in cartel theory. The majority party, if it is following its strategic premise, will have a zero roll rate whatever its size (or homogeneity or distance from the minority). However, if we take seriously the assumption that a party and its members care about majority party status, then, as I argued for CPG, the probability of gaining or losing majority status is likely to be a factor in the strategic calculations of each party. For example, the smaller is the majority party, the more important are the electoral fortunes of the members of the majority party whose electoral situation is the most precarious. Even if the majority of the majority party can win on the floor with the help of some minority party votes, it may be unwise to do so if it risks reinforcing a party record that endangers the marginal majority party members.

The more general point is that political considerations sometimes weigh heavily in party leaders' calculations about bringing measures to the floor and undermine the application of the strategic premise. Cox and McCubbins observe this in discussing presidential influence and the Senate (see below).

In addition to political pressure to take up legislation even if a loss is possible, there is a wide variety of legislation, particularly in the modern Congress, that is required, at least in some form. "Must-pass" measures are quite numerous, Budget measures and appropriations, fast-track trade legislation, and debt ceiling resolutions fall into this "must pass" category. Some law, such as key provisions of the Patriot Act, is subject to sunset provisions and so the reversion point is not simply the inherited status quo. Moreover, in some cases, the Senate has limited debate and amendments in order to facilitate action on these priority items (Binder and Smith 1997, 185–94). They are among the most prominent measures considered by Congress so the party reputation surely is at stake, but leaders' agenda-setting options are nevertheless constrained by politics to abide by rules imposed at an earlier date.

These congressionally imposed time constraints do not figure in cartel theory but alter the strategic calculations of the majority party. To the majority party leadership, no legislation may be viewed as a far less desirable outcome than the legislation that a chamber majority will pass. Agencies may close or authority important to some critical government function may expire. Cartel theory can accommodate these situations – after all, the majority party median and chamber median may still vote for the bill to avoid a calamity. But periodic legislation can force the majority party to make concessions that would not be required if the *status quo ante* was the effective reversion point. The concession can be so great that the majority party median considers it a political loss.

The dimensionality of the policy space always is a fundamental, if nagging, issue. Cox and McCubbins assume that the space can be multidimensional. The strategic premise, technically, is that the majority party does not bring a *dimension* (as opposed to a bill) to the floor unless the chamber and majority party medians are on the same side of the status quo on that dimension. The unstated assumption must be that a party can control the dimensionality of bills that are taken to the floor. If the party has such power, then a party can avoid sending a bill to the floor on which the relative location of the two medians and the status quo vary. Without that assumption, the strategic premise does not provide unambiguous guidance.

This characterization of the policy space and the majority party's strategic premise rule out packaging strategies that so many observers argue are essential to majority party success. By incorporating provisions that would not pass on the floor as stand-alone bills into larger bills, long a strategy for tax bills but now a widespread practice, and then protecting those bills from amendments, at least of certain kinds, the majority party is able to exercise potentially great influence over some dimensions of policy. Remarkably, in a theory about agenda control – and even in a chapter on the use of special rules to govern amending activity – the Cox and McCubbins analysis is silent on this possibility, apparently a victim of the underlying theory.

The Odd Treatment of the Reed Rules

In a chapter devoted to the "primacy" of the Reed rules, Cox and McCubbins emphasize that the rules and rulings under Speaker Thomas Brackett Reed (R-ME) in 1890 and 1891, and reinstituted when Reed returned as Speaker in 1895, initiated the modern agenda control regime of the House of Representatives. Their argument is that "after Reed's rules became a permanent part of House organization, over 80 percent of the bills allowed to reach the final passage stage in the typical Congress proposed to move policy toward the median voter in the majority party" (Cox and McCubbins 2005, 51). This, they contend, is the strongest argument that the foundation of majority party power in the modern House is *negative* agenda control.

The connection between the Reed rules and the exercise of negative agenda control is confused. In origin and application, the Reed rules created opportunities for a House majority to act that it may not have had otherwise. The pre-Reed House had minority obstructionism in common with the Senate of both the late nineteenth century and today. Dilatory motions, refusing to respond to the call of names under a quorum call, and other tactics were used to thwart action on the House floor. What the pre-Reed House minority could do the House majority could do, too – so a mutual veto was possible. The majority party, and Speaker Reed, found stalemate intolerable and moved to change the rules to overcome the obstructionist tactics of the Democratic minority. By creating a Committee on Rules with privileged access to the floor and dealing with dilatory motions and disappearing quorums by the exercise of the discretion of the chair, Reed made it possible to get votes on legislation that the minority had been able to prevent or postpone.

The Reed rules established a *positive*, not a *negative*, agenda control regime. It is the *positive* power that was acquired that continues to allow modern House majority parties to use their own votes to push their legislation to the floor and out the door. It is the strength of the majority party's potential positive power that distinguishes the House from the Senate.

If the Reed rules were positive in effect, then the prediction that the Reed rules would suppress majority roll rates has less solid footing. Indeed, if the Reed rules generate a higher proportion of passed bills that move in a pro-majority party direction, as Cox and McCubbins argue (Cox and McCubbins 2005, 172–89), this can be generated by the Reed rules' positive effects. When the majority party can get more of its favored legislation to the floor and approved, it increases the number of favorable outcomes just as it would decrease the number of disfavored bills that are passed. To be sure, the majority party may not bring bills to the floor that will be defeated, but in the Reed regime the majority party can get favorable votes on more legislation that it favors, thereby increasing the proportion of pro-party bills that are passed. Equally important, the Reed regime allows the majority party's central and committee leaders to package provisions in large bills, protect those provisions from floor amendments, and get floor votes on those bills. Thus, there is little in the "policy move" analysis of Cox and McCubbins that distinguishes negative and positive influence, a distinction that is central to the argument of the book.

Moreover, it would not be negative power that distinguishes the House and Senate majority parties from each other. Their roll rates *should* be similar. Rather, the strength of the positive power distinguishes the two majority parties. Unfortunately, changes in positive power are not visible in roll rates. Increasing the *number* of favored bills passed does not affect the number or proportion of bills killed – the predicted roll rate remains zero.

A Methodological Note

Much of the Cox and McCubbins analysis depends on their ability to compare the voting record across Congresses. This is vital to their analysis that the Reed rules proved critical to establishing a new regime of majority party agenda control in the House. It is worth pausing to consider the nature of the voting record that is analyzed. In Figure 5.2, the number of final passage votes (the votes on which roll rates are calculated) is shown by Congress, along with the number of bills enacted into law.

During most of the history of the House and Senate, very few bills enacted into law were subject to a record vote at final passage. The

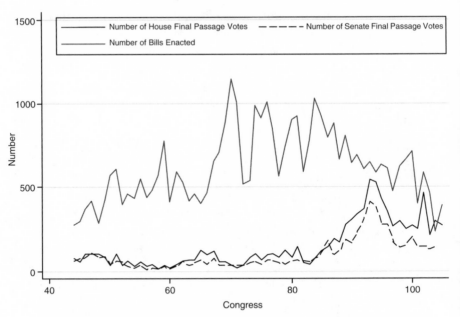

FIGURE 5.2. Number of enacted bills and final passage votes, 1875–1997.

two houses would allow key votes on amendments or procedural motions to be the only recorded votes related to bills, even many controversial bills for which the majority of the majority lost votes on amendments (a subject not addressed by Cox and McCubbins). Only in the modern period are even a majority of enacted bills subject to a vote at final passage. The House, in fact, has become vote-happy since the installation of the electronic voting system in the early 1970s. Cartel theory would predict a very low roll rate whatever the number of final passage votes, but we should be aware that the evidence on roll rates is limited to a small fraction of the legislative agenda during most of the post-Reconstruction Congresses. We cannot be certain that the majority of the majority obtained acceptable outcomes for a very large share of the floor agenda, as the low majority party roll rates might be read to imply. Worse yet, the majority party may have deliberately avoided roll-call votes on issues that would have exposed its internal divisions.

Should we merely give up evaluating the cartel argument? No. We must turn to committee records, contemporary press accounts, and floor debates to expand the range of legislation we consider in characterizing party, committee, and factional positions and strategies.

I fear that we will be surprised to find many instances of majority party losses that are not visible in the roll-call record.

THE SENATE

Missing from all but one report on CPG and cartel theory is a systematic treatment of the Senate (Cox et al. 2002). A vital proposition of CPG is that the majority party, by virtue of being in the majority, can increase the power of its partisan mechanisms more than the minority party can. In the Senate, where the minority can, and usually does, successfully filibuster or threaten to filibuster efforts to change the standing rules, the ability of the majority party to gain a substantial advantage in floor action is limited. The majority party may strengthen its leadership's resources for dealing with the internal affairs of the party and thereby gain some additional influence over fellow partisans, but, in most circumstances, the majority party cannot substantially improve its leadership's procedural control of the floor without the concurrence of the minority party. CPG arguments remain incomplete without additional qualification to account for these House–Senate differences.

As I have noted, Cox and McCubbins (2005) focus on the House and argue that modern House agenda control emerged from the days of Speaker Reed in the late nineteenth century. At that time, minority obstructionism was suppressed, the Rules Committee's modern powers were initialized, the resolutions from Rules creating special rules and other measures were granted privileged status on the floor, and the Speaker asserted the right of recognition without appeal. In the Cox and McCubbins account, the House remains in the Reed regime in most important respects.

Nothing similar emerged in the Senate. To the contrary, large minorities retained the ability obstruct, no general germaneness rule was adopted for floor amendments, and no mechanism similar to special rules emerged to limit amendments and debate. Nevertheless, and with no discussion of contested interpretations of Senate rules and history, Cox and McCubbins argue that the "nuclear option," in which rulings of the chair backed by majorities might be used to limit minorities, allows the inference that "at the end of the day, the rules in the Senate, as in the House, are determined by the majority party" (Cox and McCubbins 2005, 96). At best, this is an oversimplification of majority and minority options (Binder and Smith 1997; Wawro and Schickler 2006).

The wheels come off when Cox and McCubbins sketch an account of Senate roll rates. Having observed that Senate majority party roll rates are low, as for the House majority party, and having argued that the Reed rules were essential to the agenda control and roll rates observed in the House, they seem to be cornered into arguing that agenda control is essentially the same in both houses. They inform us that they "present evidence throughout this book that it [the Senate majority party] is . . . able to substantially affect legislative outcomes" (Cox and McCubbins 2005, 96). In fact, beyond their figures on aggregate roll rates that precede that claim and a footnote with estimates of presidential effects on minority party roll rates (Cox and McCubbins 2005, 94, 116fn), there are no additional data reported or analysis of Senate roll rates.

More important, the fact that the Senate majority *could* force the adoption of rules that strengthen its agenda control is not helpful. The Senate majority has not done so; the House majority did so. If the mere threat of doing so is enough to generate agenda control and a compliant minority, then it is difficult to explain why the Reed regime is essential to explaining majority party agenda control in the House, as Cox and McCubbins argue.

In addition to the vital claim that the majority party sets the Senate's rules, Cox and McCubbins offer a somewhat speculative list of factors that might produce the agenda effects observed in low majority party roll rates (Cox and McCubbins 2005, 95):

- The Senate majority party benefits from the House majority party's agenda control when the same party controls both houses;
- under unified party control, presidential pressure "may give the party the advantage it needs to pass policies preferred by the majority party";
- the Senate majority party may use its own specialized techniques, such as filling the amendment tree, to get what it wants; and
- the Senate majority party can use budget measures that cannot be filibustered to enact legislation.

This list of possibilities is not credible. The Senate majority party roll rates appear to be uncorrelated with unified/divided government.

If the direct influence of the president explains the Senate, then his direct influence also may explain the House and we do not need the elaborate explanation related to the Reed rules. In any case, party roll rates appear to be uncorrelated with unified/divided party control of the White House and the Senate. Filling the amendment tree may block amendments from being proposed, but it does not prevent the minority from filibustering the bill. And, finally, the packaging and filibuster protection of budget measures is a source of positive, not negative, influence and, again, is similar for both houses. Filibuster-proof measures are a development of the late twentieth century and cannot explain the full series for the Senate.

What we might have expected in Cox and McCubbins is a discussion of the way in which the possibility of needing to overcome a filibuster with cloture imposes a supermajority threshold for bills and creates the possibility of a mutual veto when a supermajority cannot be mustered. In opining that the Senate majority party sets the Senate's rules, they wish away this possibility. Still, two implications of Senate practice are fairly obvious. First, while the majority party roll rate would remain low, the minority party roll rate would be lower than we observe in the House. Second, the ability to offer nongermane amendments on the Senate floor and the absence of a means to limit amendments without unanimous consent creates the possibility that the dimensionality of a bill can be altered on the floor, which in turn makes it difficult for the majority to adhere to the strategic premise of cartel theory. And yet Senate roll rates are not too different from those of the House.

Oddly, in an earlier chapter, Cox and McCubbins make the mutual veto argument about the Senate. They imply that it explains the House–Senate difference in the frequency with which policy moves in the direction of the majority party (less in the Senate) (Cox and McCubbins 2005, 68–72). And yet roll rates do not warrant the application of the same logic. Plainly, dealing with the half of the Congress that cartel theory has not incorporated remains a subject deserving further investigation.

A CRITICAL DIFFERENCE

I hope I do not leave the impression that there is little that I like about CPG and cartel theory. To the contrary, both theories of congressional parties have enriched our understanding of the political processes that are the foundation of party activity in Congress. Scholars have a tendency to push their theories to the limits. That is a good thing. They also have a tendency to ignore the limits of their theories and rationalize disconfirming evidence. That is not such a good thing.

The strength of CPG and cartel theory is that they are theories of legislative parties. As such, they guide us to look for party influence of certain kinds in certain ways. This is a significant improvement over most of the literature reporting efforts to gauge direct party influence that I reviewed in the previous chapter.

I have cited numerous complications in developing theories of legislative parties. I rephrase four of them so that they are expressed in the intended constructive spirit:

- While both CPG and cartel theory allow multiple goals, neither CPG nor cartel theory develops the implications of these goals. Instead, both theories reduce to a spatial account of party activity that is not the only implication of legislators' and parties' goals. CPG emphasizes swings in party influence associated with the distribution of legislators' preferences; cartel theory specifies a strategic premise based entirely on the alignment of preferences.
- With respect to legislators' policy goals, both theories offer some guidance about the expected behavior of leaders and rank-and-file legislators. Proponents of both CPG and cartel theory struggle to characterize the dimensionality of the policy space in a way that allows both an unambiguous statement of the central propositions and captures the range of challenges and strategies that parties are known to pursue.
- Neither theory confronts what is likely to be a critical strategic consideration for party leaders – party size. If majority status is critical to a theory, the vulnerability of majority status is likely to be a vital factor in shaping demands placed on leaders and in leaders' strategies.
- The Senate – well, it is still there.

A critical difference between CPG and cartel theory remains. Cartel theory predicts that when a bill is passed, it is favored by the majority party median but is located at the ideal point of the chamber median (under an open rule that allows a bill to be amended to the chamber median's position). Of course, it also predicts that bills that do not pass or fail because either the majority party median or the chamber median would be made worse off than the status quo. The possibility of direct influence, from leaders or presidents, which is not anticipated in cartel theory's strategic premise, creates the possibility of outcomes shifted away from the chamber median and toward the majority median. That is the possibility that CPG asserts is present when parties are polarized. To date, no empirical analysis has been conducted to determine which theory is a better fit to the legislative record.

6

Revisiting Pivotal and Party Politics

The challenge of median voter and pivotal politics theories of legislative politics requires additional consideration. In Chapter 4, I argued that Krehbiel's 1993 challenge was misconceived and applied unpersuasively and, after reviewing the subsequent literature on direct party influence, observed that the evidence for significant party effects was beginning to accumulate (Krehbiel 1993). Krehbiel has persisted in his challenge (Crombez et al. 2006; Krehbiel 1997b, 1998, 2000, 2003, 2005; Krehbiel et al. 2005; Krehbiel and Wiseman 1999). Most of my argument about Krehbiel's 1993 challenge applies to the subsequent work. Most important, the assumption of unidimensionality, the treatment of preferences as independent of party effects, and absence of a full multivariate model of the forces at work in legislators' voting decisions remain issues in most of the follow-up efforts. Nevertheless, the more recent challenges are quite varied and, judging by the steady flow of published work, persuasive to some readers.

I cannot fully digest and evaluate this volume of commentary, analysis, and empirical analysis here, but two of Krehbiel's efforts are particularly deserving of evaluation. The first is the set of claims about minimal (direct) party influence in Krehbiel's 1998 book, *Pivotal Politics*. Remarkably, most of Krehbiel's claims about party effects in this book have not been challenged, at least not directly. In this chapter, I show that there are party effects in many of the places where Krehbiel chooses to emphasize the force of pivotal politics. The second is Krehbiel's assertion that the locations of the status quo, always difficult to measure in practice, can account for the observed patterns of individual and chamber behavior. Krehbiel properly emphasizes the importance of status quo locations in predicting outcomes, but, I argue in this chapter, his proposed solutions, which serve as the basis of his critique of cartel theory, are unrealistic (Krehbiel 2006). A more realistic understanding of how the status quo gets set and is perceived by legislators leaves cartel theory as a plausible account of one form of party influence in congressional policy making. I conclude that Krehbiel's major critiques, which address theories of direct and indirect party influence, are not persuasive.

AN INTRODUCTION TO PIVOTS AND PARTIES

It is unfortunate that some observers of the debate about party influence in Congress see pivotal politics and party politics as nonoverlapping explanations of legislative outcomes. Part of the problem may be due to Krehbiel's characterization of party politics in *Pivotal Politics*. In his first empirical chapter, his Chapter 4, Krehbiel demonstrates that winning coalitions for Mayhew's set of important legislation over the 1946–1990 period ranged fairly evenly in size from just over a simple majority to nearly unanimous, along with a large number of unanimous votes. Krehbiel concludes that the data "fail to support the party-government hypothesis of coalition sizes equal to majority-party size" (Krehbiel 1998). It is noteworthy that Krehbiel never correlates majority party size with the size of winning coalitions and rather chooses to dismiss the subject of party and winning coalition size on the basis of the pattern aggregated over 23 Congresses, House and Senate.

The subject of party effects in Congress is inherently about the marginal effects of party influence, controlling for other forces in legislative politics, as expressed in an institutional context. The institutional context is defined as a set of rules, including rules that specify decision thresholds. The Constitution specifies some decision thresholds. It is assumed, although the Constitution is not explicit, that legislation must be approved by a simple majority in each house before it is officially enrolled and sent to the president. Constitutional rules for veto overrides and treaty ratification set two-thirds and three-fifths majority thresholds, respectively. Since the Constitution was implemented, other rules that specify supermajority thresholds, such as for

Senate cloture, House suspension of the rules, Senate approval of provisions that violate its budget rules, and so on, have been adopted by the houses (by simple majorities). These rules set the bar for certain legislative motions and, in doing so, determine which legislator, or group of legislators, if any, is pivotal to the adoption of those motions.

In practice, the relationship between decision rules and party politics is far from simple. Some decision rules (and, therefore, pivots) are constitutional and essentially out of the reach of everyday party politics. Constitutional amendments, such as the proposed constitutional amendment requiring an annually balanced federal budget and a supermajority to adopt a budget deficit, generate partisan divisions and might have partisan consequences. Many state constitutions include decision rules that are conceivably the by-product of legislative party politics. And the interpretation of the Constitution's decision rules remains a contested matter in the contemporary Congress. At the moment, most Senate Republicans insist that for purposes of considering presidential nominations to the courts the Constitution implies that the Senate must cast a vote on nominations. Some of them argue that this implies that a simple majority must be allowed to invoke cloture on judicial nomination.

Other decision rules are a product of the internal politics of Congress and potentially the product of party politics. Many rules have partisan implications, at least in the short term, and so are subject to frequent argument (Binder 1977; Dion 1997). Even the threshold for setting aside other decision thresholds – that is, to suspend the rules – can be modified and influenced by partisan considerations.

In a unidimensional policy space, a decision rule – a simple majority, a two-thirds majority, and so on – allows us to identify a pivotal voter. Things become far more complicated in a multidimensional space – a different voter may be pivotal for each dimension so none are pivotal overall. Determining which, if any, of the pivots is relevant in a multidimensional space may be an important function of the majority party, but Krehbiel sticks with the unidimensional space. For the purposes of this chapter, I will let the subject of dimensionality drop.

Our task is not to determine whether pivots or parties are more influential in determining legislative outcomes, but rather to determine whether party considerations add significantly to the obvious role that pivots play in legislative decision making. It is not party versus pivots, but pivots versus pivots and party. My money is on pivots and party.

In the remainder of this chapter, I do three things. First, I demonstrate that Krehbiel's analysis of the size of winning coalitions is not helpful. Second, I elaborate on the analyses of filibuster and veto pivot effects in *Pivotal Politics* to show party effects. Third, I address the knotty problem of status quo locations.

THE SIZE OF WINNING COALITIONS

The seeming precision of decision thresholds and pivotal voters is misleading. The appropriate decision rule, and therefore the location of the relevant pivot, is more problematic than seems to be appreciated by many political scientists. The consequence of an ambiguous decision rule is that efforts to specify the expected effect of the pivot on outcomes are prone to error. This is transparent in Krehbiel's analysis of the effect of supermajority pivots on the size of winning majorities in Congress.

The Basic Pivotal Politics Model and Its Predictions

The basic pivotal politics model that Krehbiel proposes for analyzing the size of winning coalitions is provided in Figure 6.1, which illustrates a one-house legislature. Under simple majority rule, the chamber median is the expected outcome of legislative action. The status quo is not shown and can vary across the entire spectrum, but the decision rule is that the status quo prevails if the required majority fails to support the bill. A bill may be vetoed or filibustered so a bill will pass only if it is acceptable to the chamber median (m) and both of the two pivots associated with overriding a veto (v) and invoking cloture to stop a filibuster (f). If we assume that the president, who might exercise a veto, is on either the far left (a Democratic president) or the far right (a Republican president), then we know which of the veto and filibuster pivots is relevant to the outcome.

A veto pivot example: If the president is Republican and so prefers a far-right outcome (top panel in Figure 6.1), a veto will occur when the proposed bill lies on the opposite side of the status quo (not shown). To override the veto, a two-thirds majority is required. Legislators

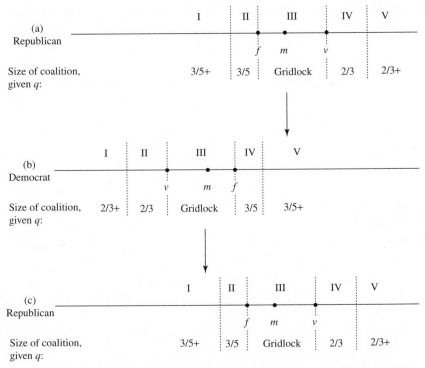

FIGURE 6.1. Krehbiel's pivotal politics model. *Source:* Krehbiel (1998), Figure 4.3.

favoring the vetoed bill would be on the left of v, which is located where two-thirds of the legislators are there or to the left. If v is to the left of (or at) the status quo, the legislature overrides the veto. If v is to the right of the status quo, the legislature fails to override the veto. Thus, to enact a bill with the status quo to the left of v is not possible.

A filibuster pivot example: Consider the top panel with a Republican president again. The threshold for cloture (Senate only) on most legislation is a three-fifths majority, which is less than the two-thirds required for overriding a veto. Consequently, if two-thirds of legislators (those at or to the left of v) are willing to override a presidential veto, the filibuster pivot (not shown) that lies between the chamber median and v is not relevant. It remains possible for a minority of senators at the far left to filibuster a bill. To invoke cloture on the filibuster requires a three-fifths majority of senators. That is, cloture would require the support of the three-fifths of senators located at or to the right of f.

If f is to the left of (or at) the status quo, then the required supermajority will favor a bill. If f is to the right of the status quo, then a sufficiently large minority will exist to prevent cloture and block passage of the bill.

Thus, in the top panel with a hypothetical Republican president, if the legislators pursue legislation on an issue for which the status quo is located in the region between f and v, the legislation will either be successfully vetoed by the president or successfully filibustered by a Senate minority. This region is labeled the "gridlock interval" to reflect the outcome of a stalemate between the president and the legislature. With perfect information about the location of f and v, legislators and presidents who are solely concerned about policy outcomes would not bother to pursue legislation with status quo locations in the gridlock interval.

Winning coalitions, therefore, would be two-thirds majorities (or larger) if the status quo was on the right or three-fifths majorities (or larger) for a status quo on the left. Smaller coalitions would suffer defeat by veto or filibuster. In a unidimensional legislative world without parties, Krehbiel proposes, the coalitions in favor of bills that actually pass should be appropriately super-sized.

Figure 6.1 also illustrates Krehbiel's point that changing the location of the president from the right side to the left side and back again alters the location of the gridlock region and where the larger coalitions are expected. Moreover, we might expect each "presidential regime" to yield a set of new policies that define the status quo in the next regime. This sequence of gridlock intervals and status quo locations will be discussed later in the chapter.

Krehbiel uses a figure, reproduced in Figure 6.2, to illustrate that winning coalitions are frequently large over the 1946–1990 period on the most important legislation (Mayhew 1991). He concludes that the record is "more consistent" with supermajority pivots argument than the view that the size of the majority party determines the size of the winning coalition (Krehbiel 1998, 84). Krehbiel's evidence is useless for sorting pivot and party effects. Many bills in the set generated winning coalitions that were less than either the veto or filibuster supermajority thresholds, contrary to the prediction of pivotal politics. Moreover, from the figure, we do not know if there is any relationship between majority party size and winning coalition size. We can infer that the

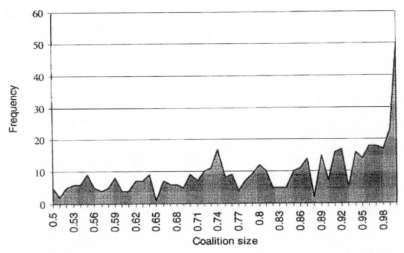

FIGURE 6.2. Distribution of coalition sizes on Mayhew's important legislation, 1946–1990. *Source:* Krehbiel (1998), Figure 4.4.

relationship is imperfect from our knowledge that party majorities seldom exceed 70 percent, but we cannot infer that majority party size is irrelevant altogether or less important than the decision pivots. Finally, House and Senate votes are included in Krehbiel's figure. The three-fifths threshold (f) is relevant only in the Senate. In the House, the gridlock interval shrinks to the interval between the chamber median and the veto pivot ($m - v$) so that small majorities can pass legislation.

The Ambiguity of the Effective Decision Rule

Essential assumptions of the pivotal politics model are that decision thresholds are fixed and political actors exploit the thresholds to their advantage. Legislators would tell us that they are not always concerned about veto or filibuster threats – even when the majority to pass a bill is not expected to be large enough to override a veto or invoke cloture. This is confirmed by the actual size of the winning majorities on conference committee reports; the last votes taken before bills are presented to the president. In Figure 6.3, I report for each house the mean size of the winning coalition on conference report votes. The horizontal line is drawn at the two-thirds threshold required for a veto override. The means mask substantial variation within each Congress,

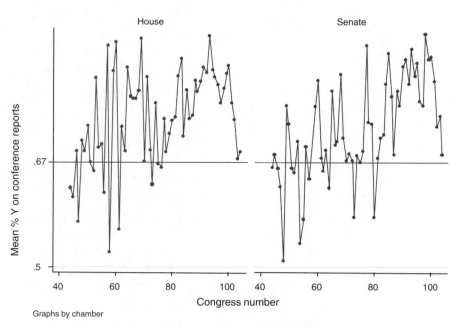

FIGURE 6.3. Mean size of winning coalition on conference report votes, 1875–1995 (proportion of chamber). *Source:* Roll-Call Voting Record.

for which the number of cases falling below the two-thirds threshold always is substantial.[1] Plainly, a very large proportion of measures are considered and passed without the winning coalition size predicted by the pivotal politics thesis. Contrary to the pivotal politics thesis, either a filibuster or veto is not feared even if it might be successful or proponents of legislation are willing to suffer losses.

Why would "small" majorities succeed when a filibuster or veto might be successful? Consider filibusters first. Naturally, the Senate votes that I aggregate in Figure 6.3 are votes that took place because a successful filibuster was not mounted against the associated motions. A successful filibuster, after all, yields no direct vote on the motion at issue. Nevertheless, a very large proportion of conference reports

---

[1] The president's position is identified by Congressional Quarterly and coded in NOM-INATE vote files at http://voteview.com. I thank Professor Keith Poole for providing the data. I thank Professor Eric Lawrence for providing data on the size of the winning majority.

appear to have been approved with minorities large enough to prevent the vote. There are three credible explanations.

First, the opportunity and transaction costs associated with filibusters are substantial (Binder et al. 2002; Binder and Smith 1997; Wawro and Schickler 2004). Not only are the filibustering senators burdened with the time and effort of organizing a filibuster, their filibuster may delay action on other legislation on which they would like to see prompt action. Opportunity and transaction costs are assumed to be zero in the pivotal politics model.

Second, there may be a disparity between the votes cast for a bill and the votes cast on cloture because some legislators may oppose bills but allow them to come to a vote. Such senators might have strong commitments to their view of procedural fairness, see their votes on cloture connected with their stance on cloture for other matters, can rationalize their seemingly inconsistent votes for important audiences, or may be subject to the influence of fellow partisans or others to allow a vote.[2] There is plenty of anecdotal evidence that the disparity between cloture votes and the subsequent votes involves partisan considerations. The phenomenon is a corollary to the observation that party loyalty is greater on procedural votes than substantive votes, as discussed in previous chapters. Again, this kind of behavior is inconsistent with the pivotal politics thesis, which holds that legislators take into account only policy considerations on the dimension at issue.

Third, it bears notice that filibusters are not possible for budget measures, fast-track trade legislation, and a variety of other legislation for which the Senate has limited debate (Binder and Smith 1997). The Senate majorities have voluntarily limited debate for these categories of legislation in order to facilitate prompt floor action. In such cases, the filibuster pivot is not present and the gridlock interval is reduced to the chamber median–veto pivot interval $(m - v)$ so the small majorities are possible even in the Senate. Mayhew's legislation did not include any such measures (as far as I can determine) so this feature of Senate procedure cannot explain the small majorities that appear in Krehbiel's figure.

---

[2] Southern Democrats in the mid–twentieth century seemed to avoid voting for cloture on any matter so that they could take an apparently principled stance against cloture on civil rights legislation.

How about voting on veto overrides? First, there is the possibility that legislators are uncertain about the president's intentions about using the veto and proceed to pass legislation that is vetoed. That uncertainty about a veto will reduce the incentive to pay the policy, opportunity, and transaction costs entailed in building a majority larger than a simple majority. Moreover, partisan and other pressures tend to be stronger on vetoes than on most other legislative issues, thus creating disparities between passage and veto votes.

Another possibility, of course, is that the president does not credibly threaten to veto when he could. Vetoes are seldom surprises – typically, presidents signal their intentions in many ways and through many administration officials – so legislators may not fear a veto in cases when no or just weak signals are sent to Capitol Hill. Why would a president accept legislation when a veto could be upheld? One possibility is that partisan political considerations enter. A veto fight between the president and a Congress controlled by his party could damage the party's reputation or otherwise harm the interests of the president or his fellow partisans on the Hill. Another possibility is that a president chooses to husband his political capital for later use, a central theme of presidential scholars (Light 1983; Neustadt 1990).

Finally, for both filibusters and vetoes, legislators are willing to suffer losses – and they often lose. Cameron reports that under divided party control of Congress and the presidency 20 percent of "landmark" legislation is vetoed, most successfully (Cameron 2000). Mayhew describes one reason legislators do not mind losing (Cameron 2000; Mayhew 1974). By forcing opponents, including a president, on the record, legislators hope to highlight differences for the public, or at least key constituencies, that they believe work to their advantage. This "loss is a win" strategy – fighting the good fight – is an everyday feature of politics that is not anticipated in a spatial theory of politics that assumes that the legislative majority engages in a legislative battle with the expectation of winning that battle without regard to other battles and goals. Another reason is that the single-play game of Krehbiel's model is not realistic. Legislation that is blocked by filibuster or veto can be reconsidered, perhaps as a new bill, perhaps in a new Congress. A supermajority may be required eventually, but there is nothing about everyday congressional politics that prevents small majorities in the initial rounds. Cameron finds that 41 percent of all vetoes and nearly two-thirds of vetoes of important legislation are part of a chain of bill–veto–bill and maybe more stages (Cameron 2000).

The lesson of these observations is that legislating is often messy in ways that violate simple models of politics. Bills must pass with majorities but invoking supermajority rules is optional and not always the best strategy for legislators and presidents. In many cases, it is likely that motivations beyond the policy motivation of the pivotal politics model are at work. Among those motivations may be partisan considerations – a tendency to support the party on procedural votes or salient presidential vetoes, a common interest in avoiding open conflict within a party, and so on. Of course, the presence of other forces does not deny the importance of decision rules. The requirement of a simple majority to pass legislation always remains in place. When policy makers are motivated to exploit their procedural advantages, supermajority decision thresholds become critical. But policy makers are not always motivated to do so.

My hunch is that partisan interests are likely to be at stake when legislators and presidents are fully exploiting their procedural rights. Consequently, the intersection of two sets of issues – the issues on which supermajority pivots are relevant and the issues on which partisan forces are active – is likely to be large. Ideally, we would identify each set independently, find the issues common to them, and measure party effects on outcomes, controlling for decision thresholds, both within and outside of the intersection.

An Alternative Explanation for Large-Sized Winning Majorities

Krehbiel's explanation for the large-sized winning majorities in Figure 6.2 is that the filibuster and veto pivots must be satisfied to enact legislation. Another explanation can be taken from Mayhew, whose data serves as the basis for Krehbiel's figure and who mentions supermajority rules as the second of two explanations (Mayhew 1991, 130–33). That explanation is that real-world conditions often create a status quo that is unacceptable to – that is, remote from – a large majority of legislators, who therefore share a common interest in enacting new policy. Mayhew emphasizes that these common perceptions of policy problems can be the product of political craftsmanship (as opposed to preexisting preferences and recognized status quo locations), but observes that "a drive toward action builds from a pervasive view that something has to be done" (Mayhew 1991, 130). The spatial implication is clear – there seem to be times when doing nothing about a problem is unacceptable to most policy makers and large majorities are readily mustered for remedial legislation. Mayhew chooses not to attribute the wide variation in winning majorities exclusively, or even primarily, to decision thresholds.

Krehbiel does not take Mayhew's first explanation seriously. Instead, Krehbiel treats the location of the status quo as a by-product of the previous "regime." A regime is a period in which the presidency changes partisan control so that the relative locations of the president, congressional median, and veto and filibuster pivots change. He does not model the possibility that the natural world of politics creates status quo locations all over the spectrum. One consequence is that Krehbiel's model is not likely to explain much of the variation in the size of winning majorities. In fact, no general empirical model of coalition size is estimated and reported by Krehbiel. In a limited model, only about 5 percent of the variance in coalition size is explained by regimes and chamber differences in decision rules.

Explaining the Size of the Winning Majorities

We cannot be optimistic about specifying an appropriate model that explains much of the variance in the size of winning majorities without some measure of the status quo locations. In this context, in fact, the everyday meaning of the term *status quo* is somewhat misleading. The changing state of the world, sometimes associated with natural, medical, economic, or political disasters, makes the status quo a moving target. Unpredictable developments, at least for legislators and presidents, seem to affect policy makers' views of the effect of inaction or stalemate and motivate a great deal of major legislative activity. The theorist's term *reversion point* may better capture the concept of the state of the world if no legislation is enacted. Reversion points are not merely inherited from previous policies; reversion points are greatly influenced by factors outside of government policy. If reversion points are widely and randomly distributed within and across Congresses, they will drive changes in the sizes of winning coalitions that will not be related to changes in decision rules, partisan forces, or other features of the internal processes of Congress. Consequently, Krehbiel's hunch that supermajority pivots are the primary determinant of the size of winning majorities is probably wrong.

Another study observes that the size of winning Senate majorities was larger, on average, after the adoption of the cloture rule in 1917 (Wawro and Schickler 2004). The inference drawn is that the rule somehow increased the difficulty of overcoming obstructionism by changing senators' expectations about obstructionism. This somewhat vague argument fails to account for the House and does not explicitly account for the opportunity costs that probably were present and variable throughout Senate history.

Figure 6.3 reports mean sizes of majorities on conference report votes – the votes taken before sending legislation to the president. The graph makes plain that majority coalitions sizes trended upward in both houses. A similar pattern is observed for all final passage votes in both houses (Lawrence 2004). These observations about the House, which never had a cloture motion and made no similar change in rules in the first decades of the twentieth century, call into question the thesis that the Senate's cloture is implicated in rising coalition sizes. The rough correspondence between the series of the two houses motivates a search for political factors that may affect both houses.

Figure 6.3 looks quite chaotic before the 1930s (before the 72d Congress) but gains greater orderliness thereafter, perhaps due to the increase in the frequency of votes on conference reports. The inverted U-shape pattern in the period starting in the 1930s is suggestive of the logic of CPG and cartel theory, which are outlined in the previous chapter. After the 1932 elections, the Democratic majority was temporarily quite homogeneous but became internally divided by the end of the decade, a pattern that extended until late in the century. Thus, from the 1940s until the 1980s, the party struggled to maintain some semblance of unity, which, according to many histories, led leaders to try to keep divisive issues off the floor. A heterogeneous Democratic majority party kept a wide range of issues off the floor so as not to expose internal divisions. When it did go to the floor, it often did so with minority party support, producing large majorities. On the other hand, a homogeneous majority party (in the 1930s and since the late 1980s) went to the floor at will but tended to win by small margins and with little minority support.

All of that is pure speculation. The roughly parallel patterns in House and Senate winning coalition sizes encourage us to look for common causes. Systematic analyses of changes in decision thresholds show effects at the margins but account for only a small part of the observed variation (Krehbiel 1998; Lawrence 2004). The CPG/cartel hunch seems reasonable but no more reasonable than a systematic change in the common reversion points and similar pivot locations of the two houses. We are stymied once again by our inability to gauge the location of the reversion points. We certainly are unable to draw meaningful inferences about the effect of partisan forces around the (variable) pivots that appear to be generated by chamber-determined decision rules.

LOOKING FOR PARTY EFFECTS IN FILIBUSTER AND VETO POLITICS

The implication of the pivotal politics model is that the focus of efforts to influence legislators is the set of legislators closest to the relevant pivot. Overcoming a filibuster and overriding a veto means modifying legislation to satisfy the legislator who will cast the last vote required to pass the legislation. Krehbiel therefore asks whether legislators who switch their votes between cloture votes on the same bill or who switch their vote between passage of a bill and the subsequent veto override vote are located in the region closest to the relevant pivot. He answers the question in the affirmative and, in doing so, argues that the pivotal politics model is confirmed.

The Krehbiel analysis in four core chapters intended to establish the viability of the pivotal model serves little purpose. Consider the filibuster switching chapter first.

For the period between 1917, when the cloture rule was first adopted, and 1995, Krehbiel identifies episodes in which more than one cloture vote occurred on the same legislation and determines which legislators, if any, switched their votes between successive cloture votes. Switchers and nonswitchers are divided into quartiles on the basis of their NOMINATE scores. The "filibuster quartile," the quartile in which the 67th or 60th senator is located (a two-thirds majority was required for cloture until 1975), is where Krehbiel hypothesizes switching will occur. The relationship between switching and several

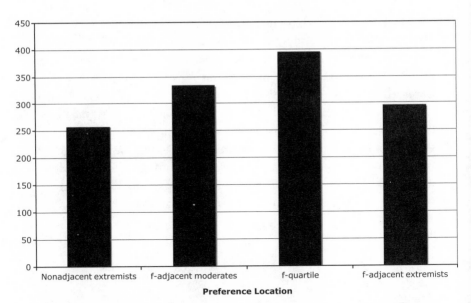

FIGURE 6.4. Location of switchers on cloture votes, 1917–1995. *Source:*
Krehbiel (1998), Table 5.5.

possible determinants of switching – location in the quartiles, being a
Democrat, divided party control of the Senate and White House, and
being a case of filibustering on the president's side – is estimated in a
multivariate model (Krehbiel 1998, Chapter 5).

On the basis of the distribution of switchers across the four quartiles,
Krehbiel finds support for the pivotal politics thesis. The frequency of
switching by quartile is presented in Figure 6.4. There is more switching in the filibuster quartile, but nearly 70 percent of the switching
takes place outside of the predicted quartile. Krehbiel concludes that
this pattern provides "preliminary support for the expectation that
switching behavior has systematic measurable components" (Krehbiel
1998, 107). My inference would be that the pivot may explain some
of the switching behavior but it is unlikely to explain much of the total
variation in switching.

Krehbiel's subsequent multivariate estimates show that being
located in any quartile other than the nonadjacent quartile yields a
higher probability of being a switcher, controlling for divided party
control of government and party affiliation. Based on these estimates, Krehbiel concludes that "the locus of bargaining over legislation that elicits cloture attempts seems consistently to be at or near

the supermajoritarian filibuster pivot" (Krehbiel 1998, 111). That is a wild exaggeration. The full equation explains less than 5 percent of the variance in switching behavior and it is plain that one-fifth of the switching occurs in the quartile most remote from the filibuster pivot. The switching and surely the bargaining are *not* consistently at or near the filibuster pivot. As Krehbiel points out a paragraph later, "an inordinate amount of variation is statistically unaccounted for and is thus best described as idiosyncratic" (Krehbiel 1998, 111). Maybe. Without a better empirical model, we will not know.

More troubling are the inferences drawn about divided party control of government and party. Neither divided government nor party should be related to the probability of switching if switching is entirely a function of legislators' policy preferences. Both show statistically significant effects, but here is what Krehbiel says:

First, is switching more likely in divided than unified government, other things being equal? The answer is yes, although the magnitude of the divided-government effect is small. Again using the most likely switcher category as our baseline (f-quartile senators), the probabilistic increment associated with divided government is only .025, or one of 40. So, to the extent that switching is a manifestation of bargaining, bargaining with senators near the filibuster pivot is slightly more common in divided than unified government.

Second, do Democrats switch more than Republicans, other things equal? Here the answer is no . . . The probability that a Democrat in the f-quartile switches is .040 less than that for an f-quartile Republican (Krehbiel 1998, 112).

I am hoping that there is a typographical error. Is the 0.025 difference for divided/unified government small but meaningful, but the larger party difference of 0.040 not meaningful? Is 1 of 40 noteworthy but 1 of 25 not so? In a quartile of 25 senators, that's 1 senator. It bears notice that proportion of switchers who are in the filibuster quartile is 0.308 and who are in the most distance quartile is 0.201 (Krehbiel 1998, 107), a difference of 0.101. The party increment of 0.040 (about 40 percent) seems reasonably large in that context and, again, the party effect in the multivariate estimates is statistically significant.[3]

---

[3] The party variable in Krehbiel's filibuster switching estimates is coded 1 for Democrats and 0 for Republicans. He describes this as an "atheoretic check" on the pivot effects. It certainly is atheoretic but it may be a meaningless check on the pivot effects. During the period for which the estimates are calculated, the Democrats were sometimes in the majority and sometimes in the minority. Under some of these circumstances, such as

The same logic applies to veto switching. In this case, Krehbiel divides the policy space into quintiles so that the veto pivot, which is associated with the legislator at the 67th percentile, is located in the fourth quintile. The analysis is restricted to the 80th–103d Congresses (1947–1995) but includes both houses. One hitch in the analysis is the strong bivariate relationship between switching and being a Democrat (Democrats switch about one-fourth as often as Republicans) and operating under divided government (switching under divided party control occurs less than half as often as under unified control). Krehbiel argues that he must include variables to capture these relationships "even though they are arguably atheoretical and certainly tangential with respect to pivotal politics theory" (Krehbiel 1998, 129).

Krehbiel's results for the House and Senate are provided in the first and third columns of estimates listed in Table 6.1. He infers that the pivot effects are about what the pivot model predicts. On the basis of these estimates, Krehbiel concludes that "the weight of evidence favors the pivotal politics theory over the divided-government-and-Democrats conjecture" (Krehbiel 1998, 133). This conjecture is that Democrats switch more in unified government than in divided government but for an unknown reason.

Again, I am perplexed by Krehbiel's inferences. Little of the variation in switching is explained. The "weight of the evidence" is that both pivot and party effects are observed, although I do not know of a party theory that predicts party differences per se. The conjecture belongs to no party theory that I can find and there is no citation to one. We might conjecture that the pressure to change positions is greatest for members of the president's party because they share a common party future, at least to some degree. Once we identify the party match between presidents and legislators, switchers are overwhelmingly of the president's party. Pivot effects remain visible. Pivots plus party, not pivots versus party.

In the end, the core chapters (Chapters 4–6) of *Pivotal Politics* that are intended to demonstrate the fundamental strength of the pivotal politics model are not entirely persuasive. Little meaningful is learned from the examination of the size of winning majorities. The relevance

when the party was in the majority under unified government, we might expect more pro-party switching, but such theorizing is about expected party effects. Similarly, we might expect party differences in switching within the quartiles. Such theorizing and empirical tests about party status are absent in Krehbiel's analysis of filibuster pivots.

TABLE 6.1. *Probit Estimates of Veto Switching, 80th–103d Congresses (Krehbiel 1998)*

Variable	House: Krehbiel (1998, 139), Col. 2	Senate: Krehbiel (1998, 132), Col. 2	Combined House–Senate Attraction: Krehbiel (1998, 173)
Constant	−0.956	−0.446	−2.304
	(−21.322)	(−3.389)	(−74.301)
Veto pivot quintile	1.086	1.009	1.358
	(34.295)	(13.659)	(30.638)
Extreme opponent quintile	0.976	0.997	1.667
	(29.715)	(12.978)	(21.913)
Moderate quintile	0.666	0.580	0.663
	(21.823)	(7.965)	(17.557)
Supporter quintile	0.214	0.046	0.261
	(6.528)	(0.562)	(6.592)
Divided government	−0.953	−1.234	
	(−19.957)	(−9.034)	
Democrat	−0.757	−1.406	
	(−13.521)	(−7.640)	
Democrat × divided government	0.610	1.031	
	(9.792)	(5.304)	
Extreme opponent quintile × president's party			0.267
			(3.736)
Veto quintile × president's party			0.267
			(7.554)
Moderate quintile × president's party			0.595
			(17.589)
Supporter quintile × president's party			0.629
			(7.885)
Extreme supporter × president's party			0.808
			(4.228)
N	59,528	10,631	56,840
Pseudo-R^2	0.092	0.133	.209

of pivots is demonstrated in the switching analysis of filibuster and veto voting, but the substantive importance of pivots is shown to be remarkably weak. The 90–95 percent of variance that is unexplained by the pivot models leaves a great deal of room for other political forces to work, including properly specified partisan forces. No meaningful partisan explanation is eliminated by Krehbiel's analysis in these chapters.

In fact, Krehbiel moves on to demonstrate that party effects are present with a more appropriate conception of possible party effects, one that was not mentioned in the initial presentation of evidence. Rather than a dummy for Democrat/Republican, an interaction term for member of the president's party and quintile is used in an analysis that separates moving toward the president on a veto override vote from being retained by the president. The attraction estimates, reported in the third and fourth columns of Table 6.1, show the predicted party effects and essentially double the explained variance over the pivot models. So it is pivots plus about as much party, not pivots alone.

Krehbiel qualifies the party effect by asserting that "the party effects are almost surely president's-party effects – not congressional majority-party effects" (Krehbiel 1998, 183). How do we know this? It comes from analysis of veto switching alone. I do not doubt that a president is important in efforts to block overrides of his vetoes, but I would guess that most of the persuading involves the president and his party congressional leaders persuading fellow partisans to sustain the veto. Sorting out presidential and party effects seems hopeless. As Truman emphasized years ago (Truman 1959), party-related behavior on Capitol Hill often blends partisan and presidential elements.

In any event, Krehbiel's veto switching findings are deceptive because they are based on the record of veto politics in just a handful of presidencies in the 1947–1995 period in which veto override votes were cast. Because no override votes were cast in the presidencies of Kennedy, Johnson, and Clinton, and only four in the Carter presidency, the analysis relies on the experience of six presidents, five Republicans and only one Democrat (Truman). So, if you were wondering why Democrats showed systematically weaker tendency to switch (in favor of the president) than Republicans, I bet you can guess now. The analysis is almost entirely dependent on Republican presidents, for whom Republicans, not Democrats, do most of the switching to support their president on a veto override attempt. This registers as a party effect for me, in this case one that melds partisan and presidential components.

Upon completing the veto switching analysis, Krehbiel summarizes his view of congressional policy making:

on balance, and most broadly, the cumulative findings from Chapter 3-8 suggest that the outcome-consequential tensions that arise and are played out in U.S. lawmaking are due, first and foremost, to politicians who straight-forwardly and individualistically express their preferences within and across two branches of government in supermajority settings. It is not disputed that majority-party leaders compete actively, aggressively, and often successfully for pivotal votes in such settings. But so do minority-party leaders and the presi-dent, and there is precious little systematic evidence supporting the hypothesis that the majority party in the Congress is disproportionately powerful at win-ning pivotal votes, much less noncentrist outcomes. Therefore, to the extent lawmaking outcomes in the United States are not approximate legislative-median outcomes, the explanation seems not to be found in a theory of party strength in legislatures. Rather, the probable cause is supermajoritarian insti-tutions which allow pivotal players to dampen only somewhat the strong ten-dencies toward policy moderation in weakly partisan voting bodies. (Krehbiel 1998, 185)

This is not persuasive, at least not based on the evidence offered. The evidence offered supports the inference that pivots and parties affect outcomes.

THE NAGGING PROBLEM OF THE LOCATION
OF THE STATUS QUO

More recently, Krehbiel has turned his attention to cartel theory, which, of course, deemphasizes the direct party influence that is the subtext of *Pivotal Politics* and focuses on the negative agenda control of con-gressional majority parties. I report my views on Cox and McCubbins's cartel theory in Chapter 5, so I will not review them here. Instead, I turn my attention to Krehbiel's hunch that the locations of the status quo, or reversion points, account for the low roll rates that are observed for House and Senate majority parties (Krehbiel 2006).

Three Models and a Simulation of Status Quo Points

The 2005 version of cartel theory provides that the status quo on any dimension is the result of the policy at the end of the previous Congress and any shock generated by nature (Cox and McCubbins 2005, 41). The size and direction of the shock is not specified. Voting on final passage motions then involves a comparison of a bill and a known status quo. The majority party brings a bill to the floor when its own median and the chamber median favor the bill over the status quo. The formal model of cartel theory's strategic premise is silent on the precise distribution of status quo points over the multiple dimensions of policy making allowed by the theory.

Krehbiel (2006) argues that the cartel model's prediction of a zero roll rate for majority parties and a higher roll rate for minority parties must be evaluated against the predictions of other spatial models – the median voter model and pivotal politics model. He requires that the status quo location for each model be based on the kind of historical series suggested in Figure 6.1. That is, the policy-making process at time t, along with a random shock, generates a set of status quo points for policy making at time $t + 1$. The status quo points are the product of each model's pivots in the last period plus a random shock that is treated in two ways. In one treatment, the status quo points are distributed uniformly over a certain range. The range is set at low, medium, and high levels to observe the effects of different assumptions. In the second, status quo points are distributed as a binomial normal distribution with a small, medium, and high variance. Thus, for each model and each treatment of the random shock to the inherited status quo, there are a certain number of status quo points at each increment along the policy space. For each such status quo point, it can be determined whether the model predicts a majority or minority roll and, by summing over the distribution of status quo points, aggregate predicted roll rates can be calculated. These are compared to the actual roll rates to determine the fit of the models.

Krehbiel finds that the cartel model best predicts majority party roll rates (Krehbiel 2006, Table 3). In fact, the cartel theory makes virtually no errors in predicting House majority party roll rates under either treatment of status quo points. The median voter and pivot models better predict minority roll rates than the cartel model, particularly for the normal distribution of status quo points. Because the minority roll rate errors of cartel theory are large, Krehbiel contends that median voter and pivot models do best overall. While he views the analysis as quite tentative, Krehbiel concludes as follows:

The cartel theory clearly provides the best account for the paucity of majority party rolls, which it should: the distances between its majority-party gatekeeping assumption, its no majority-roll prediction, and the ex ante known paucity of such rolls are razor-thin. On the other hand, the party cartel theory is clearly inadequate in predicting minority party rolls once status quo distributions are endogenized. Meanwhile, the pivotal politics theory exhibits a higher mean and lower variance in performance than the cartel theory. Yet, it is not the pivotal politics model but rather the original and simplest pivot model – Black's median voter theory – that performs best in most circumstances (Krehbiel 2006).

Some Initial Observations About the Simulation

Several questions arise in evaluating the importance of Krehbiel's "Pivots" argument. First, one fair observation is that majority roll rates determine policy outcomes so we might care more about them than minority roll rates. If the cartel model is capturing majority party strategies accurately, then the minority roll rate is irrelevant to outcomes. Thus, Krehbiel's observation that the cartel model is superior to the median voter and pivotal models in predicting majority party roll rates is significant. An equally fair observation is that cartel theory ignores the minority party (see Chapter 5), as do most party theories, so it is not too surprising that minority behavior is not well explained by the model.

Second, the simulation provides a better test of the pivotal politics thesis than we find in *Pivotal Politics*. It supports my contention that supermajority pivots often are irrelevant in day-to-day congressional policy making. Filibusters are not pursued and vetoes are not exercised as often as they could be.

Third, none of the models in Krehbiel's simulation provide a realistic view of the legislative agenda. In cartel theory and Krehbiel's models, the inherited policy remains in place until displaced by the enactment of new legislation. This parallels the actual policy-making process for some, but not all, policies. For example, under existing law, social security benefits remain in place until Congress and the president approve a new law. Unfortunately, this common, convenient, and consequential assumption is not true of all policies. Appropriations (spending authority) must be approved annually for the affected agencies and programs to continue their operations. Failure to enact the annual appropriation bill forces spending authority to zero and compels the program to suspend its activities. The reversion point of zero is far from the existing policy and is likely to be extreme relative to the ideal points of most legislators. Thus, in some areas of policy making, failure to enact legislation does not leave the existing policy in place. Rather, policy reverts to a third alternative that is seldom modeled. If these third alternatives are unacceptable to a large number of legislators, including minority party legislators, the minority roll rate will be lower than predicted by the traditional assumption about reversion points. Even winning coalitions centered in the minority side are possible.[4]

Fourth, the Krehbiel simulation of status quo points is unidimensional – the location of the relevant pivotal legislators is determined on the NOMINATE first dimension. This is necessary because the median voter and pivot models are strictly unidimensional and Krehbiel desires to compare cartel theory on the same basis. Unfortunately for Krehbiel's analysis, cartel theory does not require unidimensionality (see Chapter 5) so there is no guarantee that the relevant chamber and party medians are properly identified in Krehbiel's simulation of status quo points. Cartel theory predicts a zero roll rate for the majority party however many separate dimensions are at issue in the voting record, but its prediction for the minority party roll rate is dependent on the distribution of preferences on the relevant dimensions. This is the kind of argument implied by Krehbiel's 1993 challenge to party theories (see Chapter 4), where different interest group ratings are used to measure preferences for different committees, but Krehbiel chooses to ignore the issue here and rewrite the cartel model to fit the needs of his simulation.

My argument that cartel theory may overstate the minority roll rate is not an endorsement of Krehbiel's inclination to then find another "winner" in the competition for the single-best theory of congressional policy making. We should not accept the terms of the Krehbiel contest. As my discussion in Chapter 5 suggests, the strategic premise of cartel theory may be an excessively narrow version of the behavior expected from a majority party, one that requires more qualification than Cox

---

[4] Some legislation is reconsidered periodically as a product of multiyear authorizations so that the preferences of legislators in the immediately preceding Congress do not provide the appropriate basis for predicting the status quo points. Congress could consider new legislation at any time, but, for practical reasons, does not do so. Food stamps, higher education, elementary and secondary education, and farm subsidies are among the many such programs. The Congressional Budget Office, which provides an annual report on expiring authorizations, listed 45 programs that were expiring in 2006.

and McCubbins provide. The relevance of issues to party interests surely varies and so the strategic premise is likely to be invoked for many bills but not for many others. This is a central lesson of *Legislative Leviathan* (Cox and McCubbins 1993) that is dropped in *Setting the Agenda* (Cox and McCubbins 2005). Median voter or pivotal voter models may be a better fit to the circumstances when the cartel strategic premise is not relevant.

An Armchair Evaluation of Status Quo Points

There is an additional possibility – Krehbiel's simulation of status quo distributions may not capture the real distribution and so does not serve as a sound basis for evaluating the cartel model. In particular, a distribution of status quo points that is centered on the predicted outcome of the previous period may not capture that actual range of status quo points. To see this, I make subjective judgments about the location of the status quo for legislation subject to "key votes," as identified by Congressional Quarterly (CQ), for the 2001–2005 period. A key vote is the most telling vote, in the judgment of CQ editors, on a bill, amendment, or other legislation that represents a "major controversy" concerns "a matter of presidential or political power," or has "potentially great impact on the nation and lives of Americans." The 2001–2005 key measures are the major measures of the first five years of the Republican administration of George W. Bush and represent a different presidential regime than the previous period under Democratic President Bill Clinton. The summary is provided in Table 6.2.[5]

The first observation to be made about Congressional Quarterly's list of key-vote measures is that a key vote sometimes occurs on just one of many issues that are addressed in a larger bill. When this happens on a must-pass bill, such as on an appropriations bill, the fact that the majority party is not rolled on final passage is a bit misleading. An example is the VA-HUD appropriations bill that includes funding for two large departments and 20 independent agencies, including the Environmental Protection Agency (EPA). In 2001, Democrats, with the support of some Republicans, succeeded in getting a floor amendment adopted to prevent the EPA from weakening Clinton-era regulations

---

[5] The complete listing is available from the author.

TABLE 6.2. *Location of Status Quo Points on Key-Vote Issues, 2001–2005*

	Primary Influence on Location of Status Quo						
	Previous Policy		Mix of Previous Policy and Nature		Nature		Total
	Appropriations/ Reauthorizations	Other	Appropriations/ Reauthorizations	Other	Appropriations/ Reauthorizations	Other	
Location of Status Quo							
Far Right	11	5	2	9	0	6	33
Center Right	1	5	2	5	1	1	15
Center	2	7	0	4	0	1	14
Center Left	7	20	0	1	0	1	29
Far Left	3	5	0	3	2	7	20
Vote on Key-Vote Issue and Final Passage Vote Appear to be on Same Dimension							
Yes	13	29	2	16	2	13	75
No	9	6	2	2	1	3	23
Bill Failed on Final Passage Vote	2	7	0	4	0	0	13
TOTAL	24	42	4	22	3	16	111

Source: CQ *Weekly* reports on key votes.

on arsenic in drinking water. The vote was 218–189. Critical to the outcome was that 19 Republicans voted for the arsenic amendment with the Democrats to pass the amendment. The bill passed 336–89 with a sizable majority of both parties voting for it. We count this as a non-roll for both parties but plainly the Republican leadership, whose party opposed the amendment 19–182, was disheartened by the adoption of the amendment.

We might argue that the arsenic amendment episode is inconsistent with all three models. To be sure, the amendment may have moved the overall bill closer to the House median in a unidimensional policy space and then the bill received a large majority when pitted against the status quo of no bill. A principal components analysis generates only one statistically significant component from the 14 votes cast in the House on the bill – seemingly consistent with Krehbiel's simulation. In fact, the situation was more complex than that. The arsenic vote is not strongly correlated with the principal component. Cross-cutting divisions – at the margins, to be sure – on the arsenic amendment were sufficient cause the majority party to lose on a key vote (the vote is more strongly correlated with a minor component). In NOMINATE, a few of the legislators' votes would be unfortunate errors, but in everyday politics they make the difference between winning and losing. In this case, the *Washington Post* reports, a few Republicans in electoral difficulty were concerned about how the arsenic issue would register at home.[6] The final passage vote, therefore, was not simply a matter of a single median or pivot determining the outcome, contrary to the median voter and pivot models. Moreover, an arsenic dimension arose on which the majority of the majority party lost, contrary to the cartel model, even if a majority of the majority party won on final passage.

I infer that all three models miss an important possibility: As a package of (perhaps, individually minor) dimensions, an appropriations bill passed but with the outcome on some dimensions opposed by a majority party median. On the basis of the first dimension, we might treat this bill as an observationally equivalent and favorable result for the three models. The more appropriate interpretation is that none of the three models captured the key-vote outcome and related behavior.

[6] Eric Pianin and Juliet Eilperin, "House Backs Arsenic Rule," *Washington Post*, July 28, 2001, p. A01.

Let us return to status quo points. The arsenic episode is a case of a congressional coalition (largely a majority party coalition) attempting to change policy from a status quo point established in the previous administration, in that case policy determined by agency regulation. Another key-vote measure considered days later is an example of nature (the noncongressional world) prompting legislative action for the first time. In 1998, researchers demonstrated the ability to isolate stem cells in human embryos, which generated concerns about human cloning. In 2001, a Florida Republican sponsored a bill that was supported by most of his party colleagues that would ban cloning for any purpose, including reproduction and medical purposes. CQ's key vote occurred on an amendment to limit the ban. The key point here is that in 2001 Congress inherited no written policy. Before the new science was proven, there was no cloning issue alive before Congress and congressional inaction had no consequences. With the "shock" of the new science, the consequences of inaction became material to many people, including legislators who generated a large majority (265–162) for the bill. Out of concern that the world would change in additional unpredictable ways, a provision in the bill required the Government Accounting Office to study advances in medical technology that might require new legislation to maintain an effective ban on cloning.[7]

The complexities of the arsenic and cloning ban episodes are not unique. In Table 6.2, I report the frequency of issues for which the status quo is centrally located – as we would expect if the previous Congress merely bequeathed a policy to the current Congress – is shifted somewhat to the left or right of the chamber median, or is located to the far left or right. I report whether the status quo point at decision time was primarily the product of the inherited policy, as in the arsenic case, of nature, as in the cloning ban case, or some combination of inherited policy and new events. I also indicate whether the key-vote issue is associated with an appropriation or periodic reauthorization bill.

Several features of key-vote issues warrant attention. First, events external to government are the primary determinant of the location of the reversion point about 17 percent of the time; external events combined with the previous policy to shape the reversion point another

---

[7] Adriel Bettelheim, "House Vote to Ban Human Embryo Cloning Breaks New Ground in Regulation of Biotech," *CQ Weekly*, August 4, 2001, p. 1920.

23 percent. Second, about 28 percent of the cases involve an appropriations bill or a bill required to reauthorize a federal program. Third, 48 percent of the key-vote issues concern a status quo situated in a noncentral location. Fourth, 32 percent of the key-vote issues appear to fall on a different dimension than the one that defines the final passage vote.

The combination that is usually modeled is a case in which the previous policy sets the status quo, the bill is not a must-pass bill, and the bill and associated issues relate to a single dimension. This is the modal type – about 45 percent of the key-vote issues for the 2001–2005 period. But the modal type is not even a majority of the cases. Nature-given status quo locations, must-pass bills, or multidimensionality are evident in a majority of the cases. The variety is wide. Politics is complicated.

My tentative conclusion from this exercise is that the models we see in recent accounts of pivotal and cartel theory do not capture the strategic context of a majority of key-vote legislating. This is disheartening. It would be very convenient for parsimonious spatial models to fit the strategic context in which legislating takes place. They often, very often, do not.

CONCLUSION

Krehbiel identifies more potential than actual problems with studies that show party effects. Upon examination, Krehbiel's own work demonstrates party effects in both *Pivotal Politics* and "Pivots," but, for reasons difficult to understand, he chooses to place the emphasis elsewhere. While Krehbiel scores debating points against studies that claim to find party effects, the number of null findings for properly specified party effects is near zero in these analyses. The net effect of Krehbiel's studies is to reconfirm the presence of party influence.

The emphasis of *Pivotal Politics* is particularly deceiving. The book provides a concise articulation of the spatial model and its supermajority variant, but the treatment of party is shallow and unpersuasive. The "pivots versus party" formulation of the issue is inappropriate and directs our attention away from a useful theory of party effects. Moreover, party effects are not given a serious test in the *Pivotal Politics* analysis. The *Pivotal Politics* discussion of coalition sizes proves useless, the switching analysis shows significant party effects but is based on a very limited range of congressional behavior, and the effort to belittle the observed party effects in switching behavior is lamentable.

Characterizing status quo, or reversion point, locations remains a serious challenge for the empirical applications of spatial theory to legislative politics. For that reason, the simulation of status quo points in the later "Pivots" paper is potentially interesting. Upon investigation, it appears that the real world of legislative politics generates status quo points across the spectrum. These circumstances provide the variation that is required to allow a cartel model to fit the data. The outcome of "Pivots" simulation is that a party model, the cartel model, does a better job of explaining outcomes than the alternative median voter and pivotal models.

7

Reexamining the Direct and Indirect Influence of Party in the House and Senate

Steven S. Smith, Eric D. Lawrence, and Forrest Maltzman

The leading theories of congressional parties, CPG and cartel theory, have different emphases and both compatible and incompatible predictions for observed voting behavior. Pivotal politics theory predicts yet another set of expectations for floor behavior. The three theories have not been tested using a common methodology until recently (Lawrence et al. 2005, 2006). In this chapter, we report the results of that work.

The studies examined in the chapter differ from previous work in several ways:

- The empirical analysis considers roll-call behavior aggregated over Congresses and for individual legislators. The examination of individual legislators, as opposed to aggregated roll rates or other measures of group or party behavior, is essential to testing propositions of all three theories;
- the analysis considers both symmetric (both parties potentially exercising influence) and asymmetric (the majority party exercising influence) forms of party influence; and
- the analysis includes both House and Senate, which gives some basis for evaluating the importance of the Reed rules in the House and other potential sources of difference between the two houses of Congress.

Including the Senate requires that we give consideration to the institutional conditions that create stability in majority party agenda control. It is the interaction of institutional rules and partisan considerations that generate the kind and strength of party influence that we observe in the House and Senate. Party considerations are no more fundamental than institutional considerations. Historically, chamber rules and practices arise interactively with party mechanisms, each conditioning the development of the other. Initial conditions in each chamber had long-term consequences, so we see a stronger path dependency in the relationship between rules and party in the Senate than in the House.

MODELS OF PARTY EFFECTS

In previous chapters, it was argued that the distinction between negative and positive influence and between direct and indirect influence is difficult to make, at least in practice. Treatments of conditional party government (CPG) include all forms of party influence. Cartel theory addresses negative agenda-setting power and so seems to predict a zero roll rate for the majority party. Although we are persuaded that negative agenda control is important, a low roll rate is consistent with any party theory that gives the majority party more power than the minority party. We observe a low roll rate for the Senate majority party, too, without much of the apparatus of agenda control that we find in the House, which is the subject of the agenda control story. The result is that finding evidence in the roll-call voting record that cleanly confirms the presence of just one kind of influence (say, influence in one cell of Table 3.1) is not practical.

Preliminary Issues

With this in mind, we prefer to think of models of outcomes rather than models of causes. Let us outline some preliminary arguments that make the empirical analysis that follows possible.

First, following Clausen (1973), we can think of a legislator as having a fairly stable, long-term policy position. This policy position is a product of a wide range of political forces, including the legislator's adjustment to his or her district or state, partisan pressures from home, from within Congress, and from the White House, and personal policy commitments. Highly aggregated voting measures, such as NOMINATE-based measures, that summarize voting behavior over an entire Congress probably reflect long-term policy positions of this kind. Legislators' preferences almost certainly vary from those long-term policy positions across the many specific bills on which they vote. As for Cox and Poole (2002), we can think of short-term variation from those long-term positions as something that might be explained by party or other factors.

Second, we need to examine the behavior of individual legislators, rather than aggregate voting statistics such as roll rates, to evaluate party effects. A majority or minority party roll rate is an aggregate statistic that masks considerable variation within parties. A "roll" is an instance in which a majority of a party is on the losing side of a vote, but the party majority could be a bare simple majority or a unanimous party. As a result, a majority party can avoid being "rolled" even when nearly (but not quite) half of its legislators were on the losing side.

We prefer to consider the individual legislator's frequency of being on the winning side and to take into account the legislator's relative location in the policy space, somehow defined. Only in this way can we observe the effects of those forms of party influence that may not affect all party members in the same way. For example, we do not expect a party leader to influence legislators whose support she expects without any pressure from her, but we might expect her to seek to influence legislators who otherwise would vote against her position.

Figure 7.1 shows the mean "win rate" for legislators in the majority and minority parties. As expected, the win rate is higher for majority than minority party legislators (a mean of 84.7 and 84.5 for the House and Senate majority parties, respectively, and 61.7 and 65.2 for the minority parties). Minority party win rates vary widely but majority party win rates vary within a narrow range, consistent with the cartel model. The minority win rates for the two houses are correlated with each other ($r = 0.56$), which suggests that they have a common cause, such as electoral coalition polarization or party size. But there are anomalies, such as a few Congresses in which the mean minority party win rate is higher than the mean majority party win rate. We will return to this subject at the end of the chapter.

Third, we require a measure of legislators' long-term policy positions that can be applied over a long series of Congresses. Testing the predictions of CPG and cartel theory requires a long series of Congresses. CPG predicts that we look at the effects of variation in party

House

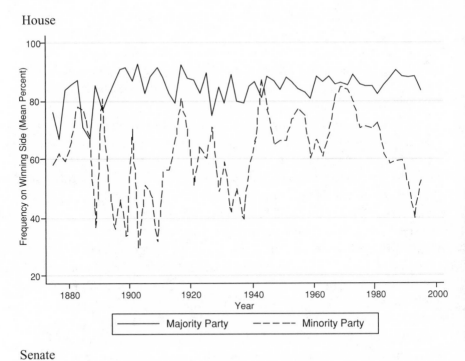

Senate

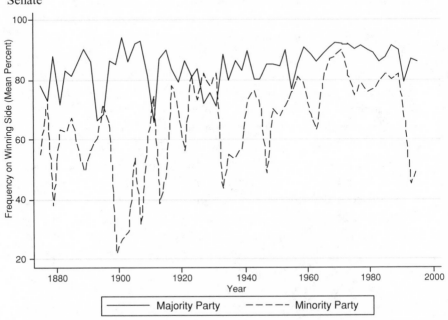

FIGURE 7.1. Mean Frequency on winning side, majority and minority party, 1875–1998.

polarization; cartel theory predicts no variation in majority roll rates over time. Pivotal politics predicts no party effect in any Congress. For the sake of argument, we use a NOMINATE measure of policy positions. By using the first dimension scores, we may be imposing a highly restrictive view of policy positions. This error in characterizing policy positions may be serious, in least for some legislative action.

Fourth, in the models that follow, we assume that legislators have single-peaked preferences as do most other theorists. A single-peaked preference is one in which the legislator's utility declines as an outcome moves away in either direction from her policy position. All things being equal, legislators seek policy outcomes that are as close as possible to their ideal policy positions. Short-term political forces, such as direct and indirect party influence, may bend policy outcomes away from the outcomes that otherwise would have been realized.

Fourth, we realize that the deck is stacked against finding evidence of direct party influence. As was discussed in Chapter 4, direct influence will be reflected in the NOMINATE scores that we use to characterize legislators policy positions. We are looking for evidence of above average influence on a subset of roll-call votes, final passage votes. If final passage votes are not distinctive in the party influence at work, we cannot gauge the effect of direct party influence.

Fifth, final passage votes are numerous, particularly in the modern Congress, and represent a comparison of a bill with the alternative of no bill. A house always can revisit an issue, reconsider a vote, or take up a modified version of an earlier bill, so it is not accurate to say that a final passage vote represents a comparison of a bill with the status quo. But final passage votes, perhaps along with conference report votes, are the closest that the houses come to choosing between a bill and the status quo, as spatial theories of legislating provide. Thus, a spatial theory really cannot be tested directly in the roll-call record. The choices legislators confront at final passage are only an approximation of the comparison dictated by theory.

Sixth, following the discussion in the previous chapter, we assume that status quo points are distributed widely across the policy spectrum. Consequently, final passage votes involve comparisons of bills with a wide variety of status quo locations. Bill sponsors sometimes need the votes of legislators to their right and sometimes to their left to win the final passage votes.

Finally, we are going to set aside an effort to account for the short-term effects of political forces other than partisan ones. This is unfortunate and should be pursued, but it will not be discussed further here.

Models

We ask, "Is a legislator's frequency of being on the winning side related to party membership, controlling for the legislator's long-term policy position?" The answer is yes, but not always. We learn more if we are clear about our conception of the consequences of policy positions and party influence. Four models capture the possibilities for the House (Figure 7.2).

The *median voter model* predicts that the median legislator determines the outcome. Because the median determines whether a majority to her left, to her right, or across the middle of the policy spectrum forms a coalition to win, the median voter will always be in the winning coalition. Legislators close are more likely to be on her side of an issue than more distant legislators. The precise form of the distribution depends on the location of status quo points – as status quo points approach a symmetric distribution, the distribution of winning frequencies will appear as shown.

The *supermajority pivots model* posits that the legislator whose vote is required to override a president's veto must favor a bill over the status quo for the bill to be enacted. In the figure, the president is assumed to be on the left end of the spectrum. The relevant legislator if a president vetoes a bill is the legislator who determines how the two-thirds of the chamber away from the president votes when a motion to override the veto is considered. A majority also must be acquired for the bill so that the veto pivot and the median pivot must agree before new legislation is enacted. Consequently, whenever the status quo is located between the veto and median pivots, no legislation can be enacted – the gridlock interval. When legislation is enacted, all legislators in the gridlock interval must favor it. Therefore, all legislators in the gridlock interval are predicted to win all the time, with distance from the interval resulting in declining frequency of being on the winning side.

The *symmetric party pressure model* assumes that each party's leaders have the resources to produce disciplined voting. The majority party, with a majority of votes, wins all the time. The minority party

Median Voter Model

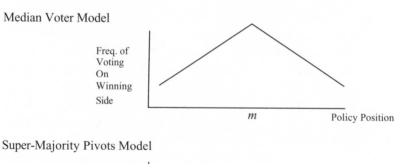

Super-Majority Pivots Model

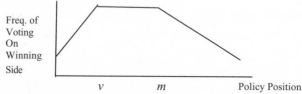

Symmetric Party Pressure Model

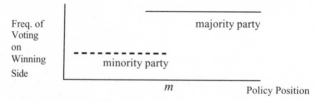

Asymmetric Party Effects Model

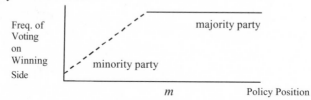

FIGURE 7.2. Models of the effects of long-term policy positions and party on frequency of winning. *Source:* Lawrence et al. (2006), Figure 1.

wins only when both parties favor a bill but otherwise loses so minority legislators have a uniformly lower rate of winning.

The *asymmetric party effects model* assumes that there is a systematic difference between the two parties. Majority party agenda control, a larger leaders' supply of incentives for gaining cooperation, or legislators' own calculations of the value of supporting the party may produce party-oriented behavior in the majority party that is not duplicated in the minority party. The prediction is that the majority party shows discipline that generates wins while minority party legislators go their own way. An additional asymmetric model could be added, but we do not show it, for the case of asymmetric party effects with a veto pivot. In that case, the set of legislators expected to always be on the winning side would extend from the majority party to the veto pivot that is farther left than the chamber median.

In the first two models of Figure 7.2, no party effect is assumed. The agenda freely allows legislators to propose legislation but only those measures that maximize the utility of the pivotal legislators will be enacted. In the second two models, a party leadership of some kind is assumed. In the symmetric case, which is the working assumption whenever a dummy variable (say, 1 for Democrat, 0 for Republican) is used, the leadership of both parties has resources to influence fellow partisans. In the asymmetric case, only the majority party leadership has such resources.

Observed Voting Patterns for the House in Recent Congresses

The voting patterns in two recent Congresses leave little doubt about which of the four models approximates observed behavior (Figure 7.3). The asymmetric party influence model closely resembles the observed win rates. The asymmetry of the pattern suggests that both party and policy positions are strongly correlated with voting behavior. A statistical estimate of the effect of party and policy position of the frequency of being on the winning side would show that both factors have a significant impact. Equally plain, the standard dummy variable for party would not capture the conditional relationships among party, policy position, and voting behavior. Party and policy position interact to produce the voting pattern.

Figure 7.3 is important for another reason. In the 104th Congress (1995–1996), Republicans controlled the House for the first time since 1954. The pattern for that Congress is the mirror image of the pattern for the previous Congress in which the Democrats controlled the House. The two patterns are consistent with the prediction of cartel theory – or another theory that predicts an asymmetry between the parties in the relationship between policy positions and voting on final passage motions.

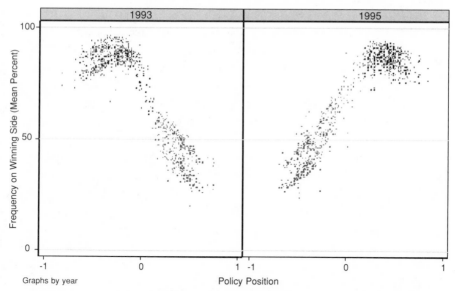

FIGURE 7.3. House scatterplots of D-NOMINATE score by frequency of winning, 103d and 104th Congresses (1993–1996), denoted by first year of Congress, majority party (black), minority party (gray).

Finally, it is worth noting that supermajority pivots are not reflected in the final passage voting patterns. If a veto pivot is the decisive legislator on final passage votes, the set of legislators who are almost always on the winning side would be extended well into the minority side of the distribution. Instead, the behavior appears to reflect a median voter pivot.

Can a nonpartisan process explain the patterns in Figure 7.3? The only possibility is that there is a systematic difference in the status quo points addressed in the two Congresses. With outcomes distributed over the minority party side of the policy spectrum, members of the majority party would be on the winning side by virtue of being on the same side of the status quo points are the chamber median. Is this realistic?

No. First, we simply do not believe that nature or the inherited policy produces status quo points in only the minority region of the policy space. We would have to believe that the House Democrats of the 103d Congress, after 40 years in the House majority, inherited status quo points entirely on the Republican side of the policy spectrum. Second, if the status quo locations are not naturally minority-shifted, then someone must be choosing which status quo policies to change. There is no obvious reason why a nonpartisan agenda setter would choose status quo points only to one side. If the agenda setter is a partisan and chooses distant status quo points, then we have a partisan process. It might make sense that a majority party agenda setter chooses to attack the more distant status quo locations but doing so demonstrates a party-based process that is denied in the median voter and pivotal models.

The argument made in Chapter 6 still serves as a better assumption about status quo points. That argument is that status quo points are widely distributed. Necessary periodic legislation, inherited policy, and the political world produce substantial variety in status quo locations in the active legislative agenda of most modern Congresses.

The Senate

At least two factors distinguish the Senate from the House. First, the possibility of a filibuster creates another possible pivot. As argued in Chapter 6, the filibuster pivot is not always relevant, but, when it is, it creates a pivotal legislator on the side of the median opposite the president. Second, majority party agenda control is not monopolistic. In the absence of a general germaneness rule, senators may offer their bills as amendments to other bills to force an issue to the floor. While an amendment can be filibustered or tabled, proponents of a bill who oppose an amendment put their bill at risk when obstructing a vote on an amendment and may face a filibuster of the bill. Thus, a Senate majority party may have to allow a vote on an unfriendly amendment in order to get a vote on its bill. Because it may be difficult to predict what amendments may be proposed, the Senate majority party may not be able to predict the content of the bill at final passage. Together, these considerations require that we anticipate that the Senate pattern of voting on final passage motions will differ from the House pattern.

Figure 7.4 shows the relationship between policy positions and winning under models adapted to the Senate, still placing a president on the left. The *Senate Supermajority Pivots Model* merely adapts the supermajority pivots model that accounts for the veto pivot (v) by adding the filibuster pivot (f). No party affiliation is relevant to this model and all senators between the two pivots always win. The *Senate*

Senate Super-Majority Pivots Model

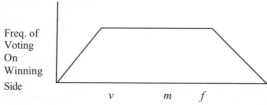

Senate Asymmetric Party Effects, Super-Majority Pivots Model

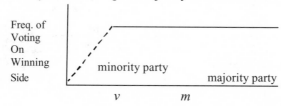

FIGURE 7.4. Senate models of the effects of long-term policy positions and party on frequency of winning. *Source:* Lawrence et al. (2006), Figure 1.

Asymmetric Party Effects, Supermajority Pivots Model accommodates the veto pivot, but direct or indirect majority party power keeps all majority party senators on the winning side. If the left party were the majority party, the predicted distribution would be the mirror image of the one shown. If the president is on the right rather than the left, as shown, the left pivot would be the filibuster pivot rather than the veto pivot.

We approach the Senate with the expectation that patterns will be considerably less clear than we see in the House. Filibusters occur but not as often as they could so the leverage of the filibuster pivot is not uniformly strong. Moreover, if the House pattern is due, at least in major part, to majority party agenda control, the possibility of a filibuster and nongermane amendments undermines monopoly agenda control of the Senate majority party. Thus, the expectations of cartel theory apply less well.

Figure 7.5 provides the Senate scatterplots of policy positions and winning frequency by party for several Congresses to show the variety of patterns present in the modern Congress. The scatterplots reconfirm the observation that the difference between majority and minority

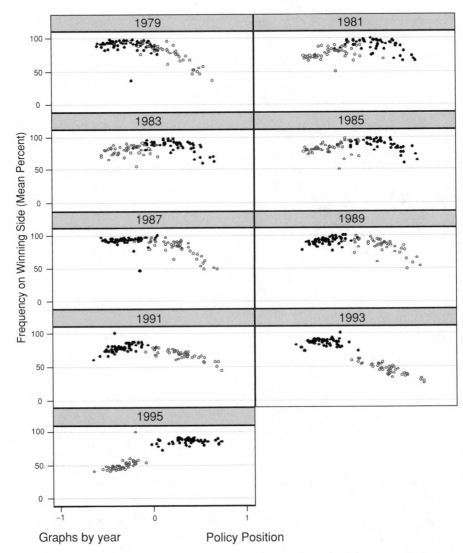

FIGURE 7.5. Senate scatterplots of D-NOMINATE score by frequency of winning, 96th–105th Congresses (1979–1998), majority party (black dot) and minority party (gray circle), denoted by first year of Congress.

party legislators in their frequency of being on the winning side is smaller in the Senate than in the House. Whereas House minority party members often exhibit a win rate of 40 percent or lower (Figure 7.3), Senate minority party members seldom fall below 50 percent and often stay higher than 60 percent. The scatterplots also show the polarization in final passage voting that occurs between the mid-1970s and mid-1990s.

Of the ten Congresses shown in Figure 7.5, six seem to approximate the asymmetric party effects model that characterizes the House in recent Congresses. The majority party senators of the new Republican Congresses – particularly for 1981–1986 period, which had the first Republican Senate majorities since 1954 – are far from a mirror image of the surrounding Democratic Senates. The majority Republicans of 1995–1996, another new majority, shows more of the asymmetric pattern, but the strong tail-off of the far right in the next Congress is not characteristic of the asymmetric pattern. The Democratic–Republican difference is particularly surprising in light of the conventional wisdom that Republicans are more cohesive than Democrats.

The scatterplots for the Senate under Republican majorities do not seem to fit any one of the models particularly well. There are similarities to the inverted V of the median voter model, which might apply if Republicans were proceeding to take up controversial legislation even if their party was somewhat divided on the bills that came to a final passage vote. This behavior is not visible for House Republicans. But the Senate patterns also are flatter, which is consistent with having to appeal to a wider range of legislators to overcome possible filibusters.

The natural place to look for a cause for differences in Senate distributions across Congresses is the location of the status quo points. We might expect that status quo points in the early 1980s were skewed to the left – an inheritance of more than a quarter century of Democratic majorities in both houses of Congress. The new Republican majority of the early 1980s would expect opposition from many Democrats and be forced to shift proposals to the left to accommodate at least those Democrats whose votes were required to avoid or overcome filibusters.

We have doubts about that explanation. We might have expected Republicans to force broader winning coalitions even when they were in the minority in the long era of Democratic control. Moreover, after six years under Republican President Ronald Reagan and a Senate Republican majority, Senate Democrats regained a majority and the Senate pattern reverts to the House-like asymmetric pattern in the 1987–1994 Congresses. One possibility is that having control of both houses is important to the observed pattern. In the 104th Congress

(1995–1996), after Republicans gain new majorities in both houses, the pattern for the Senate takes a more House-like form. Why would unified party control of the two houses matter to the Republicans? We can only speculate – existing spatial and party theories have nothing to say about this.

One speculation is that the Senate agenda is constrained to some degree by the legislation the House sends to it. The need to satisfy an opposing majority in the House may require legislation that appeals to at least some members of the other party in the Senate. If so, then some extreme majority party members may not support passage as frequently. The problem with this hypothesis is the logic should apply to the House – that is, House majorities should have to appeal to the opposition when the Senate is controlled by the opposite party. At least in the modern era, that is not the case.

A second speculation is that Senate *minority* party strategy changes when that party controls the House. This strategic change comes in the form of more frequent exploitation of Rule 22 to force the creation of supermajorities to pass legislation in the Senate. Why would the Senate minority behave this way? One possibility is that the Senate minority party's payoff for threatening obstruction is greater under divided than other unified party control of the House and Senate. Under unified party control of the House and Senate, the minority party cannot expect conference negotiations between the chambers to produce a favorable outcome even if it can force concessions in the Senate. Under divided party control, concessions made to acquire minority party votes are more likely to survive conference – or may even take certain issues off the table in conference because the House has taken the same position.

We favor the second speculation, but it remains a working hypothesis for now. After all, the twentieth century had only two other Congresses – 62d (1911–1913) and 65th (1917–1919) – with divided party control of the House and Senate, so little can be done to test the hypothesis systematically. Still, the proposition may help us to explain the Senate Democratic minority parties of the 1980s. The pivotal politics model predicts that obstructionism will always be pursued when it can affect the Senate outcome, but the model neglects the expected value of obstructionism in a bicameral legislature. Cartel theory predicts a zero majority party roll rate, but says nothing about the conditional use of obstructionist tactics. Similarly, conditional party government has nothing to say about bicameral strategies and says little about minority parties and the Senate.

Multivariate Estimates

Scanning dozens of scatterplots is not the most efficient way to summarize the relationships among policy positions, party, and frequency of winning. Statistical models can gauge the degree to which observed behavior fits the alternative theoretical models. The dependent variable is frequency on the winning side: the percentage of final passage votes a legislator is on the winning side in a given Congress. The universe of cases is all legislators in the House or Senate for the 1875–1998 period. Independent variables identify the legislators' party affiliation, policy position (DW-NOMINATE), distance from pivots, and party control of the House, Senate, and presidency.[1]

The hypotheses, in English, are as follows:

- *House Median Voter and Pivots Models.* If policy positions are the only influence on frequency of winning, then the variables that measure policy distance from key pivots should be the only statistically significant influences.
- *Symmetric Party Pressure Model.* A dummy variable for majority/minority party should show a statistically significant effect.
- *Asymmetric Party Effects Model.* The distance from the chamber median on the minority party side should have an effect but distance from the median on the majority party side should have no effect.
- *Senate Supermajority Pivots Model.* For senators external to the filibuster pivots, frequency of winning declines with distance from the neighboring pivot; for senators interior to the filibuster pivots, frequency of winning is not related to policy position.
- *Senate Asymmetric Party Effects, Supermajority Pivots Model.* For senators external to the minority-side filibuster pivot, frequency of winning declines with distance from the neighboring pivot; for

---

[1] I ignore the veto pivot because distance from the veto pivot never shows a significant relationship to the vote on final passage controlling for other features of the policy space.

senators to the majority party side of the minority side filibuster pivot, frequency of winning is not related to policy position.

Estimates for the two houses for the 1875–1998 period are provided in Table 7.1 (Lawrence et al. 2005). The results show the generality of asymmetric party effects model. In the case of the House, the estimate for party dummy effect (majority versus minority) shows no effect, a policy location on the majority side has a positive effect, and, if located on the minority side, distance from the chamber median has a strong negative effect. We would draw the same inference for the Senate when examining the same model as estimated for the House. With two filibuster pivots in the Senate, the equation is more complex, but the conclusion is the same. Weak party effects are present between the pivots where no slope for party is predicted and more sizable effects of policy positions are found external to the pivots. Overall, the median pivot model fits the Senate better than the supermajority pivots model, indicating that the filibuster pivots are not always (or even usually) a decisive consideration in the upper chamber.

Revisiting Cartel Theory and the Reed Rules

The same estimation approach can be applied to each Congress, which yields a series of estimates of party effects across the entire period. This allows us to inspect the series for possible perturbations in party effects associated with changes in parliamentary rules, as posited by cartel theory, and other factors such as polarization, as suggested by CPG, while still controlling for relevant spatial and pivot effects. We consider cartel theory first.

Cox and McCubbins devote a chapter to the rules and precedents established under Speaker Thomas Reed in the 1880s (Cox and McCubbins 2005, Chapter 4). The "Reed rules" limited minority obstructionism, created a Rules Committee with the power to report resolutions creating a legislative right-of-way for specified bills, and granted certain committees and measures privileged agenda priority. The net effect of the Reed rules was to launch an era of stronger agenda control for the majority party leadership. The authors predict that the Reed rules would move more policy outcomes toward the majority party median and away from the chamber median and produce a step-decline in majority party roll rates.

TABLE 7.1. *Probit Estimates of Party and Spatial Effects, 44th–105th Congresses (1875–1998)*

Independent Variable	House With Median Pivot	Senate With Median Pivot	Senate With Supermajority Pivots
Majority party dummy	−0.072	−0.034	−0.006
	(−1.892)	(−0.803)	(−0.117)
Majority side of chamber median	0.223	0.181	
	(7.677)	(3.727)	
Distance from chamber median, majority-side legislators	−0.267	−0.432	
	(7.677)	(−2.885)	
Distance from chamber median, minority-side legislators	−1.726	−1.461	
	(−14.597)	(−11.695)	
Senator in between pivots, on minority side			0.300
			(3.212)
Senator in between pivots, on majority side			0.269
			(3.803)
Senator on majority side of majority pivot			0.553
			(6.660)
Distance from minority pivot if on minority side of minority pivot			−1.423
			(−6.729)
Distance from chamber median if in between pivots, on minority side			−2.212
			(−4.417)
Distance from chamber median if in between pivots, on majority side			0.710
			(2.018)
Distance from majority pivot if on majority side of majority pivot			−1.205
			(−5.229)
House, Senate of opposite parties	−0.082	−0.018	0.075
	(−2.077)	(−0.320)	(0.991)
House (Senate), President of opposite parties	0.075	−0.122	0.116
	(18.821)	(−1.576)	(1.204)
Constant	1.137	1.137	0.883
	(14.909)	(14.909)	(8.675)
McFadden R^2	.091	.076	.068
N	1,575,614	253,550	224,817

Note: t-values in parentheses.
Source: Lawrence et al. (2004).

Cox and McCubbins gauge the direction and size of policy movement by calculating the correlation between DW-NOMINATE scores
(what we have used to characterize policy positions) and legislators'
votes for and against final passage of legislation (Cox and McCubbins
2005, 67). A negative correlation means left-side legislators (Democrats, generally) were closer to the bill than the status quo; a positive
correlation means that right-side legislators (Republicans, generally)
were closer to the bill than the status quo. The hypothesis is that the
Reed rules increased the proportion of bills that moved policy in the
direction of the majority party. This is the by-product of the majority party's ability to keep off the floor measures that would attract a
majority coalition composed of the minority party and a few majority
party legislators. In a visual inspection of their line graph and a corresponding multivariate analysis, the prediction seems to be confirmed.

The Cox and McCubbins observation depends on the observation
of a lower mean correlation for the pre-Reed House than the post-Reed
House. This is a tricky business. Consider these observations about the
analysis:

- There are few pre-Reed Congresses to analyze in the data series:
  1883, in just the fifth Congress in the data series, is the first year
  that simple majority of the House could adopt a Rules Committee
  resolution to set the floor agenda.
- The Reed rules were phased in over several Congresses, creating
  ambiguity about when the new regime was in place.
- One of those Congresses, the 49th, is a serious outlier. The mean
  for the previous four Congresses is not far out of line with later
  Congresses.
- There is high variance in the pre-Reed House – primarily because
  there are very few final passage votes in these Congresses. The nine
  pre-Reed Congresses average just 21 bills in the count of votes with
  statistically significant correlations with NOMINATE scores (one
  with just 6), compared with more than 100 for the last nine in their
  series.[2] Those 21 represent just a fraction of the total number of
  bills with final passage votes. Some of the other early Congresses in

[2] Data available at http://mccubbins.ucsd.edu/settingtheagenda/oda2.html.

the series include only three or four bills. This is an exceptionally thin record on which to evaluate the overall effect of rules.

- The Senate, which exhibits greater variation than the House, exhibits an average that is very similar to the House – and the Senate majority party never benefited from a Reed-like crackdown on minority obstructionism.
- Both the mean and variation in the Senate go unexplained – perhaps for good reason. The number of final passage votes on which the Senate series is based is exceedingly small. For the 1875–1950 period, the mean number of votes per Congress in the count is less than seven.
- No multivariate analysis of the Senate is offered.[3]

These concerns about drawing inferences from the Cox–McCubbins data motivate a second look based on the individual-level win-rate estimates. If the Reed rules have the predicted effect, the estimated effect of being on the majority party side of the chamber median should be insignificant in the pre-Reed House, significant in the post-Reed House, and insignificant in the Senate. The House and Senate series of the party effect, controlling for variables in Table 7.1, are in Figures 7.6 and 7.7 (using the supermajority pivots model for the Senate). A confidence interval that falls below zero reflects a weak or negative effect or a relatively large standard error that represents a small number of votes for estimating the effect.

The observed effects cast doubt on the Reed rules hypothesis. The estimated effect was usually positive before the Reed rules were adopted in the 51st Congress. The effect is negative in only two of the ten Congresses that occurred before the Reed rules were finalized in the early 1890s (left vertical dashed line). There also are five post-Reed Congresses in which the coefficient has the wrong sign, and none of these are statistically different from zero, but cartel theory leads us to expect no negatively signed coefficients after Reed.

Moreover, the Senate pattern is much like the House – and, of course, the Senate never developed rules similar to the Reed rules. In both houses, a relatively small number of final passage votes produced wide

---

[3] For my observations about the roll-rates analysis, you can return to Chapter 5 (also see Lawrence et al. 2005).

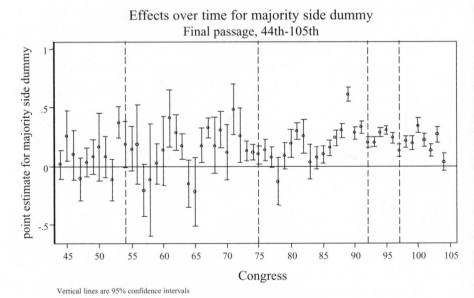

FIGURE 7.6. House estimates of the effect of being on the majority side of the chamber median, 44th–105th Congresses (1875–1998).

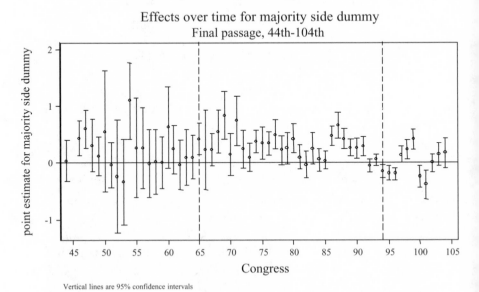

FIGURE 7.7. Senate estimates of the effect of being on the majority side of the chamber median, 44th–105th Congresses (1875–1998).

confidence intervals before the 1930s. Our inference is that the Reed rules may have the predicted effect but we have not confirmed the proposition in the roll-call record. The House track record is a flimsy basis for drawing inferences about the effect of the Reed rules. And the Senate's record of outcomes shifting in the majority party's direction is not explained by the Cox–McCubbins account. The mutual veto of the Senate majority and minority parties, emphasized in one place by Cox and McCubbins but not in another, does not seem to be consistent with the majority party bias that is explained, in the case of the House, by the Reed rules.

No significant correlation exists between polarization and the party effect estimates shown in Figures 7.6 and 7.7. We could present a complex model of the party effect estimates, but we cannot find a way to save polarization as a significant explanatory factor for these party effect estimates. But there is another possibility. The general party effects may not target the proper set of legislators. CPG may apply to party influence on legislators who are *not* on the majority party side of the chamber median but rather who are across the chamber median and prone to vote with the other party. It is the floor votes of these marginal majority party members that can extend the agenda of the majority party to more issues and win key battles on procedural motions, amendments, and bills. Therefore, we might expect fluctuating direct party influence to make the difference for these targeted majority party legislators. Consequently, we must determine whether majority party legislators in the region just on the other side of the chamber median from most of the majority party are more likely to be on the winning side once we have controlled for their policy positions.

Unfortunately for CPG, there is no relationship between polarization and the party effect for legislators in the region between the chamber median and the minority party median once the effect of policy position is controlled.[4] The bivariate correlation between polarization and party effect is moderately strong in both houses, but this is misleading. The relationship is not statistically significant once policy positions

---

[4] The effect is estimated for the 1875–1998 period for legislators whose DW-NOMINATE scores place them between the chamber and minority party medians. Frequency on the winning side is the dependent variable, with majority/minority party, distance from the chamber median, and the interaction of party and distance as independent variables.

TABLE 7.2. *Probit Estimates of Effects of Polarization and Party, Members Between Chamber Median and Minority Median*

	House	Senate
Majority dummy	−0.141	0.089
	(−2.041)	(0.629)
Party polarization	0.001	0.015
	(0.045)	(0.435)
Polarization × majority dummy	−0.000	−0.042
	(−0.013)	(−0.931)
Distance from the chamber median	−1.840	−1.618
	(−10.142)	(−6.945)
Constant	1.142	1.147
	(13.516)	(10.200)
McFadden R^2	.038	.037
N	455530	67311

Note: Asymptotic z-statistics are in parentheses.

are taken into account (Table 7.2). This seems to be the effect of the distribution of policy positions within the interval when the parties are polarized. Even within this interval, polarized parties are associated with a separation of majority and minority party members so that party and policy positions are highly correlated.

Again, this finding is not too surprising in light of the difficulty of discerning the effects of direct party influence in the voting record. DW-NOMINATE scores reflect party and other effects averaged over the roll-call record of a Congress and adjacent Congresses. We would find statistically significant party influence in the estimates presented here only if party influence was distinctively strong for final passage votes. When that "needle in the haystack search" uncovers party influence it is not correlated with polarization. The unlikely prospect of finding a relationship between party effects and polarization did not materialize, so the proper conclusion is that we cannot confirm or disconfirm CPG from these data.

ANOTHER LOOK AT THE HISTORICAL RECORD

While the statistical estimates cover a long period, they may mask important differences across Congresses that are not modeled. A hint of the importance of examining individual Congresses was shown in the Senate of the 1980s, but the importance extends to the House and across the decades since Reconstruction. In figures found in the appendix, we show a scatterplot for frequency of winning and policy positions for each party in each Congress for the two houses for the period since Reconstruction. The small size of the plots makes close inspection impossible, but our purpose is to highlight some obvious features.

The primary source of variation in the observed patterns is the location of minority party members. As we observed above, average minority party win rates vary widely while majority party win rates vary within a narrow range. The noteworthy features of the figures are as follows:

- For both houses, the "Florida" pattern is common to the years since the mid-1950s. In this pattern, the most frequently winning legislators are located somewhat to the majority party side of the chamber median and often close to the majority party median. The patterns before the 1950s are far less consistent.
- In some Congresses (the House in 1889–1890, 1895–1898, 1933–1942, the Senate of the 1930s), the most extreme majority party members (on the left with Democratic majorities, on the right with Republican majorities) are the most frequent winners. We have no model for that pattern. It may be the extraordinary influence of party or the president in these periods that leads Congress to define the agenda as the left- or right-shifted program of the party, leading legislators close to the proposals to win more frequently than other legislators.
- The world wars (1917–1920, 1941–1944) are associated with high levels of winning in both parties, which suggests that the legislative agenda during war yields majorities composed of most members of both parties. This is consistent with the view that wars are associated with reversion points that are extreme.
- Minority party legislators show high win rates in two periods when cross-party coalitions were particularly prominent. In the Senate of the late 1920s, the farm bloc of majority party Republicans and most Democrats led to many victories for minority party legislators. In the Congresses of the late 1960s and early 1970s, when the conservative coalition of minority party Republicans and southern Democrats

TABLE 7.3. *Correlates of Mean Majority Party and Minority Party Win Rates,*
1875–1998 (Pearson r)

	House		Senate	
	Mean Majority Party Win Rate	Mean Minority Party Win Rate	Mean Majority Party Win Rate	Mean Minority Party Win Rate
Relative party size	−.03	−.27	.32	−.29
Majority party standard deviation	.06	.52	.01	.57
Minority party standard deviation	.35	.28	.13	.04
Interparty distance	−.03	−.55	−.25	−.61
N	61	61	61	61

was noted to be strong, minority party win rates were quite high and the Florida pattern disappears.

To better understand the dynamics underlying the scatterplots, we would like to model minority party win rates using the minority win rates depicted in Figure 7.1 as our dependent variable. However, the most obvious independent variables, the underlying policy distance between the party and the variance within the parties, which are the components of party polarization, are difficult to measure independently of the roll-call record we seek to explain. If we use the voting record to measure interparty distance and intraparty variance, the resulting measures will be necessarily correlated with the party win rates that we displayed in Figure 7.1. We proceed in an exploratory spirit to see how interparty distance, intraparty variance, and party size interact to generate the observed patterns.

In Table 7.3, we report the correlates of mean majority and minority party win rates. Relationships to mean majority win rates, which exhibit little variance, are weak. Two exceptions are noteworthy. For the House, more variance within the minority party is related to a higher mean win rate for majority party legislators. For the Senate, a larger majority party is related to a higher mean win rate for majority party legislators but it is not in the House. This is consistent with our view that agenda control is stronger in the House than the Senate. In the House, application of the cartel model's strategic premise would yield no relationship between majority party size and floor success on final passage votes. In the Senate, weaker control over the nature of the legislation coming to a vote would make party size more important than in the House.

Bivariate relationships are stronger for mean minority party win rates, which show great variance. In both houses, a cohesive majority party is associated with a low mean minority party win rate. Great interparty distance also is associated with a low mean minority party win rate (but we must keep in mind that our distance measure is mathematically tied to the win rate measure).

The multivariate estimates for mean minority win rates are provided in Table 7.4. In both houses, a larger majority party is associated with lower mean minority party win rates, controlling for interparty distance and intraparty cohesiveness. This is noteworthy because party size is missing in action in CPG and is only implicit in the cartel model. In the House, the cohesiveness of the majority party has little net effect on mean minority party win rates, consistent with the expectation of cartel theory that the negative agenda control of the majority party is effective whatever the party's internal cohesiveness, at least most of the time. This is not true in the Senate, where a more divided majority party is associated with a higher mean win rate for minority party senators. Again, the Senate, which is given precious little consideration in applications of cartel and CPG theory, proves somewhat distinctive.

CONCLUSION

A fair inference from the analysis reported in this chapter is that party effects are significant, but cartel theory and CPG have been oversold. The circumstantial evidence for cartel theory is strong, although we have found some claims about the evidence to be unpersuasive. CPG remains unconfirmed in voting analyses. The asymmetric partisan patterns of voting on final passage motions are quite visible in the individual-level voting patterns reviewed here, but some important imperfections in that record are plain.

TABLE 7.4. *Multivariate OLS Estimates for Mean Minority Party Win Rates, 1875–1998*

	House		Senate	
Relative party size	-37.60	-33.00	-45.33	-45.72
	(-3.61)	(-3.22)	(-4.10)	(-4.19)
Majority party standard deviation	60.32	89.82	80.38	85.27
	(0.90)	(1.36)	(2.28)	(2.44)
Minority party standard deviation	-160.51	-147.82	6.21	6.94
	(-2.29)	(-2.18)	(1.01)	(1.15)
Interparty distance	-54.13	-45.35	-33.93	-32.41
	(-2.787)	(19.18)	(-3.78)	(-3.64)
World Wars I and II		12.76		9.22
		(2.30)		(1.59)
Constant	118.54	104.33	82.41	79.69
	(4.32)	(3.84)	(6.56)	(6.37)
Adjusted R^2	0.42	0.46	0.52	0.54
N	61	61	61	61

Note: t-statistics are reported in parentheses.

Still wanting is an adequate account of the Senate. Senate patterns, for the most part, are quite similar to House patterns. The asymmetric party effect is nearly as clear in the Senate as in the House. And yet our explanations of the Senate must be quite different than those weak arguments offered by scholars to date. Our speculations about the forces at work are reserved for the concluding chapter.

8

More Than a Conclusion

If you get the feeling that my commentary has been as much about my friends in political science as about party politics in Congress, you would be right. I hope they are still my friends. This set of essays would be as long as their collective works if I reviewed everything that I have learned from them. The state of theory about congressional parties is much improved for their efforts. Nevertheless, I must confess that I have not always liked the tone of the debate, the care taken in drawing inferences, or the treatment of the previous literature. We can do better. More important, even after years of effort, the study of congressional parties remains somewhat disordered and incomplete. My purpose has been to sort through the theoretical propositions and empirical claims to identify the strengths and weaknesses of the most influential scholarship. In this short chapter, I conclude with some extensions of the themes noted but not developed in previous discussion. These extensions suggest that there is a substantial research agenda for scholars of legislative parties to pursue.

THEME 1. THE CIRCUMSTANTIAL EVIDENCE OF PARTY INFLUENCE IS STRONG

Let us add it up. Here are well-established empirical regularities:

- The correlation between party and long-term policy positions varies across policy areas (Clausen 1973).

- The correlation between party and roll-call voting varies across types of votes (Froman and Ripley 1965; Roberts and Smith 2003; Rohde 1991; Sinclair 2002).
- Party has an independent effect on roll-call voting scores controlling for legislators' scales scores from a survey of their policy positions (Ansolabehere et al. 2001).
- Legislators most likely to switch their votes between a final passage vote and a vote on a veto override are legislators of the president's party (Krehbiel 1998).
- The policy positions of legislators who switch parties change in the direction of the new party (Clinton et al. 2004; Hager and Talbert 2000; Nokken and Poole 2004).
- There is substantial variation in Rice scores across issues, type of votes, and Congresses (Cox and Poole 2002).
- In individual legislative battles, the legislators switching in favor of their party is consistent with expectations from whip polls (Behringer and Evans 2006; Burden and Frisby 2004; Dodd and Sullivan 1981).
- Outcomes on key vote issues tend to produce narrow victories and substantial losses (King and Zeckhauser 2003).
- Roll rates for the majority parties are consistently low; roll rates for minority parties are consistently higher, usually much higher, than roll rate for majority parties (Cox and McCubbins 2005).
- Asymmetric party effects are strong in most Congresses (Lawrence et al. 2005, 2006).

Arguments that legislators' policy preferences, status quo points, and decision thresholds explain outcomes do not undermine the evidence that party effects are common and recurring.

THEME 2. MULTIPLE GOALS REMAIN ACTIVE INGREDIENTS AFTER PARTIES ARE CREATED

If we are to make much progress, we must move to theorizing about the effect of multiple goals. CPG accounts include references to multiple goals (Aldrich and Rohde 2000a) and provide citations to relevant literature (Aldrich 1995), but the theoretical action of CPG lies in the distribution of policy preferences (degree of polarization). An electoral story might go like this: Under conditions of polarization, party leaders are better able to force policy sacrifices out of some legislators for the overall electoral success of the party. This is not argued. Rather, party majorities empower leaders to gain policy outcomes more to their liking – as judged by policy preferences they brought with them into Congress. So electoral interests might motivate party activity, but it is never central to the dynamic posited by CPG. Instead, elections produce a distribution of policy preferences, which drive legislative politics, and electoral interests disappear as an active ingredient in policy making. Electoral interests remain a casually argued element of CPG accounts.

Accounts of cartel theory are similar. Electoral motivations are more explicitly related to the creation of legislative parties (the need to maintain and improve the party record), but the electoral interests are not mentioned in the formal model or its application. Instead, party strategy is reduced to moving legislation to the floor whenever party and chamber medians favor a "dimension" to the status quo. The possibility of bringing a dimension to the floor to benefit the party's electoral interests is not considered. Consequently, the tradeoffs between policy and electoral interests and approaches to reducing their severity – even in the use of agenda-setting tools such as special rules – are ignored. Where an electoral account might enrich the agenda-setting story by noting the positive results won by the majority party, the cartel account is unnecessarily limited to a spatial strategy and negative agenda control.

The clearer focus on parties' multiple collective interests would enrich our theory of legislative parties. In the eagerness to apply spatial theory, the field has been quick to jump from a verbal theory of party strategy to empirical propositions about voting patterns. We are missing a theory of party leaders' strategies that accounts for the multiple collective goals of parties that, among other things, force us to consider the tradeoffs among goals that are central to leaders' everyday activity.

THEME 3. COLLECTIVE PARTY GOALS REQUIRE THAT WE ACCOUNT FOR PARTY SIZE

Renewed attention to collective goals of parties surely would lead theorists to introduce party size as an important variable in driving party behavior and shaping legislative outcomes. No party theorist ignores the importance of majority party control for party influence. Majority party control is central to both CPG and cartel theory. For CPG, it is the majority party that is able to use the resources of the chamber to enhance party influence over outcomes under conditions of polarization. For cartel theory, it is merely assumed that the requisite majority party powers are in place for the party to exercise negative agenda control. Majority party control, of course, depends on the relative sizes of the parties, which are not an active ingredient in the legislative strategies of parties under either theory.

To see the importance of size, it is useful to see its relationship with the components of party polarization – the policy distance between the parties and intraparty policy variance – and to see how distance and variance fit into cartel and CPG theories. For cartel theory, the strategic premise is that the majority party brings a bill to the floor only when the party and chamber median prefer the bill to the status quo. In this way, the majority party median always wins and the outcome is at the chamber median. The policy distance between the majority party and chamber medians is the only variable in this model. The majority party roll rate is zero and the minority party roll rate is a mere by-product of the minority party members' location relative to the chamber median and the status quo points. Party size, therefore, is irrelevant to the principal finding of a zero roll for the majority party. But, I have argued, party size is likely to be important to the parties:

(1) All things being equal (such as the distribution of policy positions within each party), the distance between the majority party and chamber medians is likely to be smaller with a larger majority party. Thus, the policy sacrifice required to pass legislation is smaller.

(2) Party size affects the risks of losing majority status in the near future. The smaller the majority party the greater the incentive to favor elcetoral considerations over short-term policy considerations.

Thus, cartel theory is fine as long as we believe that congressional parties are not motivated by their positive legislative goals or the retention of majority party status.

For CPG, the components of polarization are interparty policy distance and intraparty policy variance. In applications of CPG, most of the discussion concerns policy variance within the majority party. In fact, minority party variance is ignored in the one previous attempt to measure polarization quantitatively (Aldrich et al. 2002). Distance, it is argued, affects the incentive to avoid a loss to the other party, but, under the implicit spatial model of CPG, any distance is worth fighting for and, in practice, measures of distance cannot be given any intuitive substantive meaning. Therefore, it is not surprising that distance does not figure prominently in CPG accounts about variation in centralization within the majority party.

Size, however, is another matter. A large and incohesive majority party may still win, while a small but equally incohesive majority party may not win. The incentive to exert party influence within the majority party is greater as size declines, at least for a party that is not perfectly cohesive. And as a majority party approaches minority status, the tradeoffs between influencing colleagues to support the party and allowing them to cater to home electorates can be severe. Neither cartel theory nor CPG has anything to say about this.

I could continue on the implications, but the point should be clear: size matters. In the context of cartel theory, then, party size is relevant to expanding agendas and maintaining control over agenda-setting mechanisms. A passive party would not be concerned about these things, but a party facing aggressive opposition surely would. In the context of CPG theory, party size directly affects the importance of a given level of intraparty variance for the majority party. An aggressive minority party would exploit the weaknesses of the majority party when it can, and both the size and cohesiveness of the majority party determine its strength.

THEME 4. A THEORY OF PARTY LEADER STRATEGIES IS NEEDED

Cartel theory and CPG offer some hope of a theory of leader strategies but ultimately come up short. Cartel theory specifies a simple strategic premise for the use of negative agenda control, but it really offers no more than that. CPG is less well specified and accounts of CPG cover a wide range of party activity, but the CPG accounts do not specify a theory of the strategic choices of leaders. And, as I have argued, collective party goals do not have a one-to-one correspondence with individual goals.

Elements of a theory are available in the literature. One source is Bawn's insightful treatment of leadership strategies that is motivated by the observation that leaders often allow a conference committee delegation to be composed of legislators out of step with the rest of the party on key issues (Bawn 1998). Bawn argues that "party leaders base their procedural decisions on the *intensity* of electoral impact at least as much as on the *number* of party members helped or hurt. In this sense, the procedural decisions of party members are *utilitarian*, rather than *majoritarian*" (Bawn 1998, 221, emphasis in the original). Why do leaders adopt this more complex strategy? According to Bawn, "the best way to stay in the majority is by reelecting its incumbent members. Party leaders thus have an incentive to make procedural decisions advantageous to those party members whose reelection chances are most intensely impacted by the issue in question, even when this means going against the wishes of a less-intense party majority" (Bawn 1998, 221). But violating the interests of a party majority is risky for elected leaders, creating complex calculations for leaders who must pass legislation, retain or gain a majority, and avoid alienating too many party colleagues.

In her discussion of leaders' strategies, Bawn observes that large majorities reduce the severity of the tradeoffs that leaders confront. As she emphasizes, it is sometimes difficult to expand the size of a majority without putting current incumbents' reelection at greater risk. Nevertheless, the core calculus posited by Bawn is consistent with the need to balance goals as I discussed them in Chapter 2 and that Sinclair discusses at length (Sinclair 1983; Sinclair 1995b).

We know that the Bawn formulation captures elements of the challenges party leaders confront. On the one hand, blame and credit is assigned to leaders for their ability to pass or block legislation important to party colleagues. On the other hand, blame and credit is assigned to leaders on the basis of the aggregate outcomes of congressional elections. Only if we assume that parties' electoral and policy objectives are entirely compatible can we ignore the calculations that leaders make – and are expected to make.

Careful efforts to structure the agenda can reduce the severity of the tradeoffs between competing party objectives. By allowing factions within the party to have their legislative priorities packaged in larger bills, the majority party and committee leadership can exploit the multidimensionality of everyday politics, use their procedural tools, and satisfy a range of party colleagues while pursuing potentially conflicting party goals. These gains from trade within congressional parties are modeled out of cartel theory. More direct attention to these leadership choices would push forward our understanding of party influence on legislative outcomes.

THEME 5. NEGATIVE AGENDA CONTROL DOES NOT STAND ALONE

I remain unconvinced that the primary policy effect of partisan life in Congress is negative agenda control. I am persuaded that the effects of negative agenda control are much easier to observe than the effects of direct party influence and positive agenda control. In Chapters 4 and 6, I outlined obstacles to finding direct party influence in the aggregate roll-call voting record and the necessity of developing more complete models of individual behavior to find it.

Positive agenda control, the ability of getting legislation to a vote that a floor majority does not want to get to a vote, is given inadequate discussion in recent literature on congressional parties, although it has a prominent place in theoretical accounts of collective decision making. There are two approaches to positive agenda control – packaging unpopular items with popular items and directly influencing legislators to gain their support to set the agenda as desired. These approaches may be used in tandem. The cartel model bars taking items (dimensions) to the floor without majority support and sets aside direct influence so it has nothing to say about positive agenda control. My hunch is that elected politicians and their leaders care about passing legislation and therefore devote considerable effort to devising strategies to set the agenda and directly influence colleagues to accomplish positive ends. A theory that emphasizes negative power takes out much of real politics.

Furthermore, my working hypothesis is that negative agenda control is not so strong and the strategic premise not so well established that negative, indirect party influence is constant. The cartel model's prediction is that "dimensions" are brought to the floor only when the majority party and chamber medians favor the bill over the status quo. Thus, the model identifies a necessary condition for opening the gate but is silent on the sufficient conditions. When the majority party and chamber medians favor a bill, it is guaranteed to go to the floor? The cartel model does not have an answer. If the answer is no – say, because the Rules Committee or some other committee keeps the bill off the floor – then clearly the agreement of the majority party and chamber medians is not a sufficient condition for opening the gates. Observing gatekeeping by committees at times when the party would open the gates is a finding that shows that negative agenda power by nonparty sources can undermine the implicit positive agenda power that the cartel model hints is available to the party.

This is precisely the argument that was made about the Committee on Rules in the 1940s through the 1960s (Fox and Clapp 1970a, 1970b; Peabody 1963; Price 1962; Robinson 1959, 1961, 1963; Wawro and Schickler 2006). During the 1953–1960 period, the Committee's refusal to act seemed to prevent further action on an average of 20 bills per Congress, bills that were approved by other standing committees (Robinson 1961). During the 1961–1968 period, the number was 28 bills per Congress (Fox and Clapp 1970b, 442). Observers found many of the bills blocked by Rules were of secondary importance, but the committee remained a target of reformers (Robinson 1963, 21; Fox and Clapp 1970a). In the 1960s, bills on education, civil rights, smoking and health, occupational safety, election reform, and the creation of a department of urban affairs were blocked (Fox and Clapp 1970a, 671). Adjustments in the appointments to Rules were made in 1961 and again in 1973, but, if the critics are right, the long delays in asserting stronger party control over the Rules Committee and the continuing power of its chairs had important effects on policy outcomes in the House.

Cox and McCubbins address the problem of the Committee on Rules but, of course, argue that the addition of other vetoes to the party and chamber medians does not affect the majority party roll rate. However, additional vetoes could affect *outcomes* – bills that otherwise would have been passed may be blocked at a pre-floor stage by committees. Peabody observes that a case can be made that some of the bills blocked in one Congress (the 87th, 1961–1962) would not have been supported by a majority of the House, but many observers complained bitterly about the obstructionism of the Committee on Rules and other committees. Cox and McCubbins, for reasons that are not

well developed, consider this to be a mere venal sin. In their view, the
cardinal sin for Rules, usually at the request of another committee, is
to push a bill to the floor that the Rules and the authorizing committee
favor but is not favored by a majority of the majority party (Cox and
McCubbins 2005, 129).

The Cox and McCubbins account of the threat of Rules pushing
a bill to the floor that the majority – and leadership – of the majority party oppose is incomplete. Because the twentieth-century Speaker
enjoyed the right of recognition without appeal, the Rules member
who might make a privileged motion to consider a resolution from
Rules would find it difficult to be recognized to make the motion if
the Speaker opposed the bill at issue.[1] Members of the Committee on
Rules know this better than anyone. Therefore, the deck is stacked
against finding this violation of majority party expectations. It proves
little about obligations to party to find fewer bills that Rules pushed to
the floor but were opposed by the majority party than bills that Rules
blocked but were favored by the majority party (the subject of Cox and
McCubbins 2005, Chapter 7). They are not equally likely possibilities
under the rules.

The question to be answered is whether committee obstructionism – by Rules or by other committees – blocked bills that would
have passed the House with the support of a majority of the majority
party if they had received a vote. We cannot know for certain, but
unexplored avenues for making some informed guesses are available.[2]

---

[1] House Rule XVIII, Clause 2, grants the Speaker the power to determine who is recognized and the Speaker's decision cannot be appealed to the House. By precedent,
the Speaker recognizes a designated member of the Committee on Rules who offers
a privileged motion. It is easy for the Speaker to arrange for other members to seek
recognition to take up other business, with more privileged motions if necessary, to
avoid bringing a special rule to the floor. On privileged motions, see Deschler (1977,
Chapter 21, Section 31.2).

[2] One window on the subject is the record of how Senate-passed bills fared in the House.
If the medians of the two houses of Congress were similar and the medians of the two
majority parties were similar, we would expect the chamber/majority party medians
veto to be used in similar ways in the two chambers. Thus, at least in some Congresses,
we would expect the legislative output of the two houses to be similar if the cartel model
was operating in both. If we find that the House failed to pass a salient Senate-passed
bill for which there is evidence that the bill was blocked by a committee, we have
reasonably strong circumstantial evidence that the additional veto player affected the
outcome. This is not the place to report a complete analysis, but it is easy to identify
suitable Congresses and isolate likely cases of Rules obstructionism.

THEME 6. THE SEARCH FOR DIRECT PARTY EFFECTS
WILL PROVE FRUSTRATING

The analysis of the aggregate roll-call record has severe limits for estimating the strength of direct party influence. If majority party legislators near the floor median are subject to the most regular efforts of leaders to win votes, any aggregate voting scores will incorporate the effects of party influence. Moreover, in most legislative battles where a few votes will tip the balance, the targeting is quite narrowly focused on a handful of legislators. Finding statistically significant effects for such a small group is nearly impossible. Finally, when we examine the aggregate voting record to characterize the dimensionality of the policy space, we seldom capture the dimensionality of the policy space on a bill-by-bill basis, which is required to properly gauge party influence in the policy spaces where politics is played.

More attention to basic research design issues is required. We need to be attentive to (a) the circumstances under which policy influence is most likely to be exerted (close votes, issues on which there are announced party or presidential positions, etc.), (b) the legislators who are most likely to be targets of influence efforts, (c) party actions – leadership actions, particularly – that are intended to influence legislators, and (d) the actions of other sources of influence and the factors that condition their relevance. I am not optimistic about significant progress. Access to the kind of data required to identify the legislators who are the targets of direct influence attempts and the actions taken by parties and leaders is limited. Our ability to measure and model competing and reinforcing sources of influence is even weaker.

Creative scholars will continue to find ways to isolate party effects in legislators' voting decisions and, through them, policy outcomes. But I am quite certain that *aggregate* direct influence will not be measured and weighed against the effects of indirect forms of influence, such as negative agenda control. Arguments about whether direct or indirect influence is more important will not be resolved by empirical studies.

THEME 7. THE SENATE IS NOT WELL UNDERSTOOD

I am a little sheepish about raising the issue of the Senate again. In the modern Senate, the combination of the supermajority threshold for cloture and absence of a general germaneness rule for floor amendments complicates theories based on the House experience, where cohesive majority parties can determine procedure and control outcomes. In the nineteenth-century Senate, the absence of a cloture rule creates even greater uncertainties about the effective threshold for authoritative action. The conceptual issues are beginning to be addressed, but it will be some time before the Senate is well understood (Binder and Smith 1997; Wawro and Schickler 2006).

The complications of the Senate are many. CPG accounts of the House emphasize changes in the chamber rules that a majority party can impose; similar rules changes do not occur in the Senate. Cartel theory predicts low majority party roll rates on the basis of House majority party discipline on parliamentary matters; majority party discipline on parliamentary matters does not give the Senate majority control over the floor agenda. Pivotal politics theory predicts that supermajority thresholds create special pivots who determine policy outcomes; plainly, the supermajority thresholds are not always relevant in everyday Senate floor action. No persuasive treatment of the Senate exists in this recent literature.

THEME 8. THE MAJORITY AND MINORITY PARTIES ARE NOT MIRROR IMAGES OF EACH OTHER

In Chapter 7, I demonstrated with individual-level data that the behavior of the majority and minority parties are not mirror images of each other. An asymmetry in party voting on final passage votes is common in both houses. Cartel theory offers a tidy explanation of the pattern: the majority party keeps legislation off the floor until it can win, which means holding together most of the party. This is a potentially persuasive argument, but the evidence for it is not as solid as it could be. Demonstrating that the Reed rules were critical to developing the requisite majority party agenda control in the House is difficult. Making the case that the Reed rules were critical in the House is hard to square with the observation of similar asymmetries in the Senate, where, at best, there is a mutual majority/minority veto on what comes to a vote.

We have not explored other possibilities for the majority/minority asymmetry. One possibility is that legislators' incentives to support the party are stronger within the majority party than within the minority party. Cartel theory implies that this is due to agreement to participate in a procedural cartel. I doubt that the pressure for loyalty ends there. Legislators' concern about the party record may be an even more active factor in the daily tactical considerations of the majority party, which must assume that its ability to govern effectively will influence election outcomes. That is, not only might majority party legislators empower their leaders to exercise negative agenda control, they also might be more susceptible to party appeals to help the party pass its agenda for the sake of the party record. If so, then majority parties should be more cohesive on final passage votes than minority parties. If majority party leaders also have more sources of influence, such as the ability to use positive agenda tools to package legislation and create majority coalitions, then we also are likely to see more cohesive majority parties than minority parties.

We might label this alternative view the "Truman speculation." Political scientist David Truman (1959, 92–3, 148, 278, 280–3) observed of the 81st Congress (1949–1950) that the majority party Senate Democrats demonstrated less fluidity and a more stable policy "posture" than the minority party Republicans, particularly on final passage votes. He speculated that these observed differences may be characteristic of congressional parties and due, perhaps, to the stronger tendency for the floor leader and committee leaders to accommodate each other in the majority party. He even suggests that minority party members are free to go their own way of final passage votes. If the Truman speculation is right, then it might take us some distance in explaining the similarity of House and Senate voting patterns.

THEME 9. LEGISLATIVE POLITICS IS MESSY, LEAVING OPENINGS FOR PARTY INFLUENCE

A recurring theme through the essays is the messiness of legislative politics. Here are some of the complexities I have mentioned:

- Leaders often are uncertain about what amendments to expect on the floor.
- The reversion point often is not the policy *status quo ante* but rather something much less desirable in the opinion of most legislators.
- The support of factions and individual legislators often turns on minor issues that do not recur across most legislation but frequently

expand legislators' preferences into multidimensional space for the life of each episode.

- Legislators realize that their colleagues vary in the importance they assign to different issues and so build coalitions by both compromising on the primary policy at issue in a bill and logrolling through the addition of provisions to realize gains from trade.
- Votes on final passage often are avoided once preliminary votes clarify what the outcome will be.
- Legislators often care as much or more about the electoral implications as about the immediate policy implications of their actions.

We could ignore these complexities and hope that our unidimensional, complete information, inherited status quo spatial models capture legislators' perceptions of the strategic context of policy making. We might even be right more often than with some other combination of assumptions. But my hunch is that this characterization of congressional decision making does not capture much more than the modal type, maybe not even the majority of policymaking episodes. Parties exploit, or must struggle with, these complexities to achieving their collective goals in a manner consistent with their members' interests.

CONCLUSION

There is work to be done. The evidence for the presence of party influence in congressional policy making is strong but circumstantial. Recent theories, conditional party government and cartel theories, represent important progress in the science of policy making and yet both miss important features of party influence. Recent evidence based on aggregate analyses of the historical congressional voting record shows the traces of party influence. Most persuasive are a few studies that account for specific forms of party efforts. Even a few studies that make the case that legislators' preferences drive outcomes ultimately add to the accumulating evidence for party effects. But political science has not done a very good job in sorting through the conceptual issues. In fact, I think some recent literature has muddled them. My hope is that I have contributed to clarifying what is at stake and what is to be done.

Appendix: Scatterplots of Policy Position and Frequency on Winning Side

The following pages provide the scatterplot of policy position (DW-NOMINATE) and frequency of being on the winning side for final passage votes for each Congress. In all cases, the darker markers represent the locations of majority party members and the lighter markers represent the locations of minority party members. Congresses are denoted by their first year in session.

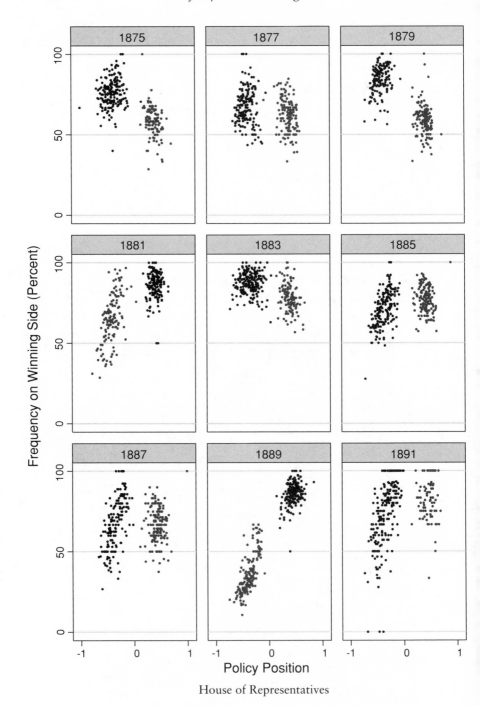

House of Representatives

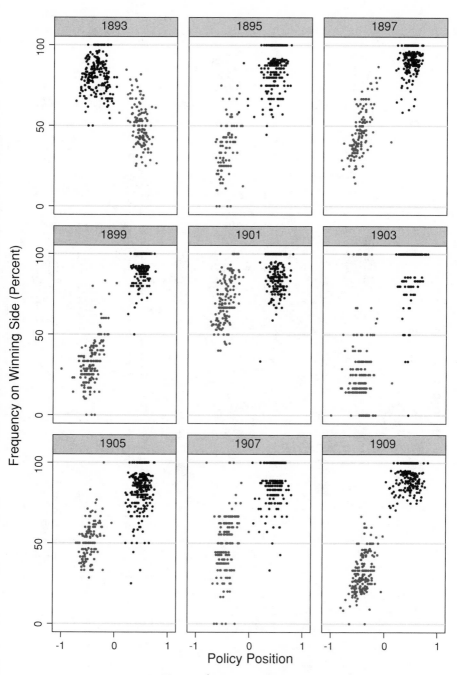

House of Representatives *(continued)*

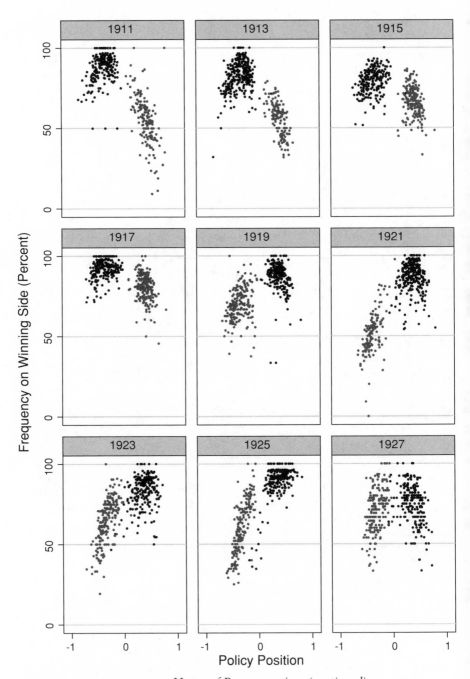

Policy Position

House of Representatives *(continued)*

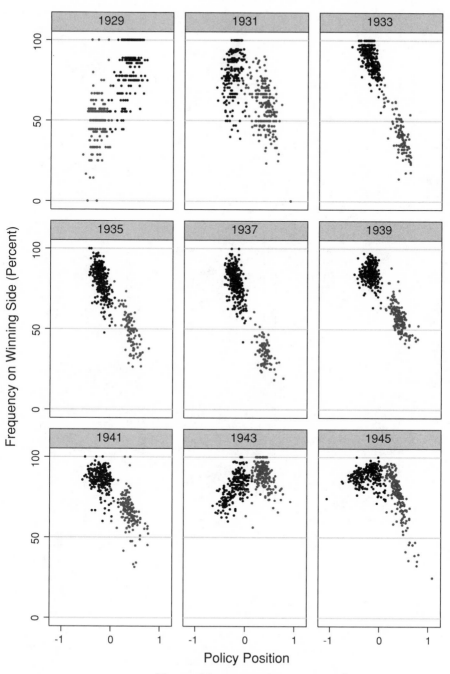

Frequency on Winning Side (Percent)

Policy Position

House of Representatives *(continued)*

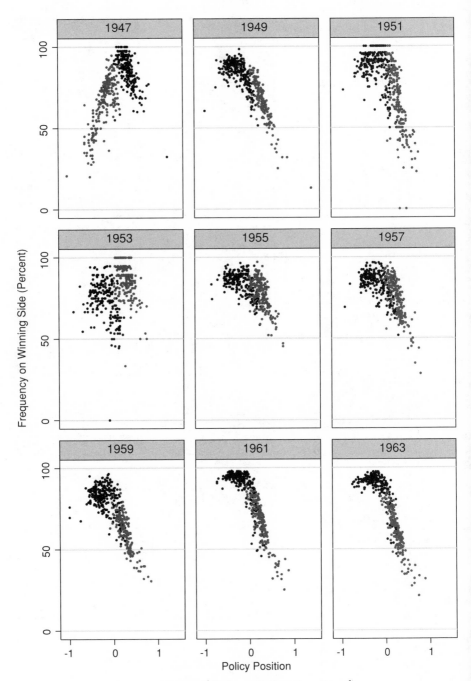

Frequency on Winning Side (Percent)

Policy Position

House of Representatives *(continued)*

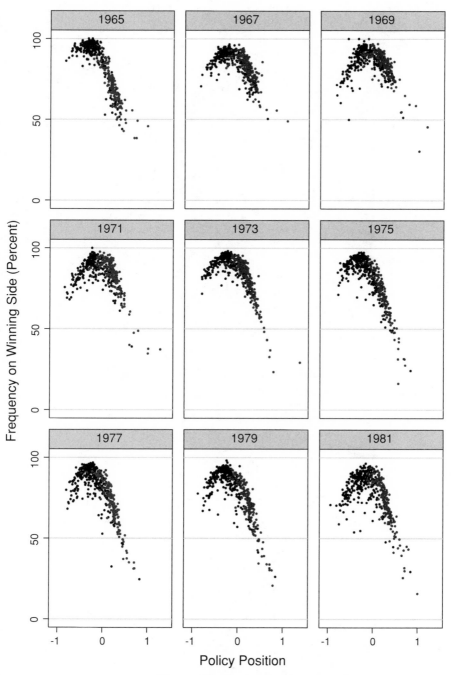

Frequency on Winning Side (Percent)

Policy Position

House of Representatives *(continued)*

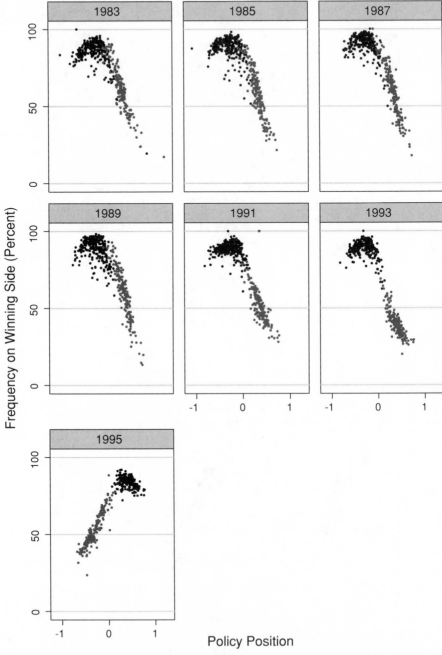

Frequency on Winning Side (Percent)

Policy Position

House of Representatives *(continued)*

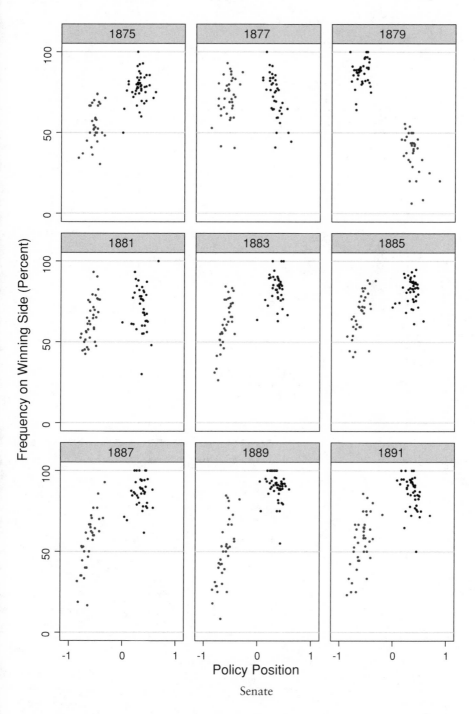

Frequency on Winning Side (Percent)

Policy Position

Senate

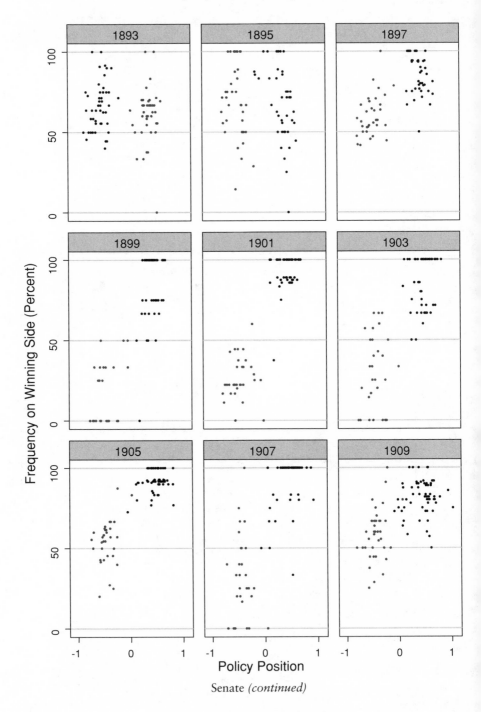

Senate *(continued)*

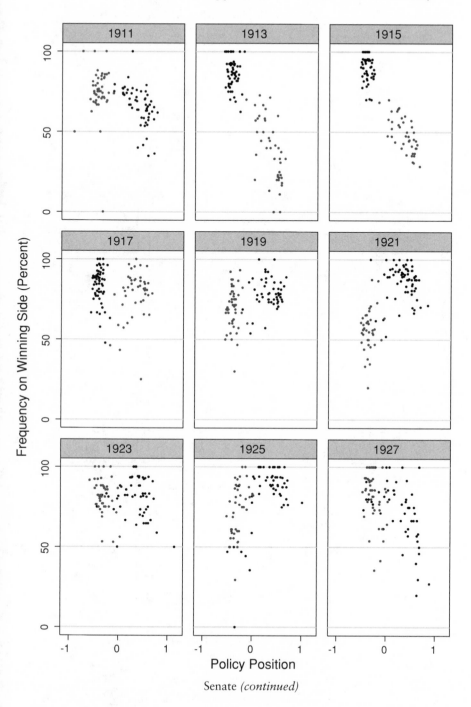

Frequency on Winning Side (Percent)

Policy Position

Senate *(continued)*

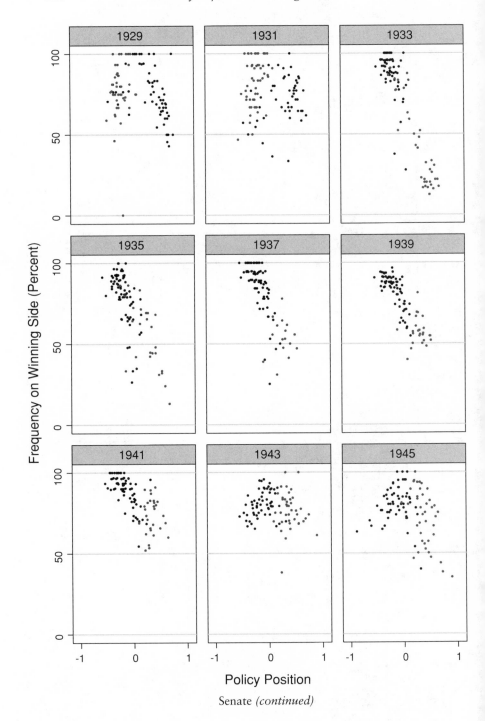

Frequency on Winning Side (Percent)

Policy Position

Senate *(continued)*

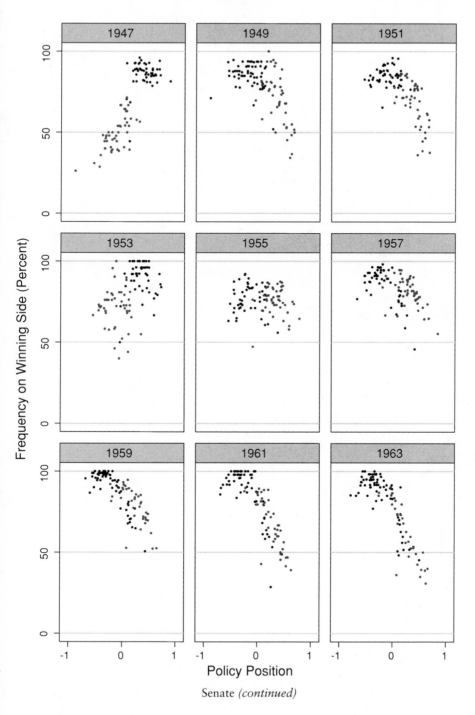

Senate *(continued)*

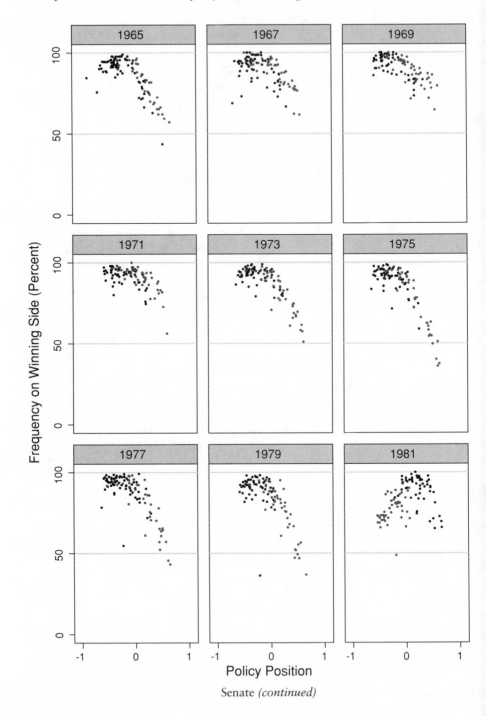

Senate *(continued)*

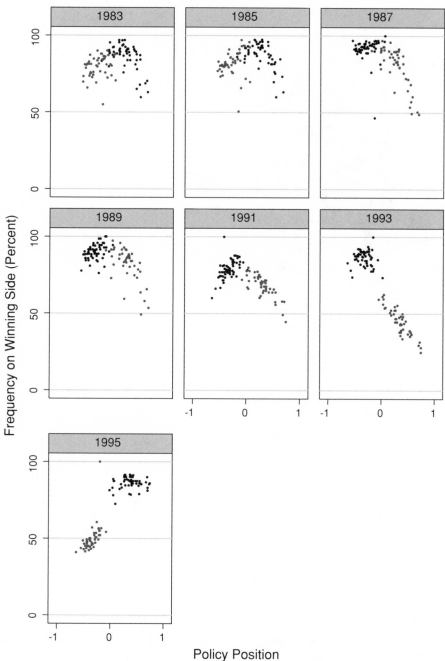

Policy Position

Senate *(continued)*

References

Abramowitz, Alan I. 1980. Is the Revolt Fading? A Note on Party Loyalty Among Southern Democratic Congressmen. *The Journal of Politics* 42 (2): 568–72.

Abramowitz, Alan I. 1994. Issue Evolution Reconsidered: Racial Attitudes and Partisanship in the U.S. Electorate. *American Journal of Political Science* 38 (1):1–24.

Agranoff, Robert. 1972. The New Style of Campaigning: The Decline of Party and the Rise of Candidate Centered Technology. In *The New Style in Election Campaigns*. Boston: Holbrook Press.

Albright, Spencer D. 1942. *The American Ballot*. Washington, D.C.: American Council on Public Affairs.

Aldrich, John H. 1995. *Why Parties? The Origin and Transformation of Political Parties in America*. Chicago: University of Chicago Press.

Aldrich, John H., and David W. Rohde. 1995. Theories of the Party in the Legislature and the Transition to Republican Rule in the House. In *Annual Meeting of the American Political Science Association*. Chicago, IL, August 31–September 3.

Aldrich, John H., and David W. Rohde. 1997. The Transition to Republican Rule in the House: Implications for Theories of Congressional Politics. *Political Science Quarterly* 112 (4):541–67.

Aldrich, John H., and David W. Rohde. 2000a. The Consequences of Party Organization in the House: The Role of the Majority and Minority Parties in Conditional Party Government. In *Polarized Politics: Congress and the President in a Partisan Era*, edited by J. R. Bond and R. Fleisher. Washington, DC: CQ Press.

Aldrich, John H., and David W. Rohde. 2000b. The Republican Revolution and the House Appropriations Committee. *Journal of Politics* 62 (1):1–33.

Aldrich, John H., and David W. Rohde. 2004. Congressional Committees in a Partisan era. In *Congress Reconsidered*, edited by L. C. Dodd and B. I. Oppenheimer. Washington, D.C.: CQ Press.

Aldrich, John H., Mark M. Berger, and David W. Rohde. 2002. The Historical Variability in Conditional Party Government, 1877–1994. In *Parties, Procedure and Policy: Essays on the History of Congress*, edited by D. Brady and M. McCubbins. Stanford: Stanford University Press.

Ansolabehere, Stephen D., Jr., James M. Snyder, and Charles Stewart III. 2001. The Effects of Party and Preferences on Congressional Roll-Call Voting. *Legislative Studies Quarterly* XXVI (4):533–72.

Arnold, R. Douglas. 1990. *The Logic of Congressional Action*. New Haven: Yale University Press.

Bach, Stanley, and Steven S. Smith. 1988. *Managing Uncertainty in the House of Representatives: Adaptation and Innovation in Special Rules*. Washington, D.C.: Brookings Institution Press.

Bawn, Kathleen. 1998. Congressional Party Leadership: Utilitarian versus Majoritarian Incentives. *Legislative Studies Quarterly* 23 (2):219–43.

Behringer, Courtney L., and C. Lawrence Evans. 2006. Parties, Preferences, and the House Whip Process. In *Annual Meeting of the Southern Political Science Association*. Atlanta, GA.

Binder, Sarah A. 1996. The Partisan Basis of Procedural Choice: Allocating Parliamentary Rights in the House, 1789–1990. *American Political Science Review* 90 (1):8–20.

Binder, Sarah A. 1997. *Minority Rights, Majority Rule: Partisanship and the Development of Congress*. New York: Cambridge University Press.

Binder, Sarah A. 2003. *Stalemate: Causes and Consequences of Legislative Gridlock*. Washington, D.C.: Brookings Institution Press.

Binder, Sarah A. 2006. Parties and Institutional Choice Revisited. *Legislative Studies Quarterly* 31 (4):413–532.

Binder, Sarah A., Eric Lawrence, and Forrest Maltzman. 1999. Uncovering the Hidden Effect of Party. *Journal of Politics* 61 (3):815–831.

Binder, Sarah A., Eric Lawrence, and Steven S. Smith. 2002. Tracking the Filibuster. *American Politics Research* 30 (2):406–422.

Binder, Sarah A., and Steven S. Smith. 1997. *Politics or Principle: Filibustering in the Senate*. Washington, D.C.: Brookings Institution Press.

Black, Duncan. 1958. *The Theory of Committee and Elections*. Cambridge, U.K.: Cambridge University Press.

Bolling, Richard Walker. 1974. *Power in the House: A history of the leadership of the House of Representatives*. New York: Capricorn Books.

Bond, Jon R., and Richard Fleisher. 1990. *The President in the Legislative Arena*. Chicago: University of Chicago Press.

Brady, David W. 1985. A Reevaluation of Realignments in American Politics: Evidence from the House of Representatives. *American Political Science Review* 79 (1):28–49.

Brady, David W. 1988. *Critical Elections and Congressional Policy-Making*. Stanford: Stanford University Press.

Brady, David W., Richard Brody, and David Epstein. 1989. Heterogeneous Parties and Political Organization: The U.S. Senate, 1880–1920. *Legislative Studies Quarterly* 14 (2):205–23.

Brady, David W., and David Epstein. 1997. Intraparty Preferences, Heterogeneity, and the Origins of the Modern Congress: Progressive Reformers in the House and Senate, 1890–1920. *Journal of Law, Economics, and Organization* 13 (1):26–49.

Brady, David W., and Naomi B. Lynn. 1973. Switched-Seat Congressional Districts: Their Effect on Party Voting and Public Policy. *American Journal of Political Science* 17 (3):528–43.

Brady, David, and Barbara Sinclair. 1984. Building Majorities for Policy Changes in the House of Representatives. *Journal of Politics* 46 (4): 1033–60.

Brams, Steven J., and Michael K. O'Leary 1970. An Axiomatic Model of Voting Bodies. *American Political Science Review* 64 (2):449–70.

Brown, George Rothwell. 1922. *The leadership of Congress, by George Rothwell Brown*. Indianapolis,: The Bobbs-Merrill company.

Bullock, Charles S. 1976. Motivations for U.S. Congressional Committee Preferences: Freshmen of the 92d Congress. *Legislative Studies Quarterly* 1:201–12.

Burden, Barry C., and Tammy M. Frisby. 2004. Preferences, Partisanship, and Whip Activity in the U.S.House of Representatives. *Legislative Studies Quarterly* XXIX (4):569–90.

Calvert, Randall L., and Richard F. Fenno Jr. 1994. Strategy and Sophisticated Voting in the Senate. *Journal of Politics* 56 (2):349–76.

Cameron, Charles M. 2000. *Veto Bargaining: Presidents and the Politics of Negative Power*. Cambridge: Cambridge University Press.

Caro, Robert A. 2002. *The Years of Lyndon Johnson: Master of the Senate*. New York: Alfred A. Knopf.

Chiu, Chang-Wei. 1928. *The Speaker of the House of Representatives Since 1896*. New York: Columbia University Press.

Clausen, Aage R. 1967. The Measurement of Legislative Group Behavior. *Midwest Journal of Political Science* 11 (2):212–24.

Clausen, Aage R. 1973. *How Congressmen Decide*. New York: St. Martin's Press.

Clausen, Aage R., and Richard B. Cheney. 1970. A Comparative Analysis of Senate House Voting on Economic and Welfare Policy: 1953–1964. *The American Political Science Review* 64 (1):138–52.

Clausen, Aage R., and Carl E. Van Horn. 1977. The Congressional Response to a Decade of Change: 1963–1972. *The Journal of Politics* 39 (3): 624–66.

Clinton, Joshua, Simon Jackman, and Douglas Rivers. 2004. The Statistical Analysis of Roll Call Data: A United Approach. *American Political Science Review* 98 (2):355–70

Coase, Ronald. 1960. The Problem of Social Cost. *Journal of Law and Economics* 3:1–44.

Cohen, Jeffrey. 1981. The Dynamics of Party Voting in Congress, 1955–78: A Cohort Model. *Political Behavior* 3 (3):211–27.

Coleman, James S. 1987. Microfoundations and Macrosocial Behavior. In *The Micro-Macro Link*, edited by J. C. Alexander, B. Giesen, R. Munch, and N. J. Smelser. Berkeley: University of California Press.

Cooper, Joseph, and David Brady. 1981. Institutional Context and Leadership Style: The House From Cannon to Rayburn. *American Political Science Review* 75 (2):411–25.

Cooper, Joseph, David W. Brady, and Patricia Hurley. 1977. The Electoral Basis of Party Voting: Patterns and Trends in the U.S. House of Representatives, 1887–1969. In *The Impact of the Electoral Process*, edited by L. Maisel and J. Cooper. Beverly Hills, CA: Sage.

Covington, Cary R. 1987. Mobilizing Congressional Support for the President: Insights from the 1960s. *Legislative Studies Quarterly* 12:77–95.

Cox, Gary W. 2001. Agenda Setting in the U.S. House: A Majority-Party Monopoly? *Legislative Studies Quarterly* 26 (2):185–210.

Cox, Gary W., Andrea Campbell, and Mathew D. McCubbins. 2002. Agenda Power in the Senate, 1877 to 1986. In *Party, Process, and Political Change in Congress: New Perspectives on the History of Congress*, edited by D. W. Brady and M. D. McCubbins. Stanford: Stanford University Press.

Cox, Gary W., and Mathew D. McCubbins. 1991. On the Decline of Party Voting in Congress. *Legislative Studies Quarterly* 16 (4):547–70.

Cox, Gary W., and Mathew D. McCubbins. 1993. *Legislative Leviathan: Party Government in the House*. Berkeley: University of California Press.

Cox, Gary W., and Mathew D. McCubbins. 1997. Toward a Theory of Legislative Rules Changes: Assessing Schickler and Rich's Evidence. *American Journal of Political Science* 41 (4):1376–86.

Cox, Gary W., and Mathew D. McCubbins. 2002. Agenda Power in the US House of Representatives, 1877–1986. In *Parties, Procedure and Policy: Essays on the History of Congress*, edited by D. W. Brady and M. D. McCubbins. Stanford: Stanford University Press.

Cox, Gary W., and Mathew D. McCubbins. 2005. *Setting the Agenda: Responsible Party Government in the U.S. House of Representatives*. Cambridge: Cambridge University Press.

Cox, Gary W., and Keith T. Poole. 2002. On Measuring Partisanship in Roll-Call Voting: The U.S. House of Representatives, 1877–1999. *American Journal of Political Science* 46 (3):477–89.

Crane, Wilder, Jr. 1960. A Caveat on Roll-Call Studies of Party Voting. *Midwest Journal of Political Science* 4 (3):237–49.

Crombez, Christophe, Keith Krehbiel, and Tim Groseclose. 2005. "Gatekeeping." *Journal of Politics* 68 (2):322–34.

Crook, Sara Brandes, and John R. Hibbing. 1985. Congressional Reform and Party Discipline: The Effects of Changes in the Seniority System on Party Loyalty in the US House of Representatives. *British Journal of Political Science* 15 (2):207–26.

Davidson, Roger, and Walter Oleszek. 1977. *Congress Against Itself*. Bloomington: Indiana University Press.

Davis, Otto A., and Melvin J. Hinich. 1966. A Mathematical Model of Policy Formation in a Democratic Society. In *Mathematical Applications in Political Science II*, edited by J. L. Bernd. Dallas: Southern Methodist University Press.

Davis, Otto A., Melvin J. Hinich, and Peter C. Ordeshook. 1970. An Expository Development of a Mathematical Model of the Electoral Process. *American Political Science Review* 64:426–48.

Deckard, Barbara. 1976. Electoral Marginality and Party Loyalty in House Roll Call Voting. *American Journal of Political Science* 20 (3):469–81.

Deering, Christopher J., and Steven S. Smith. 1983. Changing Motives for Committee Preferences of New Members of the U.S. House. *Legislative Studies Quarterly* VIII (2):271–81.

Deschler, Lewis, Wm Holmes Brown, and Clarence Cannon. 1977. *Deschler's Precedents of the United States House of Representatives.* Washington, D.Cl.: Supt. of Docs., U.S. G.P.O.

Dion, Douglas. 1997. *Turning the Legislative Thumbscrew.* Ann Arbor: University of Michigan Press.

Dion, Douglas, and John D. Huber. 1996. Procedural Choice and the House Committee on Rules. *Journal of Politics* 58 (1):25–53.

Dion, Douglas, and John D. Huber. 1997. Sense and Sensibility: The Role of Rules. *American Journal of Political Science* 41 (3):945–57.

Dodd, Lawrence C. 1977. Congress and the Quest for Power. In *Congress Reconsidered*, edited by L. C. Dodd and B. I. Oppenheimer. New York: Praeger.

Dodd, Lawrence C. 1978. The Expanded Roles of the House Democratic Whip Systems: The 93d and 94th Congresses. *Congressional Studies* 7:27–56.

Dodd, Lawrence C., and Bruce I. Oppenheimer. 1977. *Congress Reconsidered.* New York: Praeger.

Dodd, Lawrence C., and Bruce I. Oppenheimer. 1997. *Congress Reconsidered.* 6th ed. Washington, D.C..: CQ Press.

Dodd, Lawrence C., and Terry Sullivan. 1981. Majority Party Leadership and Partisan Vote Gathering: The House Democratic Whip System. In *Understanding Congressional Leadership*, edited by F. H. Mackaman. Washington., D.C.: CQ Press.

Donald, David Herbert. 1996. *Charles Sumner.* 1st Da Capo Press ed. New York: Da Capo Press.

Downs, Anthony. 1957. *An Economic Theory of Democracy.* New York: Harper.

Edwards, George C. 1984. Presidential Party Leadership in Congress. In *Presidents and Their Parties: Leadership or Neglect?* edited by R. Harmel. New York: Praeger.

Edwards, George C. 1989. *At the Margins: Presidential Leadership of Congress.* New Haven: Yale University Press.

Evans, C. Lawrence, and Walter J. Oleszek. 1999. Procedural Features of House Republican Rule. In *New Majority or Old Minority: the Impact of Republicans on Congress*, edited by N. C. Rae and C. C. Campbell. Lanham, MD: Rowman and Littlefield.

Fenno, Richard F., Jr. 1973. *Congressmen in Committees*. Boston: Little, Brown.

Fiellin, Alan. 1962. The Functions of Informal Groups in Legislative Institutions. *Journal of Politics* 24:72–91.

Fiorina, Morris P. 1974. *Representatives, Roll Calls, and Constituencies*. New York: D.C. Heath and Company.

Follett, Mary Parker. 1909. *The Speaker of the House of Representatives*. New York: Longmans, Green and Co.

Fox, Douglas M., and Charles H. Clapp. 1970a. The House Rules Committee and the Programs of Kennedy and Johnson Administrations. *Midwest Journal of Political Science* 14 (4):667–72.

Fox, Douglas M., and Charles H. Clapp. 1970b. The House Rules Committee's Agenda-Setting Function, 1961–1968. *The Journal of Politics* 32 (2): 440–3.

Frohlich, Norman, Joe Oppenheimer, and Oran Young. 1971. *Political Leadership and Collective Goods*. Princeton: Princeton University Press.

Froman, Lewis A., Jr., and Randall B. Ripley. 1965. Conditions for Party Leadership: The Case of the House Democrats. *American Political Science Review* 59 (1):52–63.

Galloway, George. 1969. *History of the House of Representatives*. New York: Thomas Crowell.

Gamm, Gerald, and Steven S. Smith. 1998. Last Among Equals: The Senate's Presiding Officer. Paper read at Annual Meeting of the American Political Science Association, at Boston.

Gamm, Gerald, and Steven S. Smith. 2000. Last Among Equals: The Presiding Officer of the Senate. In *Esteemed Colleagues: Civility and Deliberation in the United States Senate*, edited by B. Loomis. Washington, D.C.: Brookings Institution.

Gamm, Gerald, and Steven S. Smith. 2002. The Emergence of Senate Party Leadership. In *Senate Exceptionalism*, edited by B. I. Oppenheimer. Columbus: Ohio State University Press.

Greenstein, Fred I., and Elton F. Jackson. 1963. A Second Look at the Validity of Roll-Call Analysis. *Midwest Journal of Political Science* 7 (2):156–66.

Grumm, John G. 1965. The Systematic Analysis of Blocs in the Study of Legislative Behavior. *Western Political Quarterly* 18 (2):350–62.

Hager, Gregory L., and Jeffery C. Talbert. 2000. Look for the Party Label: Party Influences on Voting in the U.S. House. *Legislative Studies Quarterly* 25 (1):75–99.

Hinich, Melvin J., and James M. Enelow. 1984. *The Spatial Theory of Voting*. Cambridge: Cambridge University Press.

Huitt, Ralph K. 1961. Democratic Party Leadership in the Senate. *American Political Science Review* 55:333–44.

Hurwitz, Mark S., Roger J. Moiles, and David W. Rohde. 2001. Distributive and Partisan Issues in Agriculture Policy in the 104th House. *American Political Science Review* 95 (4):911–22.

Jackson, John E. 1971. Statistical Models of Senate Roll Call Voting. *The American Political Science Review* 65 (2):451–70.

Jackson, John E., and John W. Kingdon. 1992. Ideology, Interest Group Score, and Legislative Votes. *American Journal of Political Science* 36 (August): 805–23.

Jackson, Mathew O., and Boaz Moselle. 2002. Coalition and Party Formation in a Legislative Voting Game. *Journal of Economic Theory* 103 (1):49–87.

Jones, Charles. 1961. Representation in Congress: The Case of the House Agriculture Committee. *American Political Science Review* 55 (June):358–67.

Jones, Charles O. 1970. *The Minority Party in Congress*. Boston: Little, Brown.

Karabel, Jerome. 2005. *The Chosen: The Hidden History of Admission and Exclusion at Harvard, Yale, and Princeton*. Boston: Houghton Mifflin Co.

Katz, Jonathan, and Brian Sala. 1996. Careerism, Committee Assignments, and the Electoral Connection. *American Political Science Review* 90:21–33.

Kernell, Samuel. 1986. *Going Public: New Strategies of Presidential Leadership*. Washington, D.C.: CQ Press.

Kernell, Samuel. 1997. *Going Public: New Strategies of Presidential Leadership*. 3rd ed. Washington, D.C.: CQ Press.

Kessel, John H. 1964. The Washington Congressional Delegation. *Midwest Journal of Political Science* 8:1–21.

Kiewiet, D. Roderick, and Mathew D. McCubbins. 1991. *The Logic of Delegation: Congressional Parties and the Appropriations Process*. Chicago: University of Chicago Press.

King, David C., and Richard J. Zeckhauser. 2003. Congressional Vote Options. *Legislative Studies Quarterly* XXVIII (3):387–412.

Kingdon, John W. 1973. *Congressmen's Voting Decisions*. New York: Harper and Row.

Koford, Kenneth. 1989. Dimensions in Congressional Voting. *The American Political Science Review* 83 (3):949–62.

Krehbiel, Keith. 1988. Spatial Models of Legislative Choice. *Legislative Studies Quarterly* 13 (3):259–319.

Krehbiel, Keith. 1991. *Information and Legislative Organization*. Ann Arbor: University of Michigan Press.

Krehbiel, Keith. 1993. Where's the Party? *British Journal of Political Science* 23:235–66.

Krehbiel, Keith. 1995. Cosponsors and Wafflers from A to Z. *American Journal of Political Science* 39 (4):906–23.

Krehbiel, Keith. 1997a. Rejoinder to 'Sense and Sensibility'. *American Journal of Political Science* 41:958–64.

Krehbiel, Keith. 1997b. Restrictive Rules Reconsidered. *American Journal of Political Science* 41 (July):919–44.

Krehbiel, Keith. 1998. *Pivotal Politics: A Theory of U.S. Lawmaking*. Chicago: University of Chicago Press.

Krehbiel, Keith. 2000. Party Discipline and Measures of Partisanship. *American Journal of Political Science* 44:212–27.

Krehbiel, Keith. 2003. Asymmetry in Party Influence: Reply. *Political Analysis* 11:108–9.

Krehbiel, Keith. 2005. *Pivots*. Stanford: Stanford University Graduate School of Business.

Krehbiel, Keith. 2006. Pivots. In *Handbook of Political Economy*, edited by B. R. Weingast and D. Wittman. New York: Oxford University Press.

Krehbiel, Keith, Adam Meirowitz, and Jonathan Woon. 2005. Testing Theories of Lawmaking. In *Social Choice and Strategic Decisions*, edited by D. Austen-Smith and J. Duggan. New York: Springer.

Krehbiel, Keith, and Alan Wiseman. 1999. Joseph G. Cannon: Majoritarian from Illinois. Paper read at Conference on the History of Congress, January 15–16, at Stanford University.

Kuklinski, James H. 1977. District Competitiveness and Legislative Roll-Call Behavior: A Reassessment of the Marginality Hypothesis. *American Journal of Political Science* 21 (3):627–38.

Kuklinski, James H., and Richard C. Elling. 1977. Representational Role, Constituency Opinion, and Legislative Roll-Call Behavior. *American Journal of Political Science* 21 (1):135–47.

Lawrence, Eric D. 2004. Essays on Procedural Development in the U.S. Congress, Ph.D. Dissertation, University of Minnesota.

Lawrence, Eric, Forrest Maltzman, and Steven S. Smith. 2005. Changing Patterns of Party Effects in Congressional Voting. In *Annual Meeting of the American Political Science Association*. Washington, D.C.

Lawrence, Eric, Forrest Maltzman, and Steven S. Smith. 2006. Who Wins? Party Effects in Legislative Voting. *Legislative Studies Quarterly* 31 (1):33–69.

Lawrence, Eric, and Steven S. Smith. 1997. Party Control of Committees in the Republican Congress. In *Congress Reconsidered*, edited by L. C. Dodd and B. I. Oppenheimer. Washington, D.C.: CQ Press.

Light, Paul C. 1983. *The President's Agenda: Domestic Policy Choice from Kennedy to Carter*. Baltimore: Johns Hopkins University Press.

Lott, Trent. 2005. *Herding Cats: A Life in Politics*. New York: Regan Books.

Ludington, Arthur C. 1911. American Ballot Laws, 1888–1910, edited by N. Y. S. E. Department: University of the State of New York, Albany.

MacNeil, Neil. 1963. *Forge of Democracy: The House of Representatives*. New York: McKay.

MacRae, Duncan. 1958. *Dimensions of Congressional Voting*. Berkeley: University of California Press.

MacRae, Duncan, Jr. 1965. A Method for Identifying Issues and Factions From Legislative Votes. *American Political Science Review* 59 (4):909–26.

Maltzman, Forrest. 1997. *Competing Principals: Committees, Parties, and the Organization of Congress*. Ann Arbor: University of Michigan Press.

Marshall, Bryan W. 2002. Explaining the Role of Restrictive Rules in the Postreform House. *Legislative Studies Quarterly* 27 (1):61–85.

Martin, Andrew D. and Kevin M. Quinn. 2002. Dynamic Ideal Point Estimation via Markov Chain Monte Carlo for the U.S. Supreme Court, 1953–1999. *Political Analysis* 10 (2):134–53.

Matthews, Donald R., and James A. Stimson. 1975. *Yeas and Nays: Normal Decision-Making in the U.S. House of Representatives*. New York: Wiley.

Mayhew, David R. 1991. *Divided We Govern: Party Control, Lawmaking, and Investigating: 1946–1990*. New Haven: Yale University Press.

Mayhew, David R. 1974. *Congress: The Electoral Connection*. New Haven: Yale University Press.

McCarty, Nolan, Keith T. Poole, and Howard Rosenthal. 2001. The Hunt for Party Discipline in Congress. *American Political Science Review* 95 (3): 673–87.

Neustadt, Richard. 1990. *Presidential Power and the Modern Presidents: The Politics of Leadership from Roosevelt to Reagan*. New York: Free Press.

Nimmo, Dan. 1970. *The Political Persuaders: The Techniques of Modern Election Campaigns*. Englewood Cliffs, NJ: Prentice-Hall.

Nokken, Timothy P. 2000. Dynamics of Congressional Loyalty: Party Defection and Roll-Call Behavior, 1947–97. *Legislative Studies Quarterly* 25 (3): 417–44.

Nokken, Timothy P., and Keith T. Poole. 2004. Congressional Party Defection in American History. *Legislative Studies Quarterly* 29 (4):545–68.

North, Douglass C. 1990. *Institutions, Institutional Change, and Economic Performance*. New York: Cambridge University Press.

Oleszek, Walter J. 1985. Majority and Minority Whips of the Senate. Washington, D.C.: Government Printing Office.

Olson, Mancur. 1966. *The Logic of Collective Action*. Cambridge: Harvard University Press.

Peabody, Robert L. 1963. The Enlarged Rules Committee. In *New Perspectives on the House of Representatives*, edited by R. L. Peabody and N. W. Polsby. Chicago: Rand McNally and Co.

Peabody, Robert L. 1976. *Leadership in Congress: Stability, Succession, and Change*. Boston: Little, Brown.

Poole, Keith T. 1988. Recent Developments in Analytical Models of Voting in the U. S. Congress. *Legislative Studies Quarterly* 13 (1):117–33.

Poole, Keith T., and R. Steven Daniels. 1985. Ideology, Party, and Voting in the U.S. Congress, 1959–1980. *American Political Science Review* 79 (2):373–99.

Poole, Keith T., and Howard Rosenthal. 1985. A Spatial Model for Legislative Roll Call Analysis. *American Journal of Political Science* 29 (2):357–84.

Poole, Keith T., and Howard Rosenthal. 1991. Patterns of Congressional Voting. *American Journal of Political Science* 35 (1):228–78.

Poole, Keith T., and Howard Rosenthal. 1996. *Congress: A Political-Economic History of Roll Call Voting*. New York: Oxford University Press.

Poole, Keith T., Howard Rosenthal, and Kenneth Koford. 1991. On Dimensionalizing Roll Call Votes in the U.S. Congress. *The American Political Science Review* 85 (3):955–76.

Price, Hugh Douglas. 1962. Race, Religion, and the Rules Committee: The Kennedy Aid-to-Education Bills. In *The Uses of Power*, edited by A. F. Westin. New York: Harcourt, Brace, and World.

Ray, Bruce A., and Steven S. Smith. 1983. The Impact of Congressional Reform: House Democratic Committee Assignments. *Congress and The Presidency* (Fall): 11–22.

Rice, Stuart A. 1924. Farmers and Workers in American Politics. Ph.D. Dissertation, Columbia University, New York.

Rice, Stuart A. 1925. The Behavior of Legislative Groups: A Method of Measurement. *Political Science Quarterly* 40 (1):60–72.

Rice, Stuart A. 1928. *Quantitative Methods in Politics*. New York: Knopf.

Ripley, Randall B. 1964. The Party Whip Organizations in the United States House of Representatives. *American Political Science Review* 58 (3):561–76.

Ripley, Randall B. 1967. *Party Leaders in the House of Representatives*. Washington, D.C.: Brookings Institution.

Ritchie, Donald A. 1998. Minutes of the U.S. Senate Democratic Conference, 1903–1964. Washington, D.C.: Government Printing Office.

Roberts, Jason M., and Steven S. Smith. Forthcoming. The Evolution of Agenda-Setting Institutions in Congress: Path Dependency in House and Senate Institutional Development. In *Process, Party and Policy Making: New Advances in the Study of the History of Congress*, edited by D. W. Brady and M. D. Mccubbins. Palo Alto: Stanford University Press.

Roberts, Jason M., and Steven S. Smith. 2003. Procedural Contexts, Party Strategy, and Conditional Party Voting in the U.S. House of Representatives, 1971–2000. *American Journal of Political Science* 47 (April):305–17.

Robinson, James A. 1959. The Role of the Rules Committee in Arranging the Program of the U.S. House of Representatives. *The Western Political Quarterly* 12 (3):653–69.

Robinson, James A. 1961. The Role of the Rules Committee in Regulating Debate in the U.S. House of Representatives. *Midwest Journal of Political Science* 5 (1):59–69.

Robinson, James A. 1963. *The House Rules Committee*. Indianapolis: Bobbs-Merrill.

Rohde, David W. 1991. *Parties and Leaders in the Postreform House*. Chicago: University of Chicago Press.

Rohde, David W. 1992. Electoral Forces, Political Agendas, and Partisanship in the House and Senate. In *The Postreform Congress*, edited by R. Davidson. New York:. St. Martins Press.

Rohde, David W. 1994. Parties and Committees in the House: Member Motivations, Issues, and Institutional Arrangements. *Legislative Studies Quarterly* 19 (3):341–59.

Rothman, David J. 1966. *Politics and Power: The United States Senate, 1869–1901*. Cambridge: Harvard University Press.

Rybicki, Elizabeth, Steven S. Smith, and Ryan J. Vander Wielen. 2003. Congressional Conference Committee Bias, 1963–2002. Paper presented at the Annual Meeting of the American Political Science Association. Philadelphia.

Sabato, Larry. 1981. *The Rise of Political Consultants: New Ways of Winning Elections*. New York: Basic Books.

Schwartz, Thomas. 1989. Why Parties? Mimeo, University of California at Los Angeles.

Shannon, Wayne. 1968a. Electoral Margins and Voting Behavior in the House of Representatives: The Case of the Eighty-Sixth and Eighty-Seventh Congresses. *The Journal of Politics* 30 (4):1028–45.

Shannon, Wayne. 1968b. *Party, Constituency, and Congressional Voting*. Baton Rouge: Louisiana State University Press.

Shefter, Martin. 1983. Regional Receptivity to Reform: The Legacy of the Progressive Era. *Political Science Quarterly* 98 (Fall):459–83.

Shepsle, Kenneth A. 1978. *The Giant Jigsaw Puzzle: Democratic Committee Assignments in the Modern House.* Chicago: University of Chicago Press.

Shepsle, Kenneth A., and Barry R. Weingast. 1984a. Uncovered Sets and Sophisticated Voting Outcomes With Implications for Agenda Institutions. *American Journal of Political Science* 28 (1):49–74.

Shepsle, Kenneth A., and Barry R. Weingast. 1984b. When Do Rules of Procedure Matter? *Journal of Politics* 46 (1):206–21.

Sinclair, Barbara. 1981a. Majority Party Leadership Strategies for Coping with the New U. S. House. *Legislative Studies Quarterly* 6 (3):391–414.

Sinclair, Barbara. 1981b. The Speaker's Task Force in the Post-Reform House of Representatives. *American Political Science Review* 75 (2):397–410.

Sinclair, Barbara. 1983. *Majority Leadership in the U.S. House.* Baltimore: Johns Hopkins University Press.

Sinclair, Barbara. 1989. House Majority Party Leadership in the Late 1980s. In *Congress Reconsidered,* edited by L. D. Dodd and B. I. Oppenheimer. Washington, D.C.: CQ Press.

Sinclair, Barbara. 1994. House Special Rules and the Institutional Design Controversy. *Legislative Studies Quarterly* 19 (November):477–94.

Sinclair, Barbara. 1995a. House Special Rules and the Institutional Design Controversy. In *Positive Theories of Congressional Institutions,* edited by K. Shepsle and B. Weingast. Ann Arbor: University of Michigan Press.

Sinclair, Barbara. 1995b. *Legislators, Leaders, and Lawmaking: The U.S. House of Representatives in the Postreform Era.* Baltimore: Johns Hopkins University Press.

Sinclair, Barbara. 2000. *Unorthodox Lawmaking: New Legislative Processes in the U.S. Congress.* 2nd ed. Washington, D.C.: CQ Press.

Sinclair, Barbara. 2002. Do Parties Matter? In *Party, Process, and Political Change in Congress: New Perspectives on the History of Congress,* edited by D. W. Brady and M. D. McCubbins. Stanford: Stanford University Press.

Smith, Steven S. 1982. The Budget Battles of 1981: The Role of the Majority Party Leadership. In *American Politics and Public Policy,* edited by A. P. Sindler. Washington, D.C.: CQ Press.

Smith, Steven S. 1984. Coalition Leaders in Congress: A Theoretical Perspective. Paper presented at the Annual meeting of the American Political Science Association: Washington, DC.

Smith, Steven S. 1985. New Patterns of Decisionmaking in Congress. In *The New Direction in American Politics,* edited by J. E. Chubb and P. E. Peterson. Washington, D.C.: Brookings Institution.

Smith, Steven S. 1989. *Call to Order: Floor Politics in the House and Senate.* Washington, D.C.: Brookings Institution.

Smith, Steven S. 2005. Parties and Leadership in the Senate. In *The Legislative Branch,* edited by P. J. Quirk and S. A. Binder. New York: Oxford University Press.

Smith, Steven S., and Christopher J. Deering. 1990. *Committees in Congress.* Washington, D.C.: CQ Press.

Smith, Steven S., and Marcus Flathman. 1989. Managing the Senate Floor: Complex Unanimous Consent Agreements Since the 1950s. *Legislative Studies Quarterly* 14:349–74.

Smith, Steven S., and Gerald Gamm. 2002. Emergence of the Modern Senate Party Organization, 1937–2002. Paper presented at the annual meeting of the American Political Science Association, Boston, Mass.

Smith, Steven S., Jason M. Roberts, and Ryan J. Vander Wielen. 2006. *The American Congress*. 4th ed. New York: Cambridge University Press.

Snyder, James M., and Tim Groseclose. 2000. Estimating Party Influence in Congressional Roll-Call Voting. *American Journal of Political Science* 44 (2):193–211.

Snyder, James M., Jr., and Tim Groseclose. 2001. Estimating Party Influence on Roll Call Voting: Regression Coefficients versus Classification Success. *American Political Science Review* 95 (3):689–98.

Sullivan, John L., and Eric M. Uslaner. 1978. Congressional Behavior and Electoral Marginality. *American Journal of Political Science* 22:536–54.

Truman, David. 1951. *The Governmental Process*. New York: Knopf.

Truman, David. 1956. The State Delegations and the Structure of Party Voting in the United States House of Representatives. *American Political Science Review* 50:1023–45.

Truman, David B. 1959. *The Congressional Party: A Case Study*. New York: Wiley.

Turner, Julius. 1951. *Party and Constituency: Pressures on Congress*, Johns Hopkins University Studies in Historical and political science. Ser. 69, No. 1. Baltimore: Johns Hopkins Press.

Vander Wielen, Ryan. 2006. Conference Committees and Bias in Legislative Outcomes. Ph.D. Dissertation, Political Science, Washington University, St. Louis.

Wawro, Gregory J., and Eric Schickler. 2004. Where's the Pivot? Obstruction and Lawmaking in the Pre-Cloture Senate. *American Journal of Political Science* 48 (4):758–74.

Wawro, Gregory, and Eric Schickler. 2006. *Filibuster: Obstruction and Lawmaking in the U.S. Senate, Princeton Studies in American Politics*. Princeton, NJ: Princeton University Press.

Weisberg, Herbert F. 1972. Scaling Models for Legislative Roll-Call Analysis. *American Political Science Review* 66 (4):1306–15.

Wilcox, Clyde, and Aage R. Clausen. 1991. The Dimensionality of Roll-Call Voting Reconsidered. *Legislative Studies Quarterly* (August):393–406.

Yeomans, Henry Aaron. 1948. *Abbott Lawrence Lowell, 1856–1943*. Cambridge: Harvard University Press.

Young, Garry, and Vicky Wilkins. 2005. Vote Switchers and Party Influence in the U.S. House.

Index